The Canvas Chapel

By the Rev E Bryn Little MM

Edited by Robert Little

Little
press & public relations

Acknowledgement

Grateful thanks are due to Bryn Little's wartime friend, Bill Aish, who is still alive at the time of this book's publication. He has been able to confirm much of the content and has also supplied some of the pictures for this book.

Published by Bob Little Press & PR
23 Sherwood Avenue
St Albans
Herts
AL4 9QJ

ISBN 0-9543113-0-2

Cover design by S&W Design, St Albans, Hertfordshire
Origination by PJC Design Ltd, Northampton
Printed and bound by Falcon Press, Northampton

FOREWORD

This is the story of one man's pilgrimage in wartime. It began in the churches of Britain and led to the Canvas Chapel in Bizerte, Tunisia. The pilgrimage included the Monastery at Monte Cassino, Italy and continued to St. Peter's in Rome and later included the British Army Garrison Church in Villach, Austria. Then it came full circle to several churches in Britain.

It was a pilgrimage through many theatres of war and included humour, horror and heroics. Pathos and piety, suffering and sacrifice, comradeship and loneliness all had their place.

Spiritual and secular experiences, religious and irreligious moments played their part. Wartime experiences at home and abroad contribute to the story and yet, running through it all is the thread of Christian faith and experience. Sometimes there was the feeling of being God-forsaken, and at other times God seemed very near - which he always was - even when his presence was not recognised.

Join me in re-living the pilgrimage and enter into the humour and horrors. View the sacrifice and suffering through the eyes of one who fought fear and found courage while trying to serve his fellowmen.

In the writing of this book I am grateful to my parents who preserved all the letters I wrote to them while I was serving overseas. These provided valuable source material.

My thanks are also due to Jim Farrell for allowing me to quote from his book 'My War' and also for being able to use his diary for 1944 to confirm dates of certain events. I owe a special debt of gratitude to my son, Robert, whose help in various ways - including his advice and guidance - has been invaluable.

E Bryn Little

Bryn Little

The Canvas Chapel

Contents

CHAPTER ONE

It's different now

It was not the first time I had been dive-bombed, and it was not the last, but this time it was different. The first time I saw a German aeroplane diving towards me, machine-guns blazing and bullets flying around me, and I realised I was the target, was a very frightening experience. On other occasions, to see the bombs released and curving downwards - coming towards me - was also frightening. Sometimes, while driving a lorry in North Africa, the first sign of an attack was the sight of bullets hitting the road in front of the lorry, or to see a bomb burst nearby. At one time this was a frequent experience, and I felt that my lorry and I stood out as a huge target that could not be missed, while everything else seemed to grow smaller.

But this time it was different. Before, it all seemed so impersonal. It was just a machine trying to kill me. On this occasion, at Oued Zarga, I could actually see the face of the German pilot, and I felt it was a personal attack.

This dive-bombing at Oued Zarga was so different from the scenes in films of World War I that I had shown when I was a cinema projectionist before this war. Ever since I had volunteered for service in the Royal Army Service Corps (RASC) and had joined the Army on 7th February 1940, things had never ceased to be different.

Training camp at Herne Bay was an introduction to an existence very different from anything I had ever known before.

The scene outside Herne Bay railway station was one of utter confusion as scores of bewildered men, clutching suitcases or brown paper parcels of various kinds and shapes, milled around uncertain where to go or what to do.

Amid the confusion and chaos a voice bellowed: "Alright, look lively. Fall-in in three ranks."

More confusion - almost a stampede - but eventually some sort of order emerged, and we were told to pick up our suitcases or parcels. An optimistic sergeant, shouted: "Left turn" and, before some of the men discovered which was left, he bellowed: "Quick march."

We did our best but, nonetheless, we only shuffled out of the station approach and headed towards the town.

After a rather long 'march' we arrived at a hut and were given blankets and two linen bags, which we were told to fill with straw from an adjoining hut. This was our introduction to 'the palliasse' and 'the pillow'. With our increased burdens we were herded towards some private houses. As we arrived at an empty house, a number of men were told to: "Get inside. That's your billet."

I found myself in the front room downstairs with three other would-be soldiers. There were no home comforts. It was, literally, an empty house.

We sorted ourselves out and introduced ourselves.

Scotty was a middleweight boxer, part-time - and looked it. He was from Bournemouth. Bill was a bus driver from Weston-super-Mare. Ron was from Weymouth. I was from South Wales but had worked and lived in Bournemouth and in Weymouth. Our first night on palliasses and bare floorboards did not provide the sleep we needed.

The next morning we were marched to the Mess Hall, which had been a very large restaurant catering for the needs of happy holidaymakers. Now it was a feeding place for rather dispirited troops, and its former elegance had departed. The tables were of plain boards arranged in long lines. Each table was flanked, on either side, by a single plank bench.

On entering this mess hall, we collected a mug (enamel), one plate (metal) and cutlery. As we approached the serving table, plates were presented - carefully kept horizontal - and the meal of the moment was thrown on to the plate. Next the mug was held below table level while a tea-bucket (holding three gallons of brown liquid) was quickly tilted over the mug and the mug was filled, or over-filled. At the head of each table was a metal plate containing pats of 'butter' and we soon learned to grab a lump of this grease and two chunks of bread as we slid along the bench.

When the meal had ended, plates and cutlery were returned to a receiving point, and the men quickly escaped to the fresh air outside. It was all so very different from home cooking and comforts.

It was Saturday morning, but we quickly discovered that it was not our day off.

We spent the day marching from place to place, collecting our kit from various huts from issuers who were always in a hurry. As we came to a counter a soldier behind the counter shouted out the name of the article and the quantity we were to receive, for example: "Drawers, long, two pairs. Vests, woollen, two pairs", and so on until our arms were full. Then came the shout: "Kitbags, soldiers for the use of."

Thankfully, we dumped our collected kit into these bags.

We staggered to the next hut for, "Boots, Army, black."

As at all the other counters, we were asked: "Size?"

In our brief travels, we had learned that it was wise to answer quickly, otherwise you received the garment nearest to the issuer's hand, irrespective of size.

"Eights," I shouted quickly and a pair of boots came hurtling towards my face. As I caught them, I was commanded: "Try 'em on."

Since there were many men trying on boots in what was a very small space, there was some difficulty. I managed to put the boots on their respective feet, when a voice said: "Do they fit?"

"Yes," I replied and immediately another pair of boots came flying towards me, which I caught with some difficulty. Before I could remove the first pair of boots from my feet I was told: "Get a move on. Outside."

This was easier said than done, because I discovered that the boots I was wearing were tied together at the back. Like all my unfortunate comrades, all we could do was to shuffle forwards, three inches at a time.

Many of the men fell down as they struggled to get outside, and so lost their recently acquired kit.

Outside, we struggled to replace our civvy footwear while being constantly told: "Fall in."

We must have looked a wraggle-taggle mob as we struggled to hold all our kit and march back to our billets.

Our ordeal continued the following morning - Sunday - because we were on 'tailors' parade'. We were measured. Our uniforms were pulled and pinched and marked, and taken away for alterations. That was when I learned the Army saying: "If your uniform fits, you must be deformed."

In place of our uniforms we were issued with fatigue suits - a loose fitting battle dress type of uniform for wearing when doing dirty jobs or 'fatigues'.

There were insufficient Army greatcoats in stock, so some men were told to wear their civvy overcoats and were paid one pound a week for doing so. I received an Army greatcoat with brass buttons. One of my comrades had brown bone buttons on his greatcoat and complained because he wanted brass buttons. I suggested we exchanged buttons and he most gratefully agreed, thanking me for my kindness. I was also very pleased because I realised I would not have to clean the buttons on my greatcoat. This was a cause for continual thanksgiving during the time I wore the coat.

Another of my comrades complained that his steel helmet was too big for him because it was a size eight. I had asked for a size seven and a half and had been given a size seven, so my battle bowler was too small. I suggested we exchanged tin-hats.

He snatched my helmet from me, put it on, and said: "It's a bit small but it's better than this one", and he handed me his helmet. It was a bit big for me, but this made it possible for me to wear a woollen Balaclava helmet, or woollen cap comforter (Army issue) under the tin hat. Later, I was very glad I had taken pity on that poor soldier and exchanged tin hats with him. My battle-bowler and I went through the war together, and it proved a very good companion, shield and defender, as well as a comfortable pillow on active service. It was also a source of confidence when the shrapnel and bullets were flying around. It was worn, battered and dented when I handed it in at my demob, and I was sorry to part with it.

Since my uniform was 'almost a fit' I was told to wear it. So I did.

I found a Baptist church and attended the evening service. I maintained contact with this church while I stayed in Herne Bay and sang in the choir when they performed the cantata 'Olivet to Calvary', which I had sung several times while a member of Rosebery Park Baptist Church, in Bournemouth.

When I had joined the Army, I was determined that I would attend church services whenever possible. This intention was somewhat dented by duties and various conditions and circumstances as the years rolled by, but I always tried to attend as many services as I could.

Eventually, our first pay parade arrived.

The company office was in a small semi-detached house, and we were lined up on the pavement outside. The officer and pay-sergeant were in the dining room. The pay-sergeant called out a man's name, which was repeated by a corporal standing at the front door. The man called responded with, "Sir", followed by the last three figures of his Army number.

My name was called and I responded and marched to the front door. The corporal allowed me to enter the hall, then shouted: "Left turn"

I found myself in the dining room. As I came opposite a table, the corporal shouted: "Halt. Right turn. Salute."

The pay-sergeant said: "Ten shillings, sir."

The officer dropped some coins into my left hand, and I looked in sheer disbelief since I had been told I would receive two shillings per day and so had expected 14 shillings. But there lay the coins, four two shilling pieces and two one shilling pieces.

I was just about to inform the officer there had been a mistake when the corporal shouted: "Salute. Right turn. Quick march."

I obeyed instinctively, which was the result of four days training. As I walked through the kitchen door to the back door to return to the roadway, a hand shot out and took a shilling from my still open left hand. I instantly closed my hand over the remaining coins and asked: "What's the big idea?"

I found that I was looking up into the face of a sergeant.

"It's for barrack room damages," he said.

I faced up to him and said: "I haven't damaged any barrack rooms yet, so you can't take the money from me."

The sergeant replied: "That's the rule, so that future damages can be paid for."

I was about to continue the debate when the officer shouted: "Get out."

I obeyed, but nursed a grievance against officers, pay-sergeants, sergeants and barrack room damages.

In the evening of the following Sunday I had been unable to attend the services at the Baptist church so, late in the evening, Scotty and I went for a walk. Scotty shared the room in our billet with me and two others. We wandered around the darkened streets of Herne Bay until our attention was drawn to a notice board outside a hall, which said: 'Roman Catholic Soldiers Club'. Scotty suggested we went inside. I said: "But I'm not a Roman Catholic."

Scotty replied: "Neither am I, but I will be for tonight. Come on."

Cautiously, we entered the hall. Along one side of the hall was a long counter from which food and drink were being served. The centre of the hall was filled with tables and chairs at which sat a large number of soldiers. Scotty said he would get two cups of tea, but he returned carrying two cups of tea and two large plates containing generous helpings of beans on toast. I knew Scotty was almost without money and asked how he could afford such a feast. He replied: "Don't worry. It's all free."

I was surprised to hear that, but we soon disposed of the meal.

We had just finished our meal when a man stepped on to a platform and announced that the concert would begin. Most of the performers were soldiers and the acts were quite good. Suddenly the compere said: "Our next artist is Driver Little of the RASC, who will sing for us."

Scotty nudged me and said: "That's you. I volunteered for you; so get up there."

By this time, everyone was looking around for Driver Little; so I walked to the front of the hall and onto the stage. There was a feeble attempt at applause as I tried to find a suitable solo from among the music copies near the piano.

There was no time for discussion with the pianist so I placed a sheet of music on the piano and the pianist immediately began playing the introduction and I began singing 'Drink to me only with thine eyes.' When I finished singing the applause was a bit more spirited and the compere shouted: "Encore."

I whispered to the pianist: "Do you know the song, 'The Rose of Tralee?'"

He nodded and asked: "What key?"

I hummed the first line. He began playing before I had reached the front of the stage. After the solo, the applause was loud and long.

I made my way back to Scotty and was greeted with the words: "You sang well. I told them you could do it."

"Why did you do that to me?" I asked.

"Well, there were free eats for anyone doing a turn, so I volunteered for you and we had a free supper."

This was my introduction to singing in Army concerts and led to me becoming a member of several concert parties.

That concert led to my first press write-up. The local paper carried the report: 'The excellent tenor voice of Driver E B Little was heard to fine advantage in "The Rose of Tralee" and "Drink to me only with thine eyes".' But the next morning, on drill parade, the lance corporal called me 'Caruso' and I was a marked man after that.

Since all the men on our 'intake' had been drivers of motor vehicles before volunteering for the Army, there was no need for driving instruction, which resulted in our time of training being curtailed. Our actual training time was 17 days.

● At the WAM Tyre Company, 1937.

On our final parade at Herne Bay, a lieutenant made a rambling farewell speech, ending with the words: "I cannot say much to you. I do not know what is in store for you, but I do wish you the best of wars."

We then left by train and arrived in Broadstairs, and were billeted in civilian houses occupied by the householders. A group of us found ourselves in what had been a boarding house, and I shared a room with five others. The rule was six soldiers to a room. Everywhere stank of stale cigarette smoke and, to those of us who were non-smokers, it was horrible.

The day after our arrival we were given a lecture by a Major Temple, and discovered he was our commanding officer and we were now part of 4 GHQ Company, RASC. Much later we discovered this was the largest RASC company ever formed. Then, months later, we were told that somehow a duplicate company with the same title was in France, though this was never proved. The next day we were assigned to various platoons. Scotty and I were in the supply section of the company.

The Army tends to shatter one's illusions, and one of my cherished hopes quickly became a shattered illusion when I had an interview with Major Temple.

When I went to live in Bournemouth I entered the motor trade and eventually became the manager of shop, works and yard of the W A M Tyre Company. Later, I became the manager of the first branch shop opened by the firm. This was in Weymouth. At that time, I was considered a tyre expert and vulcaniser.

In November 1939, Sir Malcolm Campbell made an appeal on the radio for tyre experts and vulcanisers to join the Army. This had prompted me to volunteer for service.

I was told to apply for the position of tyre expert and vulcaniser in workshops when I was posted to a company. Consequently, I requested an interview with Major Temple. The major told me that vulcanisers received trade pay of seven shillings and ninepence per day but, since vulcanisers were not needed in 4 GHQ Company, I would be a driver at two shillings per day.

So much for Sir Malcolm's stirring appeal!

As if to emphasise my position, at the pay parade that afternoon, I received seven shillings (35 pence) as my wage for that week.

I had noticed that there was a Free Church of England church near our billet and I attended the prayer meeting there on my first Saturday evening in Broadstairs. The priest in charge was Bishop Mcgee, and he invited me to speak at the Open Sunday School the next day, which I did.

On the Sunday morning, I attended the service at Queen's Road Baptist Church. I also attended the evening service there and sang in the choir. It was Sundays like this that helped me to face up to Army life. It was also helpful to attend the week-night activities in the various churches I encountered on my travels.

After four weeks, we were moved to East Cliff Lodge on the cliffs overlooking the sea. We often watched air-raids on ships outside Broadstairs Harbour, in 'The Downs'. East Cliff Lodge was on the Ramsgate side of Broadstairs and we often walked to Ramsgate along the top of the cliffs.

East Cliff Lodge was an old building, square in shape, with a courtyard in the centre between the four 'wings' of the Lodge. The courtyard was our parade ground. It had all been unused for a long time and needed a lot of cleaning, which we had to do.

Soon after we took up residence, it was reported that sounds of a pipe-organ could be heard coming from the locked-up chapel. The organ could not be heard every night, although someone listened each night.

The mystery continued for weeks, until permission was given to investigate.

Nothing happened for several nights but, on the night of the full moon, the sound of music was heard again - at midnight.

A few brave soldiers opened the chapel door and torchlight pierced the darkness, disclosing dust that had not been disturbed for many years. It was obvious that the organ had been untouched by human hand for a long time and no one now sat at the keyboard.

The music sounded like a child idly running fingers over the keys. There was no sound of a bellows being worked, nor of an electrically operated wind pump, but the music continued. The soldiers were nonplussed, and withdrew.

In the morning, the chapel was closely examined. There were no signs of the organ being touched. Then we noticed that the chapel floorboards sloped slightly towards the wall facing the sea. Investigations revealed the floorboards had dropped several inches; so wind, entering a ventilation brick, went under the floorboards and came up under the organ. From there it found its way through the organ pipes. This only happened when the wind blew from the sea. So our ghostly organist did not exist.

In May 1940, German paratroops invaded Holland and everyone became nervous that a similar invasion of Britain might be attempted. This produced a severe rash of security-consciousness. Together with about 30 others from our company, I was sent to Number One Mobilisation Control, Margate. We were billeted in a large hall in what had been St Margaret's Girls School.

I was the driver of one of the lorries that carried about ten men on a patrol circuit around the area enclosing Manston Aerodrome. We began at 7pm and continued until 7am, with a break for a meal about 3am. This meal was served in a large restaurant in the centre of Ramsgate.

The whole business became very boring: continuously driving around the same circuit, with nothing exciting happening.

We watched the aircraft leaving Manston in the evening, on their way to carry out their duties. We counted them again as they returned to Manston and were relieved when they all returned. One night, as we continued our way around the circuit, we were challenged at one of the road blocks, also manned by men from our company. We faced rifles pointed at us and a demand for the password.

● With his father, William Little, on his first leave, 1940.

The corporal in charge of our section gave the password, and more men appeared, all pointing rifles at us. The corporal got out of the cab of the lorry and asked in Army language what was going on, and he was recognised and the rifles were lowered. After we had left the last checkpoint the password had been changed because of a rumour that paratroops had landed in the area, but no one had told us.

On another evening, we noticed a car parked near the aerodrome's perimeter fence. I stopped the lorry. The troops, led by the corporal, ran to the car and surrounded it, rifles at the ready. The corporal warily approached the car, and a few minutes later returned, laughing loudly. He discovered a courting couple in the car, and said: "It will take him a long time to get back to where he was when I interrupted them!"

He never explained what he meant by that remark.

We were supposed to rest and sleep during the day, and were not allowed out of the building. I had noticed the film at one of the cinemas was Charles Laughton in 'The Hunchback of Notre Dame'. I wanted to see this, so I persuaded a fellow driver, named Lionel Meech, to come with me. To get out of the building we said we were going to see our lorries, and were allowed out. We went to the lorries, looked at them, and then hurried to the cinema. As the lights were lowered two young girls came in and sat directly in front of us. We all became engrossed in the film, and when the hunchback carried Esmarelda up the outside walls of the tower, these girls became quite tense. One of them began wringing her hands and saying: "Oh! Oh! Ah!"

To help a damsel in distress I leaned forward and put my hand over her shoulder. She grabbed hold of my hand and held it tightly until the tense scene ended. Suddenly she realised she was holding my hand and dropped it, and seemed confused. Suddenly, both girls stood up and hurried to another seat. Lionel and I had a good laugh.

After a week of routine patrol, we were all recalled to East Cliff Lodge. A few days later the whole of 4 GHQ Company RASC left Broadstairs and moved to the Swindon area. Our platoon was directed to a field just outside Swindon town. We found ourselves sleeping in circular tents: 12 men to a tent and all feet to the centre pole. This was very different from the comfort of East Cliff Lodge.

CHAPTER TWO

After Dunkirk

We arrived in Swindon on Monday 27th May, 1940. The following Friday (31st May), we were roused at 3am and ate a very hurried breakfast, filled the petrol tanks of the lorries, and reported to Swindon railway station. We had not been told any details of the job we were on until we arrived there. We learned that we were there to provide transport for soldiers returning from France.

We had been told nothing of the state of affairs in France and Belgium; knew nothing of Dunkirk; nor of the evacuation of the British Expeditionary Force (BEF) until then.

We could hardly believe it. We had been told we were going to France. Then we were told it was cancelled. Now there were panic stations as our troops were pushed out of France.

When the first train pulled into the station and the troops came on to the platforms, we saw the BEF in their exhaustion and misery.

Women with tea trolleys went among the troops giving them tea and cigarettes. Civilians and railway staff helped soldiers to look after these bedraggled, weary warriors. The returning soldiers showed their exhaustion and despair. Many were dirty, their uniforms grimy and dishevelled. Some did not have complete uniforms. Some had caps; some wore tin hats; others were bare headed. One or two were wearing French steel helmets, and some had lost their boots. It was heartbreaking to look at them.

We led them to the waiting lorries and helped them to climb up into the back of the lorries. One soldier, about five feet two inches in height, carried a very large French cavalry sabre, which looked most out of place in the hands of such a short man. He used it almost as a crutch. As I went to help him up into the lorry, I said: "I'll hold your sabre while you climb up."

He clutched the sabre to him and said, quite fiercely: "That's all I have had between me and Jerry, and I ain't letting go of it now."

Not all these men had come out of France via Dunkirk, but they all presented a shocking sight: very tired, dirty, exhausted. Some were listless and bewildered and needed extra help. Every one of them needed help to get into the lorries. Some had to be lifted up: they could not make it in their own strength. Some sat glum and silent. Others talked of their experiences.

This was our first glimpse of the British Army in defeat and retreat. It was a sobering sight. We took the men to various camps that had been hastily prepared in the countryside around Swindon. As soon as we had delivered our exhausted travellers, we returned to Swindon station to await another trainload. We transported the BEF from 6am until 8pm. I returned to camp and was in bed for 8.30pm, glad my 17.5 hour day was over.

The next day, some of us were detailed to take the BEF to public baths in Swindon and to stay with them while they bathed to make sure they did not fall asleep in the water. Some were too exhausted to bathe themselves and we had to bath them.

On Tuesday 4th June, 1940, I attended a concert party rehearsal in preparation for a concert for the BEF the next evening. The concert was held in a large hall somewhere in Swindon. The Mayor of Swindon was present and so were a number of French officers and all the officers of 4 GHQ Company RASC, plus local dignitaries, the BEF and other troops.

While at Swindon, I was able to attend Sunday services and some midweek activities at the Tabernacle Baptist Church there. The minister, the Rev C H Cleal, M.A, and the members of the church made me - and the men I took with me - very welcome. Some of them even invited us to their homes for a meal, but I don't know how they could do that on their meagre rations.

While we were at Swindon, our platoon suffered its first casualty.

Driver N A V Lake, a dispatch rider, met with a serious accident on 8th June 1940, and suffered severe injuries to his spine and neck. He was in hospital for a long time and we never saw him again.

Tuesday 11th June was a day of great excitement. Seventy drivers were warned to stand-by for immediate posting, possibly to France or parts unknown. We didn't think it could be France, and speculation ran high. At the last moment the posting was cancelled and we never found out what it was all about.

The effect upon all of us was sobering, and our future looked uncertain. I sent home to my parents several of my personal things, just in case I should be posted at short notice, perhaps overseas. I learned later that the arrival of my parcel greatly upset my mother.

While at Swindon I had to report sick and was told I had fluid on the knee. This was due to a knock on the knee while I was at Ramsgate on patrol duty. I was confined to camp and told to rest my knee. I used my enforced leisure time to write letters.

Scotty Heseltine was in the same tent as I and we often had a musical time together: Scotty playing his guitar and me singing. We did not know until much later that many men came near our tent to listen to our musical efforts.

Scotty was out every day driving his lorry on various details so, one day, he asked me to write a letter to his wife because he did not have the time to do so. I knew he disliked writing letters so his letters to his wife were few and far between. For a joke, I wrote a letter to Mrs Heseltine, telling her how very busy Scotty was, while I was writing on his behalf because I was on the sick list and had time to write letters. I showed the letter to Scotty, but instead of reading it, he put it in an envelope and sealed it, addressed it to his wife.

About a week later, Scotty came to me and said: "You've got a letter from my wife. I know her handwriting. Open it and tell me the news."

I opened the envelope and began to read, but Scotty demanded I read it aloud. Not knowing what I would be reading aloud, I did as requested. In the letter was a request: 'Please give Scotty the enclosed strings.' I remarked: "I didn't know you had broken a string on your guitar."

"I haven't," replied Scotty. "Give me the strings."

I took them out of the envelope and handed them to Scotty who roared with laughter, then said: "These are harp strings."

His wife was an excellent harpist, and it was her way of suggesting his long silence indicated he had gone above to play a celestial harp.

I returned to full duties on 13th June and, the next day, 4 GHQ Company RASC left Swindon and eventually arrived at Newbury. We were billeted in tents in the grounds of Donnington Castle Hall. Some of us were in a large marquee. It was accidental but, on our side of the tent, the names of the men were in the order of our bed space: Bigg, Joslin (who had been a professional footballer), Fouracre, Heseltine, Little, Long, Small and Smallman. The sergeant thought we were being funny. Our beds consisted of three seven feet long planks, each a foot wide, and these rested on small trestles six inches high. This was an improvement, because we were now off the damp grass.

Newbury Racecourse had been turned into a vast Army dump, mainly for food. There was even a light railway used to move the stores. We often went there to move the stores or to load or unload lorries. Men of the BEF were also sent there to help in the work.

One day I heard someone shouting my name over and over again. I looked around and saw a soldier running towards me. It was Fred Bateman, with whom I had been friendly when living in Weymouth. He had been a fellow-tenor in the church choir.

Fred had been in the Territorial Army RASC and so had been called up at the beginning of the war and sent to France. While awaiting embarkation at Southampton he had recognised Mr W Allen, the owner of the W A M Tyre Company, for whom I worked, and had sent me a message that he was on his way to France. Now I knew that he had made it back in safety to England.

We were able to stay together for five hours as we worked on the stores. Fred later was sent to join the 8th Army in the desert of North Africa and, after four years out there, was sent home. He went to serve with a tank transporter unit in North Wales. One day, Fred was driving a tank transporter down a very steep hill when it went out of control. As Fred jumped out of his cab, the tank his vehicle was transporting fell on him and killed him. This happened just a few weeks before his wife gave birth to their only child.

Most of my time at Newbury was taken up with working at the Racecourse dump, with occasional visits to the local cinema and attending meetings at Newbury Baptist Church, plus digging long and deep slit trenches and filling sandbags. The weather was very hot and sunny.

While I was there, an incident occurred that was to affect me for the rest of my time in the Army.

● Fred Bateman.

When talking about what we had done or been in Civvy Street, I had mentioned that I had been a member of the St John's Ambulance Brigade. This comment had passed unnoticed, as I thought, until one night at Newbury I was called from by bed at 11.30pm and told there had been an accident at the cookhouse and I was needed. When I arrived at the scene of the accident I found one of the cooks who had spent the evening in the local public house, had tried to cut himself some slices of meat but, instead, had cut his hand very badly. I treated him and sent him to hospital. That was when I became the unofficial medical orderly for our platoon - and also for others. After that, I took every opportunity to learn all I could from medical officers, especially from those whom I helped on occasions. I had to scrounge most of my medical kit because the official issue was very small.

Tuesday 25th June was a fateful day for many of us. The whole company was vaccinated, except Scotty. He refused, despite the medical officer's attempts at persuasion, and then orders. He continued to refuse despite the demands of the company sergeant major. Consequently, his paybook was inscribed in red ink: 'Refused vaccination.' This meant that if Scotty died through lack of vaccination his widow would receive no pension.

About a week later we began to feel the after-effects of the vaccination. It was then that I was told I was to be 'E' section office clerk. Despite my protests and excuses I was told that, since I had been a manager of a tyre company, I must have some experience of keeping books, records, and writing reports and therefore I would become section clerk forthwith. The commander of 'E' section was Lt J S Dorling, who later became a major and took command of 237 Company RASC. Later still, he became Lt-Col Dorling, a deputy director of supplies and transport in Malta.

My aching arm and my new status did not prevent me being put on guard duties at Newbury Racecourse on 6th July. By Monday 8th July, I was so ill with vaccine fever that I was confined to bed - and so were most of the other men. Our marquee was like a hospital ward. We tried to help each other as best we could but Scotty was a real ministering angel to us all. By 13th July, most of us were able to get up and move around, and the medical officer came to see us and change our dressings.

On Wednesday 17th July, 4 GHQ Company RASC ceased to exist.

The company was divided into three groups. One group became 237 Company. I found myself in this company, together with many of the men I had been with in training camp. The second group became another company, while the third group were posted to a mobilisation company for redistribution to other companies. Scotty was in the third group and so I parted with a very good friend, and never heard of him again.

But it was at this time I met Bill Aish, who was batman/driver to Lt Dorling. Our duties brought us together and we continued to serve together for the rest of the war. After the war our friendship continued and we met occasionally, but always kept in touch - and we still do.

My first narrow escape from death in the Army occurred on Tuesday 23rd July. I was on guard duties at Donnington Castle Hall and was in the guard tent (in place of a guardroom). I had just picked up my rifle and tin hat to walk out to relieve my friend, Bert Matty, who was on sentry duty fairly near the guard tent. As I walked through the door of the tent I could see Bert and walked towards him. Suddenly a rifle shot rang out and Bert fell to the ground. Several of us ran towards Bert, when the guard commander shouted: "Stay where you are."

Turning to me he said: "Not you. You will be needed. Get to him as quickly as you can."

I dropped my rifle and tin hat and ran to Bert. One glance was enough to realise he was very badly wounded. The wound in his chest and the large wound in his back indicated there was very little anyone could do for him. I called for a lorry to take him to hospital and I went with him. He died very soon after entering Newbury Hospital. He was the first fatality in the newly formed 237 Company. In less than two minutes I would have been standing where Bert stood and he would have been in the guard tent.

The Local Defence Volunteers (LDV), the original Home Guard, were at the bottom of the field receiving rifle drill and musketry practice. Somehow a live round of ammunition had been placed among the dummy rounds and no one noticed. Bert Matty was accidentally shot and killed. An enquiry was held and a verdict of accidental death was returned. Bert was buried at his hometown of Stroud, Gloucestershire on 27th July.

We left Donnington Castle Hall on Thursday 1st August. We were awakened at 4am and eventually left the campsite at 6am. It was not just a straightforward move. We had to 'break bulk.' This was the name given to the normal RASC practice of dividing large quantities of rations into supplies for individual units of soldiers - often infantry battalions or support troops. The lorry drivers went to a large food supply depot and drew rations for so many thousand men. These rations were brought back to our composite platoon that divided the bulk rations into the amount required by the various units, worked out as so much per man. Then the lorry drivers loaded the unit supplies onto the lorries and delivered them to the appropriate unit. This exercise began at 11am and was completed by 11.30pm.

As section clerk, I did not drive a lorry but helped in various ways. I also attended to the paperwork, which included work tickets to enable the lorry driver to travel to his destination. I issued route cards for drivers, authorised petrol rations for each lorry, and tried to solve a variety of problems. I kept the section sergeant informed of what was happening, and also informed the section commander of numerous details, as and when requested. I was responsible for keeping records for each vehicle and ensuring that each vehicle had its monthly workshop inspection on time. I was also responsible for all sections' stores and kit replacement - plus the filling in of numerous forms and returns.

The move was accompanied by confusion, with all kind of situations to be coped with as well as the normal work to be carried out. We had breakfast at 5am and this consisted of something we were told was porridge, liver and a mug of tea. Our midday meal was a 'running buffet' and consisted of bully beef and Army biscuits, with a mug of tea. The Army biscuits were so hard that we could only break them by hitting them with the butt of a rifle. Our tea meal was in the early evening and consisted of a mug of tea, one cake and a small fruit pie (which, pre-war, usually cost three old pence). There was no supper, nor any kind of refreshment until the next morning.

Those who were not on duty slept where they could. I was able to find a place and slept from 2.40am until 4.25am, when we were all awakened. The world did not look attractive at that time in the morning. Breakfast at 4.45am was a one piece of corned beef, porridge, and a mug of tea. We moved out at 5.30am, not knowing our destination but hoping the section commander knew where we were to go. Someone recognised a part of the route and the word quickly spread: "We're heading for the south coast."

Eventually, as dawn began to break, we came to Dorking, then slowly ascended The Hog's Back. The view from the top of The Hog's Back compensated for the discomfort we had endured. At 7.30am we arrived in Crawley Down, Sussex. We halted in Sandy Lane, and the officers went ahead to inspect our prospective billets. While we waited, a very kind lady, named Mrs Warner, living at 'Mia Casa', brought out a large jug of tea and some biscuits and gave them to us. It was nectar of the gods to us.

Eventually we moved along the road to our new billet, Bankton House, Crawley Down, and the lorries were parked around the parkland surrounding the house. Immediately work began setting up the cookhouse and I set up office in a small room. I also found time to secure a sleeping place in one of the rooms.

Crawley Down was a small village, a fivepenny bus ride from East Grinstead, one and a half miles from Turners Hill and two and a half miles from Three Bridges. It was in the area over which the Battle of Britain was fought and we often watched the aerial combats taking place. Sometimes, the empty cartridge cases and pieces of anti-aircraft shell shrapnel fell among us.

One Thursday evening (15th August), we were called out to act as infantry troops to search for a German plane that had been shot down and was believed to have landed near Crawley Down. We found the debris of the plane scattered over three fields, and we also found the bodies of the crew. It was reported that, on that day, 169 German planes had been shot down and 34 RAF planes were lost.

While at Crawley Down we took part in a number of brigade exercises and, eventually, we were issued with our new brigade sign: a white circle to be sewn on the top of the battledress blouse sleeve, just below the shoulder. The same sign was painted on each vehicle.

● September 1940.

The white circle stood for 'O' for Oliver, the name of our brigade commander, Sir Oliver Leese - who later became a Lt-General and succeeded General Montgomery as commander of the Eighth Army in Italy. I saw him in Sussex and Italy, and met him socially after the war, when I lived in the Midlands.

We were now part of the 29th Infantry Brigade, which later became the 29th Independent Brigade. When civilians asked what the white circle meant we told them it represented a lifebelt because we were attached to the Royal Navy, but stationed in Sussex. This was to guard against careless talk, of which we were warned so often.

While stationed at Bankton House, a wasp stung me under my right eye. My face became swollen and I was taken to the casualty clearing station for treatment. Eventually, my eye became so swollen that it closed up.

A few days later, when the swelling had subsided, I was on guard duty. At the guard mounting parade we were inspected by the company sergeant major. When he stood in front of me and inspected me, he asked if I felt better from the wasp sting, and could I now see out of my right eye. I was touched by this unexpected show of sympathy and concern, and replied I was feeling better and could now see out of right eye. His voice changed and assumed a menacing tone, as he barked at me: "Then why didn't you see to clean the back of this button?"

Very early in our stay at Crawley Down, I paraded on the company church parade and we marched to the village church. Outside the church the order was given: "Other denominations, fall out."

I was the only one to fall out and march to the side of the parade. When the parade had moved off into the church, the sergeant major came to me and said: "Get your fatigue suit and report to the cookhouse."

I replied: "But I want to attend a church service."

"You have just fallen out of the church parade. Report to the cookhouse."

I tried again: "I am not Church of England. I am a Baptist."

A gleam came into his eye: "There is no Baptist church in the village. Get over to the cookhouse."

Again I tried: "I want to go to the Methodist church, which is the nearest thing to a Baptist church in this village."

A very stern note crept into his voice and an angry face glowered at me. He said: "You are not a Methodist, so get over into the cookhouse."

I tried one, last, desperate effort: "Very good, sir, but may I be placed on OC's Parade tomorrow morning?"

This was a most unusual request for a soldier to make. He paused.

"Why?"

"So that I may claim religious liberty, sir."

There was a pause, then: "You know too much. Go to the Methodist church."

Never again was I challenged by the company sergeant major when I fell out from a church parade, and I am sure he found out that I attended the Methodist church as often as I could. He probably heard that I conducted morning services there on several occasions. But I had established a principle, or perhaps safeguarded a religious principle. I know that, after this, other men were encouraged to make their stand and to exercise their right to worship God according to their own conscience.

Harry Waugh, our stores clerk, was told to check our reserve food stores that were kept in a wooden hut in the village. As section clerk, I had to go with him. As we moved the heavy boxes and sacks, the floor of the hut vibrated. Suddenly, a three-foot length of galvanised iron pipe slipped from its place in the rafters, and falling about three feet, landed on my head. I had just removed my tin hat so felt the full force of the blow. I was stunned for a moment but eventually carried on with the job. When he heard of the accident, Lt Dorling insisted I went to the Emergency Hospital at East Grinstead for examination and treatment.

At the Hospital a nurse tried to keep me there, but I persuaded her I felt well enough to return to my unit. This was my mistake, because the next day I had a terrible headache and suffered occasional attacks of giddiness and faintness. In 1982, an X-ray of my head revealed I had suffered at some time, a fractured skull, of which I was unaware. This had probably happened at Crawley Down, on 31st October, 1940.

The day after my accident, there was an air-raid in the evening, and bombs were dropped on Crawley Down - probably by a fleeing German pilot trying to escape. Two bombs dropped in the parkland where we kept our lorries and where the rations were divided up for each of the units in the Brigade. The next morning, we saw the effect of the bomb explosions. A large fragment of the bomb casing, measuring about 18 inches by 32 inches lay on my office desk, and several windows were broken in the stable we used for the section office and my office.

Out in the parkland, the lorry driven by Driver F S Bussell, lorry number 215124, had been blown up. The cab and chassis were undamaged and had settled down in the bomb crater. Tyres and tubes were alright but the back of the lorry, with its metal frame and canvas covering, had disappeared. The lorry had been loaded the previous afternoon with the

● 'Four Aces' in June 1941. From left: Drivers Hall, Aish, Little and North.

rations ready for delivery to one of the infantry regiments in the brigade. These rations were scattered far and wide. A bag of potatoes hung on the branches of a tree. Other foodstuffs were scattered about. A whole hindquarter of beef was stood on its end, the leg pointing forlornly to the sky. But it was not lonely. All the dogs of the village were gathered around this wonderful free feed. No one was injured, although one rabbit had, apparently, died of fright.

CHAPTER THREE

Sussex by the sea

We left Bankton House, Crawley Down, on Sunday 10th November 1940 and moved to a house near Five Oaks, a few miles from Horsham. The nearest Baptist Church was in Horsham; so I obtained a day pass on Sunday 24th November. I walked the five miles to Horsham and attended the service at the Baptist church. I was invited to have dinner with Mr and Mrs Brocker and spent the afternoon with them. I was invited to take tea with Mr and Mrs Larcombe, and went to the evening service with them and returned to their house for supper. The following Sunday I walked two and a half miles to Billingshurst and attended a service at the Congregational church there. After the service, I had a lift - by car - to Horsham and had dinner at the YMCA, where I spent the afternoon writing letters; then I went to the Baptist church for the evening service. I was fortunate to travel back to the billet by bus.

The following Sunday was a little different though. I went to Billingshurst for the morning service, but was on guard duty from 6.30pm. From 6.30pm until 3.30am we could hear the German planes on their way to London and also saw the glow in the sky of the fires, started by the bombs. Some of the bombers passed overhead on their way back to Germany.

On Christmas Eve, I decided to go to bed early, but was called at 10.30pm to attend to Driver D M Jones and took him to a hospital in Horsham. I arrived back at the billet about midnight to discover there had been a car crash outside our billet and I was immediately called to attend to two civilians, and I took them to hospital. Eventually, I went to bed at 2am. So much for my early night!

On Christmas Day, I attended a carol service at 237 Company HQ in Horsham in the morning. Our officer and senior NCOs served us our Christmas dinner. They also provided a barrel of beer for us but, being a teetotaller, this did not appeal to me.

In the evening, four of us were invited out to a social evening by Mr and Mrs Bryan. Lt

Dorling was billeted in their house and Bill Aish, as his batman, was well known to the family. Mr Bryan asked Bill to bring three friends with him for a social evening. Bill invited me, along with Johnny Jolliffe, who was our concert party pianist. Johnny had been the pianist for the dance band at the Regent Dance Hall, Weymouth, and he was a really good pianist and also piano-accordionist. He was my accompanist whenever I sang. We had a lovely evening, singing songs that were popular at that time, and chatting. Unfortunately, Johnny was posted from our company later and was sent to Crete, where he was killed.

On Boxing Day, Lt Dorling invited the section NCOs to a party at the Bryans' house. Bill Aish, Johnny Jolliffe and I were the only non-NCOs present. Johnny and I were invited to provide the musical entertainment. We sang popular songs of the time - especially by request, 'Begin the Beguine' and 'Sleepy Lagoon' - and solos from me requested by Lt Dorling.

On 31st December, we ended the year in true Army style with an inspection by a Lt-Col who was commander of the RASC for the area - usually referred to as CRASC. We spent two days cleaning everything in the billet and the surrounding area, as well as all the vehicles. The inspection lasted 20 minutes. After the inspection, the chaplain called and I had a good chat with him.

The chaplain was Padre Brown who, in peacetime, was the vicar of the village where Sir Oliver Leese lived. Somehow it was arranged that he would be chaplain in Sir Oliver's brigade.

Early in 1941 a number of men were posted to 237 Company and some of them arrived at No 1 Platoon. As clerk of the platoon office, I had to prepare nominal rolls and many other documents, and it was a hectic time. With the increase in numbers, No 1 Platoon was divided into three sections and re-named supplies wing, with Captain Dorling in charge. Lt Searle was in command of B section. Another lieutenant was in command of A Section, while Captain Butcher was in command of supplies section, which dealt with the dividing of rations according to the numerical strength of the various units in the brigade. This section was later re-named 'composite platoon' and consisted of ration issuers, butchers, clerks and various other soldiers.

I was transferred to HQ Section of supplies wing and was in charge of a small orderly room. My section consisted of Bill Aish, batman to Captain Dorling and W B Mason, a clerk, who later obtained a commission in the Middlesex Regiment. I had two despatch riders (DRs): Shorty Westlake and Harry Lintern. There were two drivers: George North, who drove a 15 cwt truck, and Frank Hall, who drove a three ton lorry. The HQ sergeant was Sgt D I Cruttenden, who later became company sergeant major.

The increase in size of supplies wing made it necessary for us to move to a larger billet - which was a mansion in its own large parkland, out in the country, between Five Oaks and Horsham. It was called Marlands. It was a beautiful house and was reputed to have a solid glass bath - although none of us ever saw it. B Section remained at Five Oaks.

After we had moved to Marlands, Padre Brown conducted a service each Sunday morning. This was a church parade and everyone had to attend. At the command, 'Other denominations fall out,' I always did just that.

One day, Padre Brown came into my office for a chat - which he often did - and asked me: "Why do you always fall out from the church parade?"

I replied that I was a Baptist, not 'Church of England'. He then proceeded to explain how, as Christians, we all belonged to the one church and that I would be welcome to attend, so could I not join in the service? Shorty Westlake burst out laughing at this point, and Padre Brown looked very hurt, and asked Shorty why he laughed.

Shorty said: "Who do you think leads the singing of the hymns in the service? It's EB."

To the original members of our platoon and those who shared training days with me, I was known by my initials, 'EB.'

Padre Brown looked surprised and said: "I have been trying to find out who has the fine tenor voice and leads the singing of the hymns from the rear of the room."

I told him that I always fell out and, when the parade was assembled and he was ready to begin the service, I would enter from the back of the room and stand at the rear of the congregation. I always led the singing because the men waited for me to start the hymn.

Padre Brown thanked me for the help I had been. He asked me not to 'fall out' but to come in with the rest of the parade. I told him: "I fall out to keep alive the principle of religious liberty so that we can worship God in the way we choose. I join the congregation to share in Christian worship, even though I may not agree with all you do or say or believe."

The padre held out his hand and said: "I admire your stand. Continue doing it, but do join us and continue to lead the singing."

I did this at every service held at Marlands.

About March 1941, 237 Company left the Horsham area and supplies wing was billeted in Bolebrook House, near the village of Hartfield, in Sussex. Bolebrook House was very old: it was believed to have been built in 1449 AD. One of the fireplaces was very large. An ox could have been roasted in it - and probably had been. The wooden panels on the walls were ancient and much of the floor was oak blocks. Naturally, it was believed to be haunted. The gardens were beautiful and the orchard was very large. It was in one of the orchards that Bill Aish taught me to ride a motorcycle. We 'borrowed' Sgt Cruttenden's motorcycle, but forgot to ask his permission first. The sergeant was mystified by the increased mileage on his speedometer readings and also by his petrol consumption, when he was not using his motorcycle very often. Since I handled petrol permits and kept records of all vehicles, I assured the sergeant I would see it was covered up.

While we were at Bolebrook, arrangements were made with a local laundry to collect our laundry and return it a week later. This led to frequent mistakes in the articles returned. One week, Shorty Westlake, who was about five feet four inches in height, received a pair of 'long john underwear' that had been made for someone at least six feet tall. Late at night, just before 'lights out', Shorty put on these outsize 'long johns' and fastened them over his head. Keeping his arms to his sides and walking in stocking feet, he silently glided out of our room and along the corridor, looking like half a man. In the dim lights of the corridor he glided slowly along. The next morning, many men swore they had seen a ghost along the corridor: the ghost of a tall man cut in half. The truth about the 'appearance' of the ghost was never told.

While at Bolebrook, I was given a stripe because of the nature of the work I did. I did not want to be a lance corporal but was told by Captain Dorling that I was to accept the promotion.

As Captain Dorling's batman, Bill Aish had been told beforehand that I was to be given a stripe. He thought I was mad to accept it. Then I explained that he and I would be due for leave in a few weeks time and I would arrange for us to go together. We would overstay our leave, I would take the blame and so lose my stripe and we would have enjoyed extra leave. He agreed to the plan.

When we went on leave, Bill went home to Nailsea in Somerset and I went to Oakdale in South Wales. I left home on the correct date for my return but left the train at Bristol and caught a bus to Nailsea, where I stayed with Bill and his family for two days. Bill and I then decided to return to our unit.

We eventually arrived at Forest Row railway station and set off to hitchhike to Hartfield and Bolebrook House. As we walked along the road enjoying the scenery and sunshine, we heard a vehicle approaching and turned towards it in the hope of a lift. Bill said: "That's torn it. That's Jack Dorling driving my PU. Now we're for it."

Captain Dorling saw us and stopped, and invited us to get in. Bill sat in the front and I climbed into the back of the pick-up, with our kit. The captain asked if we had enjoyed our leave and we said that we had. Nothing was said about being late in returning from leave. When we arrived at Bolebrook Bill and I hurried away to our room.

Next morning, at 9am, I reported to Captain Dorling - as was my daily custom - to receive orders for the day and so on. I began by saying: "I am sorry Aish and I were late back from leave, sir. It was entirely my fault and I accept full responsibility."

He looked up, studied me for a minute, then said: "That's alright, corporal. Don't worry about it."

Then he went on to deal with the business for the day.

When I returned to my office, Bill greeted me with the words: "You've still got that stripe on your arm."

I explained what had happened and Bill said: "What are you going to do now?"

I replied that we would get as many day passes as we could, chance our arm more often, and if we were caught out I would take the blame and return to the rank of driver. After that incident, Bill and I took many chances in various ways. We took a day's leave officially and unofficially but the more we chanced our arm, the more we got away with - and I did not lose my stripe.

On 29th June, I was told by Captain Dorling to pack my kit immediately because I was to report to Tregantle Fort, Plymouth, to attend a gas instructor's course. The course had begun that day and I should have left the day before to begin the course at 9am. Hurriedly, I packed my kit, remembering to take my respirator (gas mask), and was rushed to the nearest railway station to begin my journey to Tregantle Fort, where the 38 Division gas school was held. I arrived at the fort on 30th June and stayed for the full course - which ended on 11th July.

I was the last arrival and was soundly reprimanded for arriving late. My explanation - that I was not told about the course until the previous afternoon - was not believed. It was implied that I had not gone direct to the fort from my unit. Since all the squads had been formed, I had to be fitted in somehow. Apparently, a sergeant had been expected; so I was put in the squad composed of sergeants and under the command of a company sergeant major, who was the squad instructor. Since I was the only lance corporal in the squad, I was rather conspicuous.

After several lectures had been given, it was announced that each member of the squad would give a lecture on some aspect of the training so far received. The previous day we had been told the subject of the lecture we were to give, and the time we would be giving the lecture. The sergeants in the squad, who came from various infantry units, were greatly distressed at the prospect of giving a lecture, especially in the presence of the company sergeant major (CSM).

Most of the sergeants made a poor show of giving their lecture. When my turn came, the CSM made it plain that, since the sergeants had made such a mess of lecturing, a mere lance corporal would be worse than awful. I had prepared my lecture notes as I would have prepared my sermon notes: all set out and leading from one point to the next in proper sequence. My experiences as a local preacher and speaker at various church services and meetings now stood me in good stead.

I began my lecture full of confidence, speaking clearly and without nerves. I had been speaking for about ten minutes when the CSM interrupted.

"Alright, ask for questions," he barked at me. I did so and was able to answer the questions asked.

After the lecture session the CSM said to me: "You've given lectures before, haven't you?"

I confessed I had done quite a lot of public speaking, and had also been a local preacher. He seemed satisfied with my answer. Later, in the barrack room, three of the sergeants who were to give a lecture the next day, asked me to help them to prepare their lecture notes and give them tips on how to speak in public and give a lecture.

The next time I had to give a lecture, the CSM allowed me to speak for five minutes, then said: "Alright, you know how to give a lecture. No need for you to go on. Ask for questions."

After the course was completed, I learned that I had missed qualifying as a sergeant instructor in gas by only a few marks. However, as a result of taking the course, I was officially qualified to instruct in gas, and this was entered in my paybook (AB 64 Part 1) on 19th July. Whenever we had a training period in 237 Company RASC, I was the official gas instructor. I also gave lectures on first aid and associated medical subjects.

While at Tregantle Fort, I discovered that Ron Price was stationed in Plymouth and we arranged to meet. Ron and I were together in the Pontllanfraith Technical Institute and, when I went to Weymouth, I found Ron already living there, and we often met. Ron had joined up a few months before me and had been posted to an infantry regiment. During air raids on Plymouth, which severely damaged the town, Ron had been commended for his gallantry in rescuing wounded and injured people. I had been to Plymouth before the war and was shocked to see how severely damaged it had been.

The implication that I had not made my way directly to Tregantle Fort annoyed me. I had told the truth and had not been believed. On my return journey from Plymouth, I changed trains at Yeovil, leaving the London bound train and boarding the train bound for Weymouth. At Weymouth station the ticket collector told me I had come the wrong way and had to catch the next train to London. I had known him when I lived at Weymouth and so persuaded him to look the other way while I slipped out into the town. I went directly to the home of Mr and Mrs Ernie Margrie, where I had been living before the war. I was made very welcome, and I wondered how they were able to feed me on their meagre rations.

The next morning, I left Weymouth reluctantly and went to London and then on to Sussex. On arrival at Bolebrook, I discovered 237 Company RASC had moved to another part of Sussex. I eventually tracked down supplies wing to Blackboys, a few miles from Uckfield. We were billeted in a former holiday camp called Royhill.

I reported to Captain Dorling, who greeted me with the words: "What are you doing here? We did not expect you back for at least another two days."

If only I had known, I could have stayed in Weymouth, and I grieved over losing two days 'free' leave.

At Royhill, I was given another clerk for my small orderly room: a Private Richie. He was man with a great sense of humour - often very dry - and he often brightened our day.

Later, he was posted to another company and we believe he was sent to India, but no one heard anything of him.

At this time I was also put in charge of the supplies wing stores. One day, I reported to the supplies officer that the jars of rum we had received from one of regiments seemed rather light in weight. The officer and I, behind locked doors, broke the seals on the stoppers in the rum jars and discovered each jar was only two-thirds full. The officer filled the jars up to the top with water, replaced the stoppers, melted the sealing wax, spread it over the top of the stopper and pressed into the soft wax his RASC regimental button, which had the royal cipher on it. It all looked most official. There were never any questions asked about those jars of rum. Later, Captain Dorling told me that I was now in charge of the rum store. I protested that, as a teetotaller, I did not want to handle the rum. He replied: "It's because you are a non-drinker that I've put you in charge of them. You are the only one I can trust with it."

At Royhill there was a swimming pool and, since the weather was very warm, some of the men used the pool. One day, a man we called 'Uncle', a native of Sussex, who had been a farm worker all his life, had a slow way of speaking and was completely unflappable, was watching the men swimming. He was puffing contentedly at his pipe, when he slowly removed his pipe from his mouth and said: "I think that fellow over there is drowning."

His companion asked: "Why do you think that?"

"Well, that's the third time he's gone down under the water."

There was a mad dash, a quick dive, and the drowning man was rescued.

Royhill, being a former holiday camp, was ideally suited for an Army camp. The living quarters, the cookhouse, mess halls, the office block and other buildings, formed three sides of a square. Between the main living quarters and the cookhouse was a level plot of land, and this became the parade ground. It was here that the guard mounting parade was held at 6pm each evening. One very warm day I had come off duty, had my tea-meal, and had changed into my PT slippers, and had removed my jacket. For some reason I wanted to see the corporal in charge of the cookhouse, George Barnett. I left my quarters and walked to the cookhouse.

I had forgotten that the guard mounting parade was taking place until I arrived behind the guard, who were lined up awaiting the arrival of the orderly officer. I hurriedly walked behind the parade, unobserved.

I was about half way across the perimeter of the parade ground, when I sneezed. I have a very loud sneeze - especially if it comes without warning. My sneeze bellowed across the parade ground and the whole parade came smartly to attention, probably thinking the orderly officer had come up behind the parade to try to catch them out.

Suddenly, I saw the orderly officer come out of the supplies wing office and march towards the parade ground. I knew that I would be in trouble for appearing on the parade ground during a guard mounting parade and also for being 'improperly dressed' on the parade ground. Using my best sergeant major voice I shouted: 'Stand at ease' and the whole parade smartly stood at ease. I turned and ran back to my billet and the mystery of the phantom commander remained unsolved.

On each guard mounting parade, the orderly NCO inspected the guard, then the orderly sergeant inspected the guard and, finally, the orderly officer inspected the guard.

At Royhill we had somehow acquired a small dog - no one knew where he came from, but he adopted us. He was given the name Blanco, after the powder we used to colour our webbing equipment. Blanco would walk with the orderly NCO and stand and look at each member of the guard as if inspecting them as the orderly NCO did so. Blanco repeated this procedure with the orderly sergeant and again with the orderly officer. He knew his drill because he was always the last one to walk along the line of men. It was amusing to see this little dog solemnly look up and down at each man on parade. When the guard marched off to the guardroom, Blanco trotted alongside them until he wheeled off to his own quarters.

About a mile from Royhill Camp on the road to Blackboys, by a junction on the main road, was a small Methodist church. Whenever I was free on a Sunday morning I attended the service there. The circuit minister was the Rev Gordon Scott and, when he discovered that I was a local preacher, he asked me to preach at this small church. The first time I went there to preach there were five people present and no organist. I had to play the introduction to the hymn on the piano, usually with only one hand (I had neglected my piano practice), and then led the singing. The people were very friendly and I enjoyed my time spent with them. When it became known among the men that I was preaching at the Methodist church, several men came to the service. Some of them also came with me to the church when I was not preaching.

I preached at that Methodist church on many occasions, and at one service there were only three people present, and no organist. Because of transport difficulties, Gordon Scott was very pleased to have a preacher more or less on the spot. He invariably referred to me as 'the general', and I called him, 'great Scott.' When I met him later in a canteen in Souk el Arbour in North Africa, he greeted me as 'the general'. All the soldiers nearby jumped to attention and heard me reply, 'great Scott'. Gordon was a chaplain then, and later received an MBE for his services. I did not see him again, but he survived the war.

During our time at Royhill we sometimes took part in manoeuvres. Sometimes these were unpleasant but, on other occasions, they were enjoyable. We saw a great deal of Sussex and the neighbouring counties on these schemes. Often the food was not plentiful and the cooks had to work under difficulties. On one occasion we seemed to be very short of food. The cooks had built a 'field oven', which was a 40 gallon oil drum which had been well cleaned. The drum was placed horizontally on two rows of supporting stones and a shallow trench dug between the stones for the fire. Inside the drum, a grid had been fixed to hold whatever was to be cooked.

On one particular occasion, I arrived at the cookhouse the same time as the officer, who came to check that all was in order and preparations for the midday meal were in progress. Turning to the corporal in charge of the cookhouse, he asked: "What are you cooking?"

The cook made some reply. The officer opened the oven door and saw inside a chicken being cooked. He closed the door very carefully and turned around, and looking at one man said: "Where did you get it?"

Without batting an eyelid and with a serious look on his face, the cook said: "Well, it was like this, sir. That chicken was wandering around the cookhouse looking for food and I gave it a bit of corn I had found. When all the corn was eaten, and there was nothing more for the chicken to eat, it opened the oven door and jumped inside and closed the door after it."

This was too much for the men standing around and they laughed. The officer, with a very serious look on his face said: "Alright. But see I get a piece of the breast."

The man quickly replied: "You shall have two pieces, sir."

I don't know what happened to the chicken but I did not get any of it.

At Royhill, the NCOs had their own mess room, which contained a long table in the centre of the room. One mealtime, a corporal at the bottom end of the table called to a corporal at the top end of the table: "Bung my mug of tea down."

The recipient of the request waited until the mess orderly had filled the enamel mugs with tea, then picked up a mug and literally threw it to the corporal at the bottom end of

● Supplies Wing, at Royhill, 1941.

the table. It was a strange sight to see all the seated NCOs on both sides of the table lean outwards as the mug of hot tea came hurtling down the centre of the table. I don't think the corporal at the bottom end of the table caught his mug of tea.

One day, a corporal called Ben was riding his motorcycle along a country lane and saw a farm worker hedging and ditching. The worker had a red flag jutting out of the hedge to warn motorists of his presence. Ben snatched the red flag as

he passed and brought it back and hung it on the wall in the NCO's mess. This flag was the cause of many comments - mainly about the red flag of communism. The flag had been hanging on the wall for about ten days when the orderly officer noticed it during his inspection of the billets. The officer nearly had a fit. He thought all the NCOs had become communists. In no uncertain language, he ordered that the red flag be removed.

On another occasion, a despatch rider saw a man working on the roadside in country lane, hedging and ditching. This farm labourer had placed his wheelbarrow with the handles on the ground and the wheel in the air, obviously as a seat for him. The dispatch rider

drew his revolver and fired a couple of shots through the bottom of the wheelbarrow. The farm worker was standing some distance away, but at the sound of the shots he leapt over the hedge, and from a standing start, cleared the top of the hedge with room to spare.

After a long time at Royhill, I asked to be relieved of clerical duties and to return to a working section. I was transferred to the relief driver increment of supplies wing. The section NCO was Phil Joslin, who had been a professional footballer. He was often away from supplies wing playing football, usually for Arsenal FC. After the war, he was goalkeeper for Cardiff City for many years.

The summer of 1941 was warm and sunny, and it was very pleasant to walk along the country lanes. We were also able to obtain leave passes to visit Tunbridge Wells

● As Guard Commander at Royhill.

for the day, and were able to visit many other places within easy reach.

One of our main leisure activities was playing 'Monopoly'. A Monopoly set had arrived in a 'comforts for the troops' parcel, and the donor could never have imagined the pleasure it gave to the troops. Every time a game was played, the players were surrounded by a crowd of onlookers.

CHAPTER FOUR

Hertfordshire to Scotland

2 37 Company RASC remained in Sussex until the end of October 1941, and then moved to Ware, in Hertfordshire. 'A' platoon, under the command of Lt Cheeseman, was billeted in a large house on the Hertford Road, called Chadwell House. After the War, this house was demolished and a housing estate built on the site.

We had been in Ware for a few weeks when men from the Beds and Herts Regiment who were unfit for infantry duty were posted to our company. This involved setting up a driving school, which was billeted in Hertford. It also prompted the setting up of a training programme for the company. I was the instructor for gas training and first aid lectures, among other things. It also meant a great deal of marching, foot drill and arms drill.

We were heartily sick and tired of all the foot drill and marching - and of repetitious rifle drill. One morning, I was told to take a section of men and give them drill for half an hour, and to do so on the wide drive just in front of the billet.

The large room downstairs in Chadwell House was the officer's office and he looked out of the window at intervals to see that the drill was being carried out. I marched the men up and down in front of the window until the officer became engrossed in his paperwork. Then I marched the men to the end of the billet and told them to go around the corner and keep out of sight and have a smoke and a chat, but to fall in quickly if I called them. Then I went to the corner of the building and at intervals shouted out orders as if the men were really hard at their training. When it was time for me to hand over to another NCO, I marched the men in front of the officer's window. At that point, the officer said he thought the men had had enough foot-drill and I could dismiss them.

The whole company used the Drill Hall in Ware as its mess hall, and every section marched regularly from their billet to the Drill Hall.

For our platoon, it meant marching down the main Hertford to Ware road and over the railway level crossing. We felt rather silly when the level crossing gates were closed and we had to stand there until the train went through.

When I was Orderly NCO, I would try to get to the Drill Hall in an afternoon when no one was there and stand on the stage and practice singing. Sometimes Johnny Jolliffe, who was a cook but had been a dance band pianist, would come into the hall and play the piano. This was great fun and served as a singing lesson. Sometimes, civvies would come into the hall to listen to us practising.

While in Ware I attended the Methodist church as often as I could. I sang in the choir - singing solos on special occasions - and preaching on Sundays or speaking at midweek meetings. I made many friends at Ware, especially with Mr and Mrs Wiggall and family, who appropriately, were hairdressers.

During our stay in Ware, the company was used as a general transport company. This usually meant that a driver would be called at 5am. There was breakfast in the Drill Hall at 6am, followed by a trip to the vehicle park to collect a lorry and leave at 7am. The journeys varied, but they usually involved driving 200 or so miles in the day and returning to the billet about 11pm, or later. Much of the driving was during the hours of blackout, with practically no lights. Often, during the winter months, we were driving in rain, snow and fog. One day, I left Ware at 7am and drove to Colchester, collected equipment for Home Guard units and delivered it at various places - the last of which was the Drill Hall at Watford. We often went to Poplar, London, to collect rubble from bombed buildings, and take it to Army depots, camps or aerodromes in the making. I once took a load of rubble from Poplar to Cambridge.

In January 1942, while at Ware, I was sent on detachment to Waddesdon, near Aylesbury, in charge of a transport section. We were attached to a petrol depot, which was in a field alongside the main road from Waddesdon to Aylesbury, about a mile from Waddesdon and five miles from Aylesbury.

The place was a sea of mud, except where the surface had frozen solid. We were billeted in a Nisson hut, in which almost all the windows were missing or broken. Most of the holes were stuffed with sandbags or rolls of paper - or anything else that would help to reduce the draught. In the centre of the hut was an old-fashioned iron stove, with the chimney going up and out through a hole in the roof. The stove was fed with coke, and the many draughts wafted the fumes around until they escaped through one of the many holes in the windows. Everything was covered in frost, snow and ice, and it was exceedingly cold. At about 8.30am, we would fill a topless four gallon petrol can with water and leave it on top of the stove until 6pm, when about ten men would share the warm water. The water would be poured into a bowl and this was not thrown away until at least four men had used it. The road conditions were also very bad, and often we had to drive along country lanes and narrow secondary roads, which were usually covered with snow or ice.

Recreation was very limited at Waddesdon, so I arranged for a lorry to be available most evenings for anyone who wanted to go to Aylesbury to visit the canteen or cinema. This was used by members of the staff of the petrol depot as well as by my own section. Life was rather grim at the depot because of the living conditions and the extreme winter weather, so that any diversion or temporary comfort was greatly appreciated.

One Saturday morning, I decided to give myself a 36 hour pass. I had agreed for some of the men to have a leave pass each weekend, as duties permitted, but had not taken advantage of the privilege myself. I now decided to visit my friends Fred and Dolly Hammett, who lived in Shipton-under-Wychwood. I had known Fred and Dolly in Weymouth, where we had become very good friends. Fred was a manager for a grocery firm and had been transferred to Shipton. I hitchhiked from Waddesdon and eventually arrived in Shipton about 5pm and was warmly welcomed by Fred and Dolly.

On Sunday, after an early tea, Fred took me by car to Oxford and I found the train from Oxford to Aylesbury had been cancelled. Eventually I found a bus going to Thame, where I arrived at 10pm. There were no buses to anywhere at that time of night, so I set off to walk eight miles to Waddesdon along a route I had never travelled. There were no sign-posts, but a few people I met gave me directions. After walking for a very long time I met a man who advised me to turn down a lane and go through a wood, and that would save me walking several miles. This was at 2am.

I followed his directions and floundered through snowdrifts, grateful for a clear path-

● Fred and Dolly Hammett, with their son, Raymond.

way now and again. Eventually I heard voices and discovered a small outpost with soldiers guarding something or other. They gave me directions to get to Waddesdon and I trudged on. I arrived at the depot at 4am and was glad to fall into bed to sleep until 6.30am, when we began another day.

At the end of February, my section and I were recalled to Ware. In March, 237 Company RASC left Ware and travelled to Scotland. We travelled in convoy, which must have disrupted traffic all along our route. We halted outside Doncaster racecourse for our night's rest, with our lorries spaced out along the road. We slept in our lorries and we were very grateful for the civvies who brought us hot water in the morning, so that we could wash and shave. After breakfast, we continued our journey, and halted for the night at a transit camp in Carlisle, about 6pm.

After a meal and a wash, most of us went to the NAAFI Canteen. There were several hundred men in the camp, apart from our company, and the canteen was full. After a while, Johnny Jolliffe and I went to a piano on a stage and a group quickly formed around us. I realised there was no entertainment available, so I sent messages to members of the 237 Company Concert Party to come to canteen. We gave an impromptu concert that the troops seemed to appreciate, although it comprised only our usual items.

I was soloist and compère and a young girl in the ATS asked if I would sing the song, 'I'll be with you in apple blossom time.' I was not sure I could remember all the words, so I invited the girl to join me in singing it, and she quickly joined me on the stage. We held a quick conference with Johnny to make sure we were all in the right key, and we began singing. After the first verse and chorus, with my confidence increasing, I began to har-monise while the girl sang the melody. This must have sounded impressive because, when we finished singing, the applause was deafening. After that, we had to sing many more songs. When the concert was over, words or appreciation poured in and the NAAFI manager said that it was the best concert they had had in months.

The next evening, when we went into the canteen it was packed with troops, and I was greeted with shouts of: "When's the concert going to start?"

● February 1942.

Apparently, word had gone around about our concert the previous night and it was taken for granted we would do another show. The NAAFI manager hurried over to me and said: "Get the show going quickly. They've been waiting a long time for you to come in."

He would not accept my explanation that we had not planned a repeat concert so, again, I sent messengers to members of the Concert Party to get to the canteen in a real hurry. We gave another concert with slight variations from the previous night's programme and, again, our efforts seemed to be greatly appreciated.

The Transit Camp was called Hadrian's Camp. We left it at dawn the next morning and went on our way to Scotland. I travelled in the cab of a lorry driven by Archie McLelland who, in peacetime, had been a farm worker in Scotland. As we drove along, Archie explained what was happening on the land and why certain things were done in certain ways. I found the journey both interesting and informative.

Eventually we arrived at our destination. Company HQ and Workshop Section were billeted in an old jam factory in Coupar Angus. Supplies Wing was billeted in Meigle, with 'A' Platoon and the Relief Driver Increment billeted in Belmont Castle. This was not as grand as it sounds, because we occupied the lofts over the empty stables.

Once we settled down in our new billets, the usual 'spit and polish' programme started. We became fed up with the repeated orders to scrub our sleeping quarters; so when we received yet another command to 'scrub out', a bucket chain was formed and the water was poured on a certain part of the loft floor, until it seeped, trickled and eventually cascaded into the room below. That was the room that had been made into the Platoon Office, and in which the Platoon Officer sat. The reaction to the deluge of water was both swift and dramatic. There were no more commands to scrub out the sleeping quarters.

CHAPTER FIVE

Wedding Bells

The reason for our transfer to Scotland soon became known. We were now part of the 1st Guards Brigade, under the command of Brigadier F A V Copeland-Griffiths, DSO, MC. The infantry regiments in the 1st Guards Brigade were the 3rd Battalion Grenadier Guards, 2nd Battalion Coldstream Guards, and 2nd Battalion Hampshire Regiment.

I later discovered that Len Addoo was a clerk in the Quartermaster's Stores in the Hampshires. I met him when I delivered stores to the Hampshires in Forfar. Len and I were friends when we both attended Rosebery Park Baptist Church, in Bournemouth. I met him several times in Scotland, and then saw him during the battle of Kasserine Pass in North Africa. He was later killed in Italy.

The 1st Guards Brigade, with the 36th Infantry Brigade and the 11th Infantry Brigade along with other units, formed the 78th Division. The Divisional sign was a yellow battleaxe on a black square. Later this caused the German radio announcer 'Lord Haw Haw' to refer to us as 'Churchill's Choppers'. It became a famous Division, one of the best in the British Army, renowned for its skill in mountain warfare. The foundation for this skill was laid in Scotland in the many schemes and training exercises we endured.

Gradually there built up a tremendous esprit de corps: a very strong sense of comradeship between men in the division. If a vehicle bearing the sign of the Battleaxe was in trouble, other vehicles of the division would never pass by without offering help. This began in Scotland and continued until the division was disbanded. Any man wearing the Battleaxe could depend on help from anyone wearing the same sign. Irrespective of which regiment or unit one belonged to, the sign of the Battleaxe bound everyone together in comradeship. This was exemplified at the end of the war, when all men serving with the division made a voluntary financial contribution to enable the formation of the 78th Division Battleaxe Club.

This Club has met for a reunion dinner annually in London each November since 1947. It has also established branches in other towns, such as Leeds, and a town in Scotland. The same comradeship still exists between the survivors of 78th Division, and any man who has served in the division may join this elite club. The History of the 78th Division, 'Algiers to Austria' by Cyril Ray, was published in 1952 and reprinted in 1982.

We were told - though I cannot vouch for the truth of the statement - that 237 Company RASC had been especially chosen to serve with the 1st Guards Brigade because of our efficiency and smart turn out. We had always been a 'spit and polish' company with a high standard of smartness in appearance, a high degree of skill in foot drill and so on, plus an excellent record as a working company. This may have been flattery, but it was very encouraging at the time to be told this.

Any sense of pride we may have had was quickly checked. We were to begin a training programme. Of course, that is not an unusual practice but, this time, it was to be very different. Our training instructors were to be sergeants from the guards with a guards' drill sergeant in charge.

Drill Sergeant Knight was of fearsome appearance. He was about seven feet tall - a very big man - with a very big voice, and a fierce manner. His hands were huge and, when he saluted, his hands looked enormous. His badge of rank was a work of art. It was a circular badge about ten inches in diameter and was emblazoned with the Royal Coat of Arms. The guards' sergeants who were to train us thought they would treat us like a half-witted, untrained, inferior class of beings who had to brought up to the guards' standards in everything.

The training included everything being learned and performed the guards' way. We had been a general transport company for almost six months so that marching and exercises soon found muscles we had forgotten about. They had been at ease for such a long time. We marched up and down the roads of Meigle until we knew every stone in the road. We saluted every telegraph pole in Meigle. We did rifle drill, we were re-taught musketry as per the guards. The only thing we were not taught was ceremonial guard duties as for Buckingham Palace. Then we were taken on 'schemes' and became infantrymen.

Part of the platoon went first and took up positions on the mountainside, and the rest of the platoon had to charge up the mountainside to capture the positions. We charged up and down the hillsides until even in our weariness we recognised almost every bush and clump of heather. Sometimes thunder flashes were thrown very near us. They exploded with a loud noise and a bright flash of light. We were made to handle and throw live hand grenades. In fact, we became infantrymen almost up to guards' standards.

One of the schemes we went on covered a very wide area of action and was codenamed 'Dryshod'. The rain did not stop from the time we set out on the scheme until long after we had returned to our billets. We were grateful when we were back to transport duties and not playing soldiers. On these schemes we slept rough and meals were not always regular or attractive. One night, ten of us just lay down on the wet ground and pulled a large tarpaulin over us. It seemed a very long night.

On 'Operation Dryshod' we were hungry, wet through and very fed up. The captain who was responsible for training in our company came to a group of us and we complained about the conditions under which we were living and also about the lack of food. He had been a peacetime soldier and had risen to the rank of regimental sergeant major before being commissioned as a captain. He listened to our complaints and then disappeared in his car. After a while he returned and took from his car a large quantity of potatoes, telling us to boil them and make the best of the meal. Then he warned us not to go near a certain spot on the road in case the farmer had discovered some of his potatoes had joined the Army.

Another of the schemes took us around Loch Ern and Loch Tay. On this occasion, I was assigned to the party who looked for suitable sites for the overnight camp and set up the cookhouse and so on. This was, for me, a very pleasant job and I was able to enjoy the scenery. I was also medical orderly and attended casualties and also treated sore and blistered feet. I remember one site I chose on the banks of Loch Tay, with a stream of lovely clear mountain water flowing into the Loch. In the evening I arranged for the men to sit on the banks of the stream and soak their feet in the cold mountain water before I did my nightly foot inspection.

On returning from one of these schemes, Bill Aish told me there was a parcel for me in the platoon office. The parcel was from my mother and in it were Welsh cakes. These were always very much appreciated but, on this occasion, they were doubly welcome. Later, I received a parcel from Mrs Margrie, my landlady in Weymouth. I opened the parcel very carefully and found a bread-pudding still in its dish. I had hardly looked at the pudding when someone saw it and shouted: "A bread pudding."

I just had time to fall over the pudding, guarding it with my body, as an avalanche of hungry soldiers fell on me like a rugby scrum. I was allowed to sit up after promising that they should share in the pudding. I then cut the delicacy into small pieces and shared it with my comrades. Silence descended on the room as I think we all thought of home and of previous bread puddings that we had enjoyed with our families.

Our platoon canteen was a disused and almost derelict chapel. Bill Aish and another batman slept in one of the vestries. The first night they slept there, Bill was awakened by a blow in the chest. Switching on the light he could see nothing unusual, but almost as soon as he switched off the light something landed on his chest. Using a torch Bill shone the light into a hole in the wall when he heard a noise. A rat jumped out of the hole on to Bill's chest and down to the floor and scurried away.

During one of the schemes, a section of drivers found ourselves in Motherwell. Someone told us to drive to a certain road on a housing estate and wait there for further orders. It had rained all night and we were wet, tired and fed-up. About 10am, a middle-aged woman opened her front door and offered to boil water for us to make tea. We all had the necessary ingredients except for the boiling water. This kind lady allowed two of the men into her kitchen to make the tea and, when she saw how wet they were, she offered the use of her bathroom to anyone who wanted a hot bath. Several of the men accepted the kind offer and, while they had their bath, the woman dried their clothing. Others were glad just to have a wash in hot water. That woman's kindness was remembered for a very long while and, when I see the name Motherwell, I think of her with gratitude.

In April 1942, some of us were selected to go with the 1st Guards Brigade to the Isle of Wight, on a special secret mission. I was detailed to go as Medical NCO. We were not told where or why we were going. We were put on a train and the engine driver, fireman and guard were changed at various intervals on the journey to ensure no one knew where we were from or where we were going. No one had a complete picture of the journey, except us, and we did not know our final destination. Eventually we arrived on the Isle of Wight and the various units were spread over the island. The RASC were stationed at Freshwater.

The second night we were on the island there was a massive air raid, the first the island had suffered. During the raid, a naval gun in the field next to our camp opened up. We did not know it was there and the vicious crack of the gun firing gave us a fright, while the recoil of the gun shook the ground around us. In the midst of all the noise of planes diving, machine guns firing, anti-aircraft guns firing and this naval gun making such a frightening row, I heard a nightingale singing in a nearby tree.

The next morning news began to reach us of the damage done to towns and villages on the island and of civilian casualties, and also of casualties to our own units. It appeared that 1st Guards Brigade HQ was the main target and there had been heavy casualties. One report stated Brigade HQ had been wiped out, but this was never confirmed.

We also learned the reason for our visit to the island. We were intended to take part in a raid on the French coast. Eventually, we learned that it was a trial run for the later Dieppe Raid. Our effort was cancelled and the survivors returned to Scotland. Guardsmen later told us they were shown photographs of the French town, together with detailed photographs of the streets and buildings and special targets that they were to attack.

A special enquiry was instituted to discover the cause of failure of our secret mission. It was later established that, because of careless talk in a public house on the island by a member of the advance party - believed to be an officer - the enemy was prepared for our raid. We were told that the area where we were to land had been reinforced with troops and anti-landing devices. Where there had been one German division there were now three. Various types of barricades in the sea had been extended seawards by about 100 yards. Everything was set to give us a warm welcome. The German planes raided the Isle of Wight for the first time in an attempt to destroy both us and our equipment and so prevent the raid. One result from all this was the making of the film 'Next of Kin', a propaganda film about the dangers of careless talk.

While in Meigle, I was sometimes attached to Company HQ in Coupar Angus to take over the duties of Eddie Biscomb, the Company Medical Orderly NCO, while he went on leave. To live in a small town was always a welcome change from the isolation of a small village. The company workshops for the repair of vehicles were in what had once been a jam factory. Company HQ was in a large house. There were shops in the town and a restaurant, which became a teashop for the troops. Most of the staff there were Italians.

During one of my periods of duties at Company HQ, it was decided to give a concert in the local cinema-cum-hall. Most of our Company Concert Party were involved. It was suggested that, in addition to my regular solos, I should also perform my 'celebrated' potted version of a visit to the opera. In this skit on an opera, I sang three voices: tenor, baritone and soprano (falsetto), plus a voice to represent the chorus. I had a set type of sketch that I adjusted to suit local conditions or recent incidents in the company. There were always remarks poking fun at the company sergeant major, and, if possible, something aimed at the officers. They all took it in good part. This version of the opera was usually very popular and I was often asked to do it - and even received shouted requests from the audience during a show.

The day after the concert I went into the restaurant for the evening cup of tea and, as I walked to the counter, one of the Italian girls screamed out: "There he is."

Everyone looked around, including me, but it slowly dawned on everyone that the remark was aimed at me. The girl shouted again: "There he is."

I was getting worried and wondered what it all meant. Then the girl turned to the other members of staff and said: "He is the opera singer I told you about."

Then she came to me and said how very much she had enjoyed my efforts and that it was so true to opera. She asked me where I had studied singing, in which operas had I sung and a lot more questions. I had difficulty in persuading her that I had never had my voice trained, I had never sung in an opera, I was a self-trained singer but liked to go to the opera whenever I could. After that, whenever I went into the restaurant, I was greeted as 'the opera singer'.

Meigle was a small village and the only church was the Episcopalian (Church of England). The vicar was a very nice man. I met him a number of times and enjoyed talking with him, but I did not attend the services he conducted. I arranged to be guard commander on alternate Saturday nights so that the other NCOs could enjoy an evening in Dundee, which was 14 miles away. The reason for my actions was that, by being on guard on the Saturday evening, I was free on Sunday and could then attend the evening service at Alyth, at the Barony Church - the Church of Scotland. This meant that I had to catch a bus on Sunday afternoon about 4pm, arriving in Alyth about 4.30pm and waiting around until the service started at 6.30pm. Unfortunately, there was no cafe open on a Sunday. After a few visits to the Barony Church, I was invited to sing in the choir and, at the Harvest Services, I was asked to sing the solo, 'Thanks Be To God', which I did.

It was the custom, after the service, to go to the hall near the church that was used as a canteen for the troops and the Land Army girls who worked in the area. I usually had a belated tea meal, which consisted of beans on toast and a cup of tea. I was asked to conduct the community hymn singing, which began at 9pm. After hymn singing for about 20 minutes, someone - often me - gave a short talk on a Christian subject. One of the ladies who helped in the canteen was a very gracious lady, and she was godmother to Vivien Leigh, the film actress.

Bill Aish and his girlfriend, Yvonne, decided to get married in July 1942.

Yvonne was a sergeant in the ATS and was stationed somewhere in Yorkshire, attached to the Yorks and Lancs Regiment. I had met Yvonne when she came to Ware and spent her leave there to be with Bill. Bill was now a lance-corporal because he was batman/driver to Major J S Dorling, who was now the Officer Commanding 237 Company RASC.

The wedding day was arranged for 18th July, 1942. Yvonne travelled - alone, since none of her family could be present - to Meigle the day before the wedding. None of Bill's family could come from Nailsea in Somerset. I was the only person in Scotland that Yvonne knew, apart from Bill; so it was arranged that I would look after Yvonne on the wedding day until we arrived at the Episcopalian Church in Meigle. At the church, I would leave Yvonne with Corporal George Barnett, who would act as 'father' and give the bride away. Bill and I had talked with the vicar several times and all seemed to be safely arranged. George, Bill and I applied for leave passes. Bill's leave was for seven days, while George and I had 'day passes'.

The wedding day weather turned out fine.

Yvonne was billeted with a Scottish couple who lived in the staff quarters of Belmont Castle. At the appropriate time, I called for Yvonne, who was nervous and excited, although the good lady of the house did her best to reassure her. I opened the door and allowed Yvonne to step out into the courtyard of the castle, and then I joined her. A group of soldiers who belonged to 'Composite Platoon', plus members of 'A' Platoon, surrounded us immediately and began to bombard us with rice. I guess many Army units in the brigade went short on their rice ration the following week. Apparently it is the custom in Scotland to throw rice on the bride as she leaves her home to go to the church for the wedding. Neither Yvonne nor I were aware of this custom and were caught totally unprepared and had to run the gauntlet until we were outside the entrance to the courtyard. Bill was popular with everyone and the lads had decided to give Yvonne a real send-off, which I thought was a very nice gesture. It showed the wonderful spirit of comradeship that existed in our platoon and in the company.

Yvonne and I walked to the church, trying to remove the rice from the necks of our tunics and other places where it had penetrated. At the church door, I introduced Yvonne to George Barnett, and warned them not to hurry as they walked down the aisle. I went into the church to find Bill, and took him into the vestry to see the vicar and to check all the entries for the marriage register. I asked the vicar: "Where is the organist?"

The vicar hesitated for a moment and said: "We have no organist."

Panic stations. I said: "Stay where you are until I come back."

I made a hurried exit from the vestry and was pleased to see a large number of our fellows occupying the pews. I was especially delighted to see Sergeant Vic Eales sitting in the back row. I went to Vic and said: "Vic, there is no organist, so get up on the organ stool as quickly as you can, and be ready to play the Wedding March."

Vic turned pale and began to make excuses for not playing the organ. Vic did not read music but could play a large selection of tunes from memory. I cut short his excuses by saying: "There is no time to argue. It is time the service began, so do your best."

Taking his arm I almost dragged him to the organ console, pushed him onto the organ stool with the advice: "Try to find the right knobs and switches to make it work and I will delay the vicar until you let me know you are ready."

The vicar was looking concerned when I entered the vestry; so I said: "One of our sergeants will play the organ, if that is alright with you."

He nodded agreement. There was not much else he could do in the circumstances. A quick look through the vestry doorway; an appealing look at Vic, and a small flood of relief as Vic nodded his head. He was ready.

I looked back into the vestry and said: "Come on, let's go."

The vicar led the way, followed by Bill, and I followed him. As I passed Vic I had a quick word with him: "Wait for the bride to come through the door before you start playing."

Bill and I took our places before the vicar and looked to the front, and waited.

Suddenly the organ flooded the church with the strains of the Wedding March. Bill obeyed my instructions and looked straight ahead, but I glanced over my shoulder and saw Yvonne walking slowly down the aisle arm in arm with George. The organ music died away as Yvonne stood by Bill's side and the ceremony began. Afterwards we went into the vestry for the signing of the register. When all this was complete, I went to the vestry door and signalled to Vic that the bridal couple were about to emerge. Again, the strains of the Wedding March filled the church as Bill and Yvonne walked slowly from the vestry, down the aisle and out of the church. George Barnett and I slowly followed them.

It was grand to see so many of our fellows present at the ceremony. They had supported Bill and Yvonne, trying to make up for the absence of members of families and friends from Yorkshire and Somerset. Outside the church, someone produced a camera and photographs were taken, with the vicar included in the group, and many good wishes were expressed to the happy couple.

I went to Vic and thanked him for being the volunteer organist. Then I asked him: "What happened to the second and third lines of the Wedding March?"

Vic quietly answered: "Well, I could only remember the first bit so had to keep playing that bit over and over again."

I assured him that was fine.

Eventually the bridal party - Bill, Yvonne, George and I - managed to get away from the well-wishers and caught the bus to Dundee. On our arrival in the town, we made our way to the YMCA canteen. We were fortunate to find a vacant table to seat four people and Bill

went to order 'the wedding breakfast.' He came back with four portions of beans on toast and four cups of tea, with the necessary cutlery. I think we had something for desert, but cannot remember what it was.

After much talking, laughter and eating, we left the canteen and went to Green's Theatre to see a variety show. Bill had bought the tickets and we found ourselves in the front row. I don't remember much about the show but there was one number in which scantily clad chorus girls were dancing and coming very near the footlights. This was when I turned to Yvonne

● Wedding day at Meigle. From left: The vicar, Bryn Little, Bill and Yvonne Aish, and George Barnett.

and had a conversation with her. Bill interrupted our conversation by leaning in front of Yvonne and saying to me: "I bought these tickets for you to look at the dancing girls; not for you to chat-up my wife."

When the show ended, the four of us made our way to the bus station.

Bill and Yvonne were to stay for a few nights with some people Bill knew in Dundee, while George and I were to return to Belmont Castle, Meigle. We stood in the bus station chatting; then moved to the appropriate bus stop and waited for the bus to Meigle. When the bus arrived, George and I bade farewell to the happy couple and moved towards the bus. I was about to climb into the bus when Yvonne ran to me, and putting her arms around me said: "Oh, Bryn, don't leave me now!"

I had been with her all day and had shepherded her through the pre-ceremony fuss and through the ceremony, but I knew my place, and replied as I stepped into the bus: "Yvonne, you do not need me now,"

As the bus pulled away, George and I could see Bill and Yvonne, holding tightly to each other and we knew they would be alright.

During 1942, I had three periods of

● In Dundee, after the wedding.

leave at home. The first leave was in April.

Going on leave was a real experience and an occasion for much anxiety. We could never be sure that leave would not be cancelled at the last moment, that leave passes would not arrive on time, or that ration cards would be correct. The morning we were to go on leave was nerve-racking. We would try to persuade the sergeant to give us our leave passes as early as possible. But the leave passes always had to be issued by an officer. We would be ready - kit packed - ready to fly the moment we grabbed our leave passes and, all the time, anxiously watching for the sergeant bearing the precious bits of paper. We would grab the papers, give a quick look to see that everything was correct and then run to the waiting lorry, which would take us to Alyth Junction to catch the train the Glasgow Central Station. There would always be one person who would be late and a lorry load of anxious soldiers would be shouting encouragement or abuse to the luckless individual.

● With Bill Aish, on leave, 1942.

At last, the lorry would move and the driver would be encouraged in no uncertain language to put his foot hard down on the accelerator. Arrival at Alyth Junction was the signal for a mad rush out of the lorry and a scramble to the station platform. The train always seemed to take an age to arrive. If the train was late, we would not be able to make it to Glasgow Central Station in time to catch the London train. Eventually the train would arrive and we would struggle to get into the already crowded compartments and corridors, and then try to relax.

When the train arrived in Glasgow station, we all scrambled towards the main road, and there was a race to get on a tram going to the Central Station. How the civvies must had dreaded the periodic mad scramble by hordes of people in uniforms. On arrival at the Central Station, there was another race to find the right platform; then a struggle to get through the ticket barrier, followed by a search to find a place on the already crowded train. If you found a vacant seat, you were extremely fortunate - except for the fact that more people crowded into the compartment until it resembled a tightly packed sardine tin. Sometimes small men were lifted up onto the luggage rack and left there until they reached their destination. The corridors were packed with service personnel, plus stacks of kit.

The train on which I travelled left Glasgow about 5.30pm and I stood in the corridor until we reached Crewe, where I sometimes changed trains. I studied the countryside and watched the evening shades deepening in colour and enjoyed the sunset. Then came the seemingly solid blackness of night. It was a relief to get out of the train at Crewe, but the emptiness and desolation of Crewe station in the early hours of the morning was enough to sap the resolution of the stoutest heart. The arrival of another train meant another struggle to get aboard, followed by continued standing in the corridor in a close encounter with other bodies. The longing to reach home became intense. But we survived and still looked forward to leave. The discomforts of the journey only served to make the leave more enjoyable. The return journey was just as bad, but it was less pleasurable looking forward to our billet, because you often found you were on guard duties on the same evening you arrived back.

My second leave from Scotland was in August, when I had nine days leave. The special joy of this leave was that I was at home with my parents for my father's birthday. This was the first time we had been together for Dad's birthday since 1934, so the three of us greatly appreciated this.

The third leave from Scotland was seven days embarkation leave, which began on 18th November. This meant that I was home for my birthday for the first time since 1934. While I was at home we heard, on the radio, of the landings in North Africa, and I realised where I would be going. I told my father of the probability and said that if I went overseas, I would begin numbering my letters - starting at number one each time I arrived in a new country. I explained that I would not be able to give any details of where I was but he would be able to know by the Army address on my letters and by newspaper reports. We decided not to tell my mother while I was home, but Dad would tell her after I had returned to Scotland. That was a most enjoyable leave and I looked at my family, my home and the local countryside with keen eyes and very mixed feelings.

I arrived back in Belmont Castle, Meigle, on 25th November. The lorries had been waterproofed and had already left for loading on to ships. We prepared ourselves and our kit, for we realised where we were going. On 2nd December, 237 Company, RASC were moved by train to Greenock and embarked on the troopship 'Circassia'. This ship had been used in peacetime almost exclusively as a passenger ship in the Indian Ocean, but had been converted into a troopship.

Before we finally left Scotland, the troopship anchored in the Clyde for several days while the convoy assembled. We would soon know if our training and previous service and experience would be any use to us.

CHAPTER SIX

Life on the ocean wave

The troop train came to a halt somewhere in the docks area of Greenock. We climbed down from the carriages and walked along the railway lines towards the quayside. The usual uncertainty existed and we said: "General Confusion is in charge again."

Eventually, kitbags were collected and stowed somewhere in the lower depths of the ship. Each man was given a small square piece of green cardboard as we began to walk up the gangplank. This was mess deck information: the place where we were to live for the period of our voyage. Carrying our kit, we stumbled along corridors, down steps, through hatches, going ever lower into the ship. Eventually we emerged into a low vaulted area in which there were very long tables set at right-angles to the ship's sides, These were bolted to the deck. As each man came opposite to the end of a table, he was told to slide along the fixed seat running the length of the table. When the maximum number of bodies had been packed into the space on the seats, we were told to sit down and get sorted out because that was our space for the rest of the voyage. Kit was dumped on the table, under the table and under the seat. Behind this plank-like seat was a clear gangway along which we could walk, but our dwelling area was rather confined.

When it was time for a meal, we discovered that four to six men from each table went to the galley (cookhouse) to collect the food for the table. This was a long walk and, at times, was quite hazardous - especially when the ship was out in the open sea. Later we ventured onto the deck - or the parts of the deck that were open to the common soldiers - and we watched the activities on shore. After the tea-meal, we were shown where the hammocks were stored and told to collect a hammock and to hang it from hooks in the ceiling above our living space. This was another new experience for most of us.

We found the special hooks above our living area, and managed to fit one end of the hammock to it. Then we had to trespass onto another person's living space to fix the other end on another hook. This was done by standing on the table.

Tempers began to flare. Language became more lurid and insults hurled more frequently but, at last, the hammocks were slung. Someone tried to climb into his hammock and promptly rolled out again. This was greeted with gales of laughter, but the laughter ceased when almost everyone did the same thing. Somehow, by trial and error, we learned how to stay in our hammocks.

I found sleeping in a hammock very comfortable but, since we slept 'head to toe', it was quite difficult. To find a pair of feet on either side of one's head - and in very close proximity, in a hot, stuffy atmosphere because the hatches were closed at night - did not suggest cool sea breezes. The hammocks were lashed and stowed soon after reveille so that we could use the tables and living space.

Certain men were appointed 'meal orderlies' and it was their duty to carry the meals from galley to table. This was easy while the ship was in dock, but it became a real achievement once the ship got underway. The food was good, and the white bread was always fresh, soft and delicious. Drinking water was rationed; so washing and shaving were done in salt water. We soon found this made shaving very painful.

The practice was to try to shave before everyone had finished breakfast, and then catch an unthinking soldier with his cup of tea unguarded. A quick dip of the shaving brush into the tea - and a resultant brown lather - made shaving a little easier. We soon learned to keep one hand on top of our cups. It was a colourful session to see men with brown lather on their faces, and colourful language from those whose tea had been used. I often drank most of my tea and used the last inch of liquid for shaving. Once a shaving brush had been dipped into a cup, everyone around tried to make use of the now undrinkable tea.

While we were anchored in the Clyde, life on board was quite pleasant. We were assigned to our lifeboat stations, made aware of many rules that governed life aboard ship, and learned to find our way about. Those who had medical orderly experience were assigned to various posts on the ship where it was thought we would be most useful in the event of the ship being attacked. I was appointed to look after a machine gun crew (anti-aircraft defence), which was on the highest part of the ship's superstructure.

One of the things we all disliked was the fetid heat on the mess decks, especially when the hatches were closed at sundown which, at this time, was about 4pm. The hatches were re-opened at dawn, although it was possible to get out from the mess deck and walk around the deck or go to other parts of the ship until lights out at 10pm. I used every possible moment to get on deck and stay there as long as I could. I did this throughout the whole voyage, even in the worst of the weather.

During this pre-voyage period, auditions were held with a view to forming as many concert parties as possible. Our 237 Company Concert Party was distributed around the three concert parties formed, and I became part of 'A' Concert Party. Rehearsals were held in the lowest portion of the ship's hull. It was so far down that we could see both sides of the hull, and a short walk took us from one steel wall to the other. Later, when the ship was moving, we could hear the sea swishing past the hull - which was not very comforting. It became very frightening when we realised we might be the target for an enemy submarine and its torpedoes. Our confidence received a shock when one of the infantrymen in the concert party did his party piece, which was a recital of Binyon's poem: "If I should die, think only this of me, That there's some corner of a foreign field that is forever England."

The day dawned when the 'Circassia' sailed down the Clyde to join the convoy. We were on our way. As the ship slowly took us down the Clyde, we looked at the scenery and buildings with mixed feelings. As we moved towards the open sea we passed the Isle of Arran, and then we knew we were really on our way.

The voyage was marked by extremely bad weather. It was so bad that some of the experienced sailors on board were seasick. For eight days we suffered from severe gales, lashing rain, heavy seas and mountainous waves. It was rather frightening to stand on deck holding tightly to the rail, and see a 30 foot wall of bottle-green water towering above us, with little bubbles of foam sliding down the glassy looking surface; then, the next moment, to be on top of such a wall of water and look down into the trough of the wave so far below. In the brief moments the ship rode on top of the wall of water we would look for any other vessels in the convoy, and very often we would not see another ship.

This very rough weather had its advantages. It helped to protect us from enemy submarines. At one time it was reported we were only 400 miles from Greenland.

During the voyage many men were severely ill with seasickness. One of our men spent the whole voyage curled up in the area reserved for stowing hammocks and refused to move, and had no food at all. He was so ill he vowed he would walk home. Some men were flung against the ship's rails or other parts of the ship as it tossed up and down, or rolled from side to side, so that many broke arms, legs or ribs.

I was very pleased to find that I was a good sailor, and I enjoyed being on deck as much as I could, watching the waves and breathing fresh air. One advantage for those of us who were well was that, with so many men ill and the same amount of rations being issued to each table, some of us were eating too much and enjoying it.

During the daily lifeboat drill, the duty officer inspected the mess decks, and we sat on the deck beside our particular lifeboat. To make use of this enforced idleness, Frank Davis and I played chess on a small traveller's chessboard with peg-in pieces, which enabled the pieces to remain on the board despite the movements of the ship.

Before we had left the Clyde we were allowed to write letters for posting on shore. I was very careful what I said in my letters to my parents and to my grandmother, yet both letters were censored, and the censor literally cut out the word or words he didn't like. The result was that my letters arrived with long holes in them. My grandmother wanted to write to her MP because someone had cuts bits out of a letter addressed to her. My parents kept all the letters I wrote to them while I was overseas, and since they were numbered as well as dated, they were in chronological order. These letters are now very useful for recalling incidents and sights from my travels, and will provide material for this story of my pilgrimage.

The voyage was rough until we reached Gibraltar. We passed 'The Rock' just after dawn on 10th December, 1942, and I was on deck to see it. The Mediterranean was flat calm, just like blue glass - a striking contrast to the seas we had travelled through. We all enjoyed the brilliant sunshine and calm sea. Concert party shows were given on deck and, in one of these, I was just about to sing a solo when two enemy aircraft appeared. It was all excitement for a few minutes, but the planes did not attack, and flew away, probably to report our position.

The coast of North Africa appeared and we looked at it with interest and wondered where we would land. On 11th December, we entered Algiers' harbour and almost immediately the ships in our convoy were attacked by three German dive-bombers. The 'Circassia' immediately put to sea again, followed by the troopships 'The Stratheden' and 'The Strathallan', and went on to Bone. On this last part of the voyage 'The Stratheden' and 'The Strathallan' were attacked and damaged by enemy aircraft action and a submarine. It was later reported that 200 nurses had perished in the attack. The 'Circassia' was also attacked but, thanks to the skill of the captain, the ship was not damaged, although

● Bone, 1942.

members of the crew assured us that, just before dawn, only the captain's skill saved the ship from being hit by a torpedo. We were all below decks at the time, so we knew nothing about it until a few hours later.

We arrived safely in Bone harbour on 12th December. After the usual chaos, we disembarked on the quayside and stood on North African ground for the first time. Then we had to find our kit, which had been unloaded from the holds.

Chapter Seven

Algeria to Tunisia

Amid the chaos on the dockside we found our kit, which had been unloaded from the ship's hold. With all our kit hung around our bodies and our rifles clutched in our hands, we slowly made our way out of the dock. We had almost reached the outskirts of the town when we came under sniper fire. We all dived for cover on the roadside. Since there were no German troops in the town, we suspected that the sniper fire came from Arabs sympathetic to the Germans or supporters of the Vichy French. When the sniping ceased, we continued our way out of the town, looking suspiciously at the houses and trees.

It was with relief that we halted at a large building on the outskirts of the town, which we discovered was an empty tobacco warehouse. We were told to settle in as best we could. The light was fading and there were no lights, so we hurriedly found a place to sleep and dump our kit. The floor was bare concrete and bore the stains of whatever produce had been stored there. We each had one blanket, so we placed our ground sheet on the concrete and folded our blanket in half, lengthwise, and then crawled between the two surfaces of the blanket and pulled our greatcoats on top. I used my tin hat as my pillow. None of us slept much: the concrete was too hard and too cold. How I longed for my hammock. During the night there were several air raids, mainly on the docks in Bone and on the ships in the harbour.

Breakfast the next morning, 13th December, consisted of Army 'compo' rations, and this included Army biscuits. We longed for the soft, white fresh bread from the 'Circassia'. When we wandered to the doorway of the warehouse and looked out, we saw that it was a beautiful sunny day with blue skies. Opposite the warehouse was a convent, in the grounds of which we could see a large number of trees, some of them loaded with fruit, especially tangerines. We went to the gardens and the nuns told us we could buy the tangerines at one franc for a kilo, which worked out at ten pence (pre-decimalisation value) for about

● Bone, 1942.

30 tangerines. Oranges were 18 for 10d. Since we had not tasted oranges or tangerines for several years we greatly anticipated tasting these fruits.

As soon as it was possible, we went to the convent gardens and picked the fruit. We discovered that a tin hat full of tangerines weighed about a kilo. We took our fruit to a table where the nuns weighed it and took the money, and we returned to our billet. I warned the men not to eat too many oranges or tangerines because their stomachs would not now be used to them. Some did not heed the warning but savoured the fruit until they were all gone: eating too many in a short space of time. They had to pay the inevitable penalty by having to make a very hasty retreat from our presence.

We stayed in the factory warehouse for a few days and were then moved a short distance out of Bone, to live in tents pitched beneath some very large eucalyptus trees. These trees were about 30 feet high. There was a stream nearby and, beyond that, an open space covered with green grass. It was too large to be called a field and it had no hedges. In the distance, a small ridge ran from our right until it met another ridge coming in at an angle from our left. When the sun set, at about 5.30pm, the sun sank quickly behind the ridges and, as it disappeared, the 'field' gradually filled with shadows, beginning at the farthest end under the ridges. The shadow was grey to begin with, deepening to purple; then turning black. Each evening we watched the changing colours as the deepening shadows crept toward our encampment. We had no lights so, at sundown, we sat beneath the trees, or lay down on our blankets in our tents, and talked or sang.

We spent some time under the eucalyptus trees and were introduced to the first of the creatures of North Africa.

The laughing hyenas soon announced their nearness. After sundown we sometimes saw these dark forms moving in the shadows and, on a moonlit night, we would see the moonlight reflected in their eyes. They never came into our camp - at least, not when we were awake and active. The other creature we met we could not name. It was like a very large

The Canvas Chapel

milk-white maggot. It was about four inches long and its body was just over half an inch in diameter. It moved in a rhythmic manner, each segment of the body and the tiny legs moving in progression. The front end was a disc of brown skin with what we thought was a mouth and a pair of eyes. This creature lived in the earth under the eucalyptus trees and, sometimes, in the floor of our tents. Every morning we emptied our boots before putting them on, in order to make sure that no creepy-crawly had taken up residence there during the night.

The reason for our stay among the eucalyptus trees was that we were waiting for our lorries to arrive. They had travelled on a different convoy. However, we were not allowed to be idle in this waiting period. Apart from the usual guard duties, we were used as labourers at the docks in Bone, unloading ammunition and other stores. German aircraft frequently attacked the docks, both during the day and by night. Sometimes, when we had loaded a lorry with ammunition, we travelled with the lorry to the large ammunition dump outside of Bone.

On one occasion, Frank Davis and I were working together and travelled to this ammunition dump on a tank transporter that we had just helped to load. On the return journey, we lay down on the deck of the transporter and looked at the stars. Against the black sky, the stars sparkled like jewels, and Frank told me the names of the stars and the constellations. This subject was one of his interests.

On 23rd December, I was working on the docks in Bone with other men from our platoon, when a small box of ammunition fell over and the end of the box landed on my left foot. Some of the fellows carried me into the railway station and placed me in a room in which there were some French soldiers. They were preparing a meal and, when it was cooked, they shared the food - some very sweet coffee and an omelette - with me. I greatly enjoyed this treat.

I was carried to a truck and taken back to our billet. It was too dark by this time for me to examine my foot, except by feeling it. Next morning, I carefully examined the foot and was relieved to find no bones broken; just severe bruising and some swelling.

Although it was Christmas Day, it was work as usual. The officer considered that I was fit to work, so I went with others to the docks, where we worked until 3.30pm. No lorry arrived to take us back to our tents so we had to walk the four miles back to our camp. On our arrival at camp we were served our Christmas Dinner, which was stew followed by a 'substitute' Christmas Pudding. No one asked what was in the portions we had eaten.

Christmas Day evening we sat in our tents, about 20 men to a tent. In our tent there were three good bass singers and three good tenors; so we began to sing Christmas carols, and the rest of the men in the tent joined in. We were the only ones in camp to sing carols but, next day, we learned that all the other men in the other tents just lay there listening to us.

New Year's Eve 1942 saw us again working on the docks at Bone. We finished work about 3.30pm and I went to the Bone Railway Station to see the French soldiers who had been so kind to me. They invited me to join them for a meal and we had cold turkey, lettuce, French omelette and brown bread, followed by French puff pastries. The French soldiers were surprised and a little mystified when I declined their offer of champagne, whisky and beer. They could not understand anyone not wanting to drink alcohol.

While we were at the docks one day, one of our men needed to look for a toilet and set off to find one. He went into the railway station and eventually returned to us. It was clear that he was extremely annoyed. He burst out with: "Those rotten so-and-so Germans have pinched the lavatory pans."

We tried to explain that the continental lavatory furniture differed from the English, and two pads for the feet either side of a central hole was the usual way of things. I don't think he really believed us and was often to be heard saying very nasty things about "those so-and-so Jerries."

In a letter written on 9th January 1943, I wrote: 'I have just finished dinner. Weather is quite cold and the wind is very cold. A few fields away there is an Arab ploughing, and he is using two oxen and it all looks very ancient. They all use oxen for ploughing here. It looks like some scene from the Bible to see a man behind a plough and a boy walking alongside the oxen. The oxen are yoked in pairs and there are often four oxen to a plough. They plod onwards, looking stupidly in front of them, seemingly unmoved by the cries of both man and boy - or by the lash of the whip, usually applied by the boy. It seems a very slow way of ploughing but they carry on as if there is no hurry.'

From the same letter, under the heading of 'Saturday', I wrote: 'As I looked over the hills this morning the low clouds were wrapped around the tops of the hills, I wished I could adequately describe all I could see. The little hovels of the Arabs dotted here and there over the side of the mountain, with the blue smoke of their fires curling upwards; the sun shining over one mountain to give a bright patch of green on the opposite mountain; the stunted trees and bushes, and what grass there is looks like an English hillside in spring. At my feet, the stream runs swiftly by, swollen by last night's rain, bearing with it many objects - some of which are foreign to this part of the country: empty bottles and tins. Here and there, sailing gaily along, are pieces of orange peel. Then a wind sprang up and some of the clouds cleared away from the mountain top and patches of blue sky appeared. Then a voice shouted: "On parade" and my musing was turned to the more immediate things of everyday life.'

In a letter dated 20th January 1943, I recorded how I met my cousin Victor Little, a corporal in the Royal Army Medical Corps (RAMC).

I had signed the sick report because I was orderly corporal for the day. When the men reported to the medical inspection (MI) room in Bone, the corporal on duty recognised my signature and asked a few questions about me and then told the sick men that he was my cousin. Victor had arrived at the MI Room only that morning and was to stay there for only one week. I managed to obtain permission to have a few hours off duty in the afternoon and went to Bone. I met Victor and we spent the afternoon together.

We moved from the Bone area and camped among the olive groves on the outskirts of the Arab town called Tebasouk, which was on the road to Medjez el Bab - where the front line was. There was a shallow valley between our location and Tebasouk, and we could see the white houses on the rising ground opposite. The Roman Catholic church stood out, glistening white. Not far away was the Arab mosque with its minaret, like the spire of the Catholic church, pointing to the sky. We could hear the Arab calling the faithful to prayer. We did not have time to visit the town. We were kept busy taking ammunition and other supplies to the forward areas, and so began our new existence of driving by night without lights and to the forward areas.

While at Tebasouk we were known as 1st Guards Brigade Company, RASC, and worked mainly with the 1st Guards Brigade units, but we also worked with other units as required. During this time it was part of our duties to take ammunition to the Royal Artillery units of the brigade and to supply any units in the area needing food; ammunition; petrol and diesel for the tanks. This often involved us in some exciting experiences.

As part of 78th Division, we were also used as general transport as required. I often went to or through Beja, Oued Zarga, and Medjez el Bab. I had an exciting time at Beja one night and also ran into trouble and excitement at Medjez el Bab when talking supplies to the Royal Engineers.

One day I was at Oued Zarga with some of the men from our platoon and we had parked our lorries beneath some trees in an attempt to hide them from the German airforce. The only aeroplanes we saw seemed to be from the Luftwaffe - except for two spotter planes which we called 'flying compo boxes'. I think that these were Lysanders. These two Allied planes flew over at regular intervals and were nick- named 'Gert and Daisy' after two popular comediennes on the radio.

The general rule was, if you heard an aeroplane, you dived for cover because it would be a German.

The first time I saw a German plane diving at me - and I realised that I was the target - was a frightening experience, but it was to become a frequent experience too. I was often alone when the attack came and felt very exposed. It was as if everything else decreased in size but my lorry and me became a target too big to be missed. Nonetheless, somehow I survived.

Oued Zarga was a small village with a railway station, and it was also the junction for three main roads: so it was an important place. Near the road junctions there were groups of trees. An Army unit had camped among one of these groups of trees. The small group of us from our platoon had parked our lorries under another group of trees and we were eating the bully beef sandwiches, which were our rations for our midday meal.

Suddenly we heard the familiar noise of a German plane diving. We scattered, seeking cover. I did a rugby tackle on the base of a tree, and slid down into a hollow. I looked up and saw the plane screaming down in a dive. Then I saw the pilot's face, and his helmet and goggles in clear detail. It was the first time I had ever seen the face of my enemy.

This seemed to make the attack all the more personal. As the plane swooped down, I saw the bomb leave the plane and hurtle down among some trees, and the pilot pulled the plane out of the dive and flew away.

The bomb curved downward towards the group of trees and it exploded as it hit the tops of the trees, showering death and mutilation over a wide area. The noise of the explosions drowned the noise of the enemy plane zooming away.

I got up and saw a man with his face covered in blood, I went to him and asked where he was wounded. He said he was not wounded. He had hit his nose on trunk of a tree and had a nosebleed. I did what I could for him and then ran to the scene of the explosion.

The first man I came to was lying, face downwards, and I could see he was very badly injured. As I examined him, a medical officer came along, looked at the injured man and said: "Leave him. He will be dead in five minutes. Find someone you can help."

I protested but was curtly told: "Help someone else."

I felt awful. It was the first time I had left a dying man. I hurried away to another man, but knew I could do nothing for him. He had mistakenly chosen to seek cover under a lorry, and had chosen to lie beneath the petrol tank. The lorry had been set ablaze and his charred corpse bore testimony to his bad judgement in seeking shelter where he had.

I moved on, helping another man who was wounded. Eventually the injured were attended to, and transport arrived to take them to a field dressing station. I cleaned my hands and walked slowly back to the other group of trees. There, I found one of our lads - a 19 year old boy - very upset by what he had seen. He was sat by a tree, obviously distraught, with the shock of the attack still evident on his face. It was his first experience of warfare in action. I spent some time trying to comfort him. Then I sat down and continued eating my bully beef sandwiches. It was the only thing to do.

During my time in the Army, I gave medical assistance to many men. Some of their injuries were horrific. One or two, however, had their humorous side.

One of our men was unloading ammunition when a shell burst nearby and he fell to the ground. Upon examination he was found to have a piece of shrapnel in his buttock. When told the extent of his injury his main concern was how to explain to his children why he was wounded in his backside when he was not running away.

It was about this time I was given a special job, called 'forward recovery and salvage'.

I was given a three ton Bedford lorry and a 'roof-spotter', who was to stand in the back of the open lorry and keep a look out for enemy planes or enemy troops. If he saw any of these, he was to bang on the cab roof to warn me. Unfortunately, when men knew they were to come with me they all seemed to develop some illness that needed a visit to the medical officer. This meant that, in practice, I rarely had a roof spotter. The only man who came with me was Jeff Plant, who was a very quiet and polite man.

The job was to recover enemy equipment from forward positions before the enemy could counter-attack and recapture both the positions and the equipment. This meant that I followed the infantry and, when they advanced, I collected the enemy equipment in the dugouts and trenches or what had been their forward positions. Whatever I found I was to take to a dump behind our lines. This included all types of German equipment, arms, ammunition, hand grenades, booby traps and a variety of items, some of which were lethal. There were also useful items that could be called 'souvenirs'. While no one wanted to come with me, they were all eager to come to see what souvenirs I had when I returned to camp. I usually handed out these souvenirs to anyone who wanted them. But I wondered what tales were told about how these men had obtained them!

I quickly learned how to defuse German hand grenades and various types of explosive items. One particular little terror was about the size of an egg and painted a brilliant blue. On one end was a white cap like the cap on a toothpaste tube. Attached to the underside of the cap was a short piece of white string and when this was pulled the device exploded, blowing off the hand. These were often left upside down with the white cap wedged into something so that anyone picking it up detonated it. I soon learned how to handle them and render them safe. There were, of course, many other types of booby traps left behind by our departing enemies.

It was strange, at first, to go into the enemy dugouts and defensive positions and realise these places had been the 'homes' of men like myself, but who wore a different uniform and fought for different ideals. Sometimes there were half-eaten meals left behind, obviously abandoned during a sudden attack. Personal items were scattered about. Sometimes there were signs of casualties. Not all were pleasant sights.

One day, I found a large anti-tank mine. It was about 18 inches in diameter and was painted a dull yellow. The detonator was in the centre, and there was a carrying handle on the rim. When I took it back to the dump no one would take it or handle it, despite the fact I had removed the detonator. Anyway, it required the weight of a tank to detonate it. Eventually I had to carry it to the outskirts of the fenced area and place it on the ground. Even then, no one would go near it.

One day, when Jeff Plant was with me as spotter, I was driving along a winding track when Jeff thumped the cab roof. He had seen a German aeroplane - and the German pilot appeared to have seen us. I stopped the truck and jumped out of the cab. Jeff and I dived into a wadi alongside the road. The wadi was like a long trench, about five feet deep. The German plane fired at us and missed. It also missed hitting the lorry, so the pilot returned and fired again, and we ducked down below the rim of the wadi.

As we crouched there waiting for the aeroplane's next run, I noticed that Jeff had his right hand on the wall of the wadi, almost covering a hole in the wall. As I looked I saw

something move in the hole and shouted: "Jeff, move your hand, there's a scorpion in that hole."

Jeff snatched his hand away and a scorpion immediately appeared where his hand had been, with the scorpion's tail in the 'attack' position. We were glad when the German plane flew away and we could continue our journey.

Another day, when Jeff was my spotter, I was driving along a twisting track. Unfortunately, on this occasion, Jeff did not see the German aeroplane

● Tunis, 1943.

come out of the sun towards us. The first we knew we were being attacked was when we saw the machine-gun bullets from the plane hitting the road in front of the lorry. As the plane banked and turned to come at us again I accelerated and swerved the lorry around a bend in the track, and the bullets passed overhead and ploughed into the road behind us. We had escaped again.

We were frequently dive-bombed and machine-gunned, but were never hit. For me, Oued Zarga was a place of excitement.

Chapter Eight

With the Guards

Just after the Oued Zarga incident I was attached to the 1st Guards Brigade Headquarters and put in charge of a small transport section. Os Redgate, from our platoon, came with me and a driver from another unit joined us. We carried land mines and coils of dannet (barbed) wire and, as required, food, ammunition, petrol or troops.

At the end of February, the rainy season began and lasted all through March. This caused the ground to become a sea of mud and bogged down transport and tanks, thus preventing any advance or even any large scale attacks. This meant that we were static - but we knew that, once the rain stopped and the ground dried out, we would be in action again. I often heard the guardsmen saying: "Send it down, David," - meaning 'send down the rain and prevent any action taking place'. This was especially so on St David's Day (1st March).

The transport drivers were fortunate in that they could live in the cabs of the vehicles, while the infantrymen had to find what shelter they could. I suggested that some of the men could sleep in the back of the lorries but, when they found out that they would be lying on a load of landmines, they all declined.

Living in the cab of a lorry is rather cramped, but at least it is dry. We ventured out into knee-deep mud to fetch our meals and hurried back to the shelter of the cab to eat whatever we had been given. We drank the rainwater that collected on the food as we moved from the cookhouse to the cab.

When the rain eventually stopped and the ground became dry, we prepared to go into action. Every day, at least once - sometimes more - an Arab in white robes, and sitting on a white, lovely looking horse, would appear on the hillside a fair distance from us. After studying the area for a while, he would turn his horse to point in one direction or another and that was when we took cover.

He was indicating to the Germans in which direction to fire their shells. It never failed.

The Arab always remained out of range of our rifle fire and so remained unhurt while he carried on his spying for the Germans.

When the ground dried out, we frequently saw our commander, Brigadier Copeland-Griffiths walking about in carpet slippers. He appeared to have trouble with his feet. He also appeared to be a friendly man - often chatting to the men around him.

Another very friendly man at Brigade HQ was the chaplain.

I came to know him quite well and, whenever I could, I attended the services he held. On one occasion, the chaplain held a service and we gathered around him. He used the gun-layer's seat of a two pound anti-tank gun as the altar, placing the wine and wafers on a cloth draped over the seat. He announced the first hymn and said: "I cannot sing very well, so will one of you please start the hymn?"

I started singing the hymn and the chaplain looked across to me and smiled his thanks.

● Os Redgate.

When the service was ended and the Communion Service was about to begin I went to the chaplain and explained that I was a Baptist and had not been confirmed in the Church of England but had been baptised by immersion, as is the practice of the Baptists.

He asked if I was a member of a Baptist church. I replied that I was and that I was also a lay preacher for the Baptists - and was still considered to be a lay preacher even though I was serving in the army. In reply, he told me that I would always be welcome to share in any Communion Service that he conducted. A group of us then knelt down on the sun-baked earth and shared in the Communion Service. It was a time of real Christian fellowship and blessing.

One day, as we were queuing for the midday meal at 1st Guards Brigade HQ, the motor transport sergeant called me out of the queue. He told me to take Os Redgate and his lorry and go to a certain place - map reference supplied - and there meet another driver with a lorry. We were to leave immediately.

I protested strongly that we had not yet had our midday meal. The sergeant took me away from the other men and told me I was on a secret detail that required the utmost urgency and that I was to leave at once. The sergeant gave me a map and showed me an oasis at a certain map reference and told me to get there as quickly as possible. He then showed me another map reference where I was to find the other driver and lorry. I was instructed not to tell anyone where we were going, not even Os Redgate and the other driver. At the oasis, I was to contact an officer and exchange passwords and then do whatever the officer told me. The sergeant then took the maps from me, so I had map references but no map to use them on.

As Os Redgate and I drove away from HQ, we passed infantrymen digging in on the side of the road we were on. We stopped and asked what was going on. One infantryman told us to get out as quickly as possible because the Germans had broken through and were less than a mile away. They were expected to attack at any moment and the road we were on was the new front line. We left in a hurry.

Later, we found the other driver and his truck. He was full of complaints about being sent on this job. I cannot now remember the route we followed but, about 5pm, we arrived at the designated oasis. A British armoured car stood near a well and a British soldier stood near it. Some distance away stood a British officer.

I halted the two lorries about 20 yards from the well and slowly approached the officer. The officer watched and, as I came up to him, I passed a few words with him and mentioned the password. The officer gave the answering password. I then introduced myself and said I had been told to obey his orders. He introduced himself as Major Gill of the 17th /21st Lancers. When I told him we had not had anything to eat since 8am that day, he waited while we had a meal that his batman/driver had cooked.

After this hurried meal, Major Gill spoke to me about the route we were to take and the need for haste. It was dark by the time we set of, with Major Gill leading in his scout car. We travelled for hours until Major Gill stopped and we had a break. The Major suggested we should have an hour's sleep and then continue. I suggested it would be better to continue our journey. He said that he needed sleep because he had not slept the previous night. He said that he was afraid that the drivers would fall asleep if they did not rest now. I assured him that drivers in the RASC were accustomed to driving through the night and for long periods.

I could see the Major was very tired, so I suggested that he allowed me to lead the convoy while he slept in the back of our lorry. Reluctantly, he agreed. Then he gave me his map and told me we were going to a desert area near Tebessa. I agreed to wake him when we were in sight of the map reference he gave me.

On we went through the night. I was in Redgate's lorry. The other RASC lorry followed us, with the scout car in the rear.

About 4am, I halted the small convoy and woke Major Gill. I showed him on the map where we were and pointed out that we were near our destination. The Major then told me to meet him at our destination and he got into his scout car, which sped away. Scout cars could travel at 60 mph, while Bedford lorries were governed down to only 30 mph. We eventually came to the camp, which was our destination, and the Major had gone inside. He came rushing out.

The Major then told me the reason for our secret mission.

The Lancers we being trained in the use of American Sherman tanks and had received very little training up to that date but, because of very heavy losses in tanks by the Americans, the Americans intended using the partly-trained Lancers in an attack that morning. Major Gill was to prevent this and find the Lancers very quickly. The major had discovered that the Lancers had left the camp on the previous evening and had already moved into pre-battle positions. Unfortunately, the major had only hazy instructions as to the possible position of the battle form-up area.

Quickly we sent off: the major leading the way. We headed in the direction of the desert. When the major saw the tanks in the distance, he told me to bring the trucks as quickly as possible while he speeded ahead in his scout car.

Fortunately, we caught up with the tanks just in time. The tank engines were running, the men were on board and everything was set for the move forward into battle positions. When we arrived the major was already in conference with a group of officers.

When Major Gill saw us he gave orders that we were to be given food. While we were eating our breakfast, the Lancers were ordered out of the tanks and told to get aboard the Lancers' own lorries and the two lorries we had brought.

One of the Lancer officers said we were to move out immediately, but Major Gill said: "Not until the RASC corporal and his drivers have eaten their breakfast. They have driven almost non-stop since yesterday lunchtime and, thanks to them, we arrived in time to save you. When they are ready we will move off."

When we had eaten our breakfast, I reported to Major Gill that we were ready to leave. So, the 17th /21st Lancers moved off, leaving the Sherman tanks standing in the desert.

Slowly the convoy moved away from the battle form-up area and began its journey to 'Happy Valley'. It was a long journey, and I cannot now remember its exact location, but it was given its name because it was a place of green grass, trees and a peaceful atmosphere.

It was on this journey that I first met Jim O'Mara. He was a captain in the Royal Artillery and was a gunnery instructor training tank crews. After the war, be became the sub-editor and chief reporter for the weekly newspaper for the Halesowen and Stourbridge area in Worcestershire. When I went to live in Halesowen in 1948 I met him again and we became friends.

During the journey I told my two drivers to put tins of stew on the exhaust manifold of the engine of each lorry for us to have a hot midday meal. This was a custom for RASC drivers and ensured that we could have a hot meal when on our travels. When we stopped for our midday meal break, my two drivers and I opened our hot tins of stew and began eating the contents straight from the tins.

A captain of the Lancers saw us and gave me a real telling-off for allowing my drivers to eat a meal without an officer's permission. I was annoyed, so I told him that we had driven all through the night with Major Gill to prevent him being committed to battle, and it was my duty to see that my drivers were fed and looked after - and I had given them permission to have a meal. In reply, the captain threatened to put me on a charge for insolence and insubordination.

This was too much for me to stand, so I walked away from him and went to Major Gill and explained what had happened. The major came back with me to the captain and said I was correct in what I had done, and the convoy would not continue its journey until 'the RASC corporal and his drivers had finished their meal'. The major also told me that, if I had any more trouble or interference, to inform him immediately.

On our arrival in 'Happy Valley', Major Gill thanked me for all that I had done to help him save the Lancers from being committed to battle in Sherman tanks when they were not fully trained in their use. He also thanked each of the drivers.

Later, I learned that Major Gill had been killed in Italy, near a place called Piumerola. At that time, Major Robert Gill was a squadron commander of the 16/5th squadron. He was climbing out of the turret of the tank when a sniper shot him. Major Gill was a true officer and a gentleman in the best sense of the words.

When we left 'Happy Valley', we had great difficulty in finding 1st Guards Brigade HQ. Because of fierce fighting which had occurred after we left Brigade HQ, the HQ had moved its location several times. Nonetheless, we found it eventually. A few days after our return to Brigade HQ, Os Redgate and I returned to our platoon.

During the ensuing months I had a number of adventures - some of which had their humorous side.

One of our jobs was to take ammunition to the battery of 25 pounder guns at Chaouach, which was in a forward area. It was a dangerous place because it was on top of a set of hills and among the rocks. When German shells exploded on the rocks, the result was flying shrapnel and also flying pieces of rock. The noise of the lorry engines labouring up the hillside always warned the enemy that we were on our way to the gun positions and this resulted in us receiving a warm welcome.

One night, on a trip to Chaouach, a driver called Tosh was with me. While waiting to unload the ammunition, Tosh said that he was going to light a cigarette. I told him how very dangerous it would be to light a cigarette in our present position, because the glow would be seen by the enemy. I left Tosh for a few moments, and when I returned, he was missing. I called quietly but no answer. Eventually, he returned and I asked where he had been. He replied: "I could see a fellow over there smoking so I crawled over to him and said, 'Give us a light, mate' and I put my cigarette up to his. Then he moved it. I said, 'Hang on, mate, and keep it still' and again put my cigarette up to his, and again he moved it. This happened a few times before I discovered it was a firefly."

In a letter dated 2nd March 1943 I told my parents: 'As I write this, I am surrounded by trees - almond trees, peach trees, pomegranate, apricot, figs, apple, and pear trees. The almonds are formed but are small and unfit to be eaten yet. What a feed if I am here when they are ripe! The wet weather has ended and it is hot now. We are all turning brown. The earth is drying out and the number of flies and other insects is increasing. I expect the mosquitoes will soon be about. Tortoises are now awake and may be seen 'dashing' from bush to bush, and in the grass. Locusts are a familiar sight and so are lizards."

At one place, a lizard lived in a bank near my tent and he became so friendly that I could pick him up. To be able to recognise him among the other small lizards I put a very small spot of yellow paint on his tail. I called him 'Oscar' and often talked to him. I would pick him up and put him on my arm, and he liked to lie in the folds of my rolled up sleeve.

Sometimes he would walk up my arm to my shoulder and lie on the divisional sign - a yellow battleaxe on a black square - which we wore on the shoulder strap on our khaki drill shirts. He would also walk along the back of my neck or collar of my shirt and rest on the other shoulder, or descend down my arm to the fold of my rolled up shirt. Oscar was most useful because he prevented flies and insects settling on my neck and shoulders.

One day, while our platoon officer, Lt Douglas, was talking to me I saw his eyes open wide and he stopped talking and looked intently at my right arm, and his gaze travelled slowly up my arm to my shoulder, then darted to the other shoulder. I realised that he was staring at Oscar and so explained about my pet. The look on the officer's face showed more than surprise. He was amazed. I fed Oscar on corned beef, which he liked very much. When we moved, I had to leave Oscar behind and often wondered if he missed me as much as I missed him.

A registered letter was brought to me at 10pm on Tuesday 25th March, 1943. This was most unusual. Then I saw it was from Bill Aish's mother and I feared the worst. Bill had not received any mail from his mother or his wife for several weeks, but we knew Yvonne, his wife, was ill. Mrs Aish began her letter: 'I know you will help my son in this time of great sorrow for him...'

Then came the news that Yvonne had died at the beginning of March. This came as a terrible shock because we had no idea that Yvonne had been so ill.

Bill was batman/driver to Major J S Dorling, the officer commanding our company: 237 Independent Brigade Company, RASC. The Company HQ was billeted a short distance away from our platoon. I saw our platoon officer, Lt C R Douglas, and explained that I had to see Bill and tell him the news. Then I went to Major Dorling and explained why I had to see Bill. The major knew that Bill and I had been very close friends for many years, and I had been clerk to the major when he was captain of supplies wing in Sussex.

I found Bill walking with Driver Nichols, another batman/driver who looked after our adjutant. Bill had received no mail for 23 days, so I told him I had just received a letter from his mother. We walked away from 'Nick' and wandered among some olive trees. Bill sensed something was wrong, and I then had the unpleasant task of breaking the news to him of his wife's death. When I was with Yvonne on her wedding day and acted as best man at their wedding I never imagined I would have to tell Bill this news. Bill was greatly shocked and I stayed with him for two hours. When I left him alone, I went to see Nick and told him the news too.

It was now quite late and I had to return to my own platoon. Nick told me afterwards that he was so afraid that Bill would try to do something terrible because of his grief, that Nick took his and Bill's rifles and put them under his blankets and lay on them all night. Bill was so popular with all the fellows that everyone felt sorry for him. He received a letter from Yvonne's father on 27th March and a letter from his mother on 29th March. Both letters had been posted before the one I had received on 25th March. Bill felt unable to write letters, so I wrote letters to Mrs Aish and to Yvonne's father. I went to see Bill every evening, but it took Bill a long time to recover from the shock.

Major Dorling arranged for Bill and me to go to a rest camp at Ain Draham. The major sent for me and told me he had made the arrangements. He said he knew that Bill and I had been friends for a long time and that I was trying to help Bill, so he was sending me with Bill to look after him.

● Yvonne and Bill Aish.

We arrived at the rest camp on Thursday, 1st April 1943. The camp was in the usual Army style, but the village was set among the cork forests. From a nearby road we could look down on the blue waters of the Mediterranean. We had a lovely view of a beautiful horseshoe-shaped cove at the foot of the cliffs. It reminded me of Lulworth Cove in Dorset, as it had been before the War. It was really a secluded village called Le Calle on the North African coast and the area seemed completely untouched by war. The local inhabitants were harvesting the cork from the trees and life seemed to be tranquil. It was ideal for a rest camp.

Officers at the camp were billeted at the local Hotel Belle Vue, but other ranks, such as Bill and I, were allowed to have evening dinner at the hotel - if we could afford the cost. We lived in barrack room type accommodation, but it was clean and comfortable. In a letter to my parents, dated 3rd April, I wrote: 'We sleep on beds, have our meals on a plate and sit at tables to eat our meals. We are in a building; not in tents.'

I continued: 'On Saturday evening, Bill and I, in company with some of the other boys, went out to dinner at a French hotel. Dinner was to have been at 7pm but, because of the sudden and unexpected influx of guests, it was not served until 7.45pm. The majority of those present were servicemen from the rest camp and we whiled away the waiting time by singing.

'The French people present seemed to enjoy our efforts. I was asked to sing a solo and, eventually, sang five. I sang these solos in this order: 'The Holy City' (by special request from one of the boys), 'Land of my Fathers' (also by request), 'Because' (by request), then 'Vienna, city of dreams' and, as an encore, 'Smilin' through'. The boys applauded with enthusiasm, and the French people clapped and called out something.

'As we were leaving, a French lady asked me to sing for them on Sunday evening but, when I told her I would be leaving on Sunday morning, she was disappointed. When we reached camp I was told by those who understood French that the French people thought I had a lovely voice. The lads were pleased too, so I, helped, once more, to bring pleasure to others.'

When the meal was eventually served at the French hotel near the camp that evening, it looked very appetising. It was a 'meat and two vegetables' type of meal. A serviceman sitting next to me complained that the meat was very tough and I replied: "Well, goat meat is always like trying to eat rubber."

This man stopped eating, stared at me in sheer disbelief, then clapped a hand to his mouth and ran from the room.

A further extract from my letter of 3rd April reads: 'On Sunday morning, there was a church service in the camp, conducted by Colonel Victor Pike, a Church of England padre. He used as his text and theme Galatians 5, verses 16 to 23, and Revelation 21, verses 1 to 6. He was really great and held everyone's attention for almost half an hour, with a challenging address. He spoke plainly and with understanding.'

The Rev Victor Pike once played rugby for Ireland, and he went on to become Chaplain General of the British Army.

After our time at Le Calle, Bill and I returned to our unit and resumed normal duties.

During this time, our washing facilities were often primitive. We got hold of used, non-returnable, four gallon petrol cans, which were made of thin tin. We cut open one side and dubbed over the ragged edges where we had cut the tin, and, in this way, we made a washbowl.

Whenever we were able to obtain enough water and the weather was warm enough to strip off, we used our washbowl as a bath. This meant stripping to the waist and washing the upper parts of the body. Then, the lower garments were removed and one foot was placed in the bowl and one leg was washed and up to the waist. This operation was repeated for the other leg. The whole process was, of course, carried out in the open air and we hoped there would not be an air attack while we were in this position!

It was an exciting piece of news when a 'bath parade' was announced but, even so, it was sometimes quite an ordeal. The mobile bath unit would set up the equipment in an open field and those allowed the pleasure of a bath stood under a shower. These shower units were fitted into a long metal pipe, about one inch in diameter, and this pipe was suspended on two tripods, also made of one inch metal pipes. There were usually three shower sprinklers on the main pipe. A large boiler heated the water, but it was rarely hot and would often turn cold while men were under the shower. The water was pumped by hand from boiler to sprinkler and, if the man operating the pump became tired or wanted to light a cigarette, the water supply stopped until a chorus of cries prompted its renewal.

Since the showers were erected in an open field, bath time was usually windy and often in sight of Arab villagers. Some of the female villagers in particular seemed to enjoy the sight of these white figures performing their strange ritual. Sometimes we could get clean clothing from the bath unit. This was clothing, left by previous bathers, which had been laundered. This was our luxury bath under normal conditions.

On Thursday, 15th April 1943, I had returned to our platoon camp about 2am, after taking ammunition to the front line artillery. I was awakened at 5.30am and told that I was one of the lucky ones to be allocated to a special bath parade. About 20 of us were told to get aboard a lorry and we could have breakfast when we returned. We left at 6am and no one seemed to have any idea where we were going or why we had to have a bath so early in the morning.

Eventually, we arrived at a small Arab village. Just outside the village was a Roman bath, still in good working order. A natural hot sulphur spring had been harnessed to supply hot water for three separate baths. Each bath was about ten feet long by four feet wide and about four feet deep. The water level almost reached the top of the bath.

Eight of us were in the bath together, but we had plenty of room to enjoy our bath. Once we became used to the smell of the sulphur we began to enjoy the real luxury of a really hot bath and the pleasure of soaking ourselves. This was our first real bath for about six months and we made the most of it. This was generous luxury after being used to bathing in a few inches of water in a petrol tin. Reluctantly, we left the baths and returned to camp, arriving about 8.30am, just in time for breakfast.

Some weeks after our visit to the Roman baths - when we had moved to a different part of North Africa - we were billeted in a sloping field. The weather was now a lot warmer and the luxury of a good wash or a primitive bath was greatly appreciated.

Tosh - of the firefly incident - a Londoner, decided he would have a real bath, not in a petrol tin. He dug a hole about four feet long and 18 to 24 inches wide and about 12 inches deep. He placed his waterproof groundsheet in the hole and then filled the depression with water. He quickly sat in his 'bath' and was soon enjoying himself and singing lustily.

We kept him talking so that he did not see three Arab women coming towards him. Arabs never completely undress and do not expose their bodies to the sunshine, so the sight of a British soldier lying, naked, in a hole in the ground and singing loudly attracted their attention. Tosh did not notice them until they were about five feet from him. They had stopped and were leaning on the handles of the wooden shovels they had been using in the fields.

When Tosh saw the women, all grinning and goggle-eyed, he waved his arms to indicate he wished them to leave and shouted: "Go away."

The women smiled broadly and waved their hands in greeting and said: "Hi, Johnny."

They showed no intention of moving away. Instead they showed a intense interest in Tosh and his undressed state. We all laughed - except Tosh. After a while, we encouraged the women to leave. I don't think Tosh ever took a bath in that fashion again.

In a letter I wrote in April 1943 I said: 'We are pestered by flies, and they bite. When they bite, it feels like someone sticking a needle into you. We made fly-swatters, that is, a piece of tin nailed to a piece of stick, but it does not seem to have much effect on the number of flies, even though we are swatting all day. Many queer insects and animals have appeared since the warmer weather began: lizards, small snakes, frogs, hundreds of ants - some small black ones and others about half-an-inch long, with big red ones - and all sorts of little insects. There are crowds of flowers, some like English flowers - marigolds, daisies, poppies and marshmallow plants with purple flowers. Some of the flowers are strange to us. Geraniums grow wild here. There are bushes of wild thyme. We see eucalyptus trees, fir trees and various forms of cacti.'

About this time, it was fairly common to see green parrots flying around. They seemed to live among the trees and could often be seen resting on the telephone wires. We often saw snakes crossing the roads. They were usually too fast for the lorries to run over them, although a few met their end beneath lorry wheels. Lizards were also a common sight, varying in size from a few inches to thick-bodied ones about 18 inches long. We also saw storks flying about, but they kept out of our way and nested in the tops of tall trees.

Any moments of humour were cherished, however slight the comedy, and these incidents were often recalled when light relief was needed. Remembered now, they may not seem so funny but, then, they were appreciated to the full.

One such incident involved the frying of an egg. How the eggs were obtained is not now clear. Probably they had been bought from an Arab. Eggs were a luxury to be enjoyed as soon as possible before we were ordered to move to a new location, to take ammunition into the line or take petrol to some unit in need. We decided to fry our eggs in a dixie over a small tommy-cooker. A tommy-cooker was the British Army's patent cooker. It consisted of a round tin, about four inches in diameter and two inches high, with a raised perforated guard around the top of the tin which supported the object to be heated. This tin was filled with a wax of methylated spirits which, when ignited, burns long enough to boil one pint of water, and a bit longer.

One egg had been fried. Frank Davis then began frying his egg, but the cooker was used up before the egg was properly cooked. To keep his egg cooking until someone could bring a new cooker into operation, Frank held his dixie over a candle flame.

To the onlookers it was comical but, to Frank, it was a very serious business. This incident provided material for many letters home. Items of news suitable for inclusion in letters - that is, news that could not give away details of our position, strength or plans and so would not attract the attention of the Army censor - were scarce and so writers seized eagerly upon anything that was suitable.

CHAPTER NINE

The end of the campaign

The arrival of an Easter Card from my parents was a timely reminder of a way of life very different from the way we were living at that time. On the Good Friday, it was duties and details as usual but, by some miracle, Corporal George Barnett - who was in charge of our cookhouse - was able to make some hot cross buns. There were enough buns for each man to have one.

On Good Friday, a voluntary church service was held, conducted by the Rev Melfyn Powell, a Baptist chaplain who was able to come and see us occasionally. About 40 men attended the service and 17 of them remained for the Communion Service that followed. It was a simple service but was greatly enjoyed by all who attended. The men sat on the sloping sides of a wadi and on the sun-baked earth, where a few stunted bushes struggled to grow. The sun blazed down from a clear blue sky. Overhead, the birds sang. Insects buzzed and, at intervals, an RAF plane flew over. We could hear the sound of the artillery firing in the distance.

Peace descended on the little wadi as the Padre's voice led the men in worship. We sang the hymn, 'There is a green hill far away' and its melody was carried by a gentle breeze to those still on duty. Then followed prayers, a reading from the New Testament and a talk. The service ended with the singing of the hymn, 'For all the saints', and some of us remained for the Communion Service.

No one seemed to want to leave the wadi. We all lingered there, as if the place had been hallowed by our worship. Our thoughts were on the service, the hymns, the sermon - and of our loved ones and of Easters long ago. Then, all too soon, it was back to duty. I am sure there were others who, like me, carried with them the Easter message and a peace that the world cannot give. As we moved from the wadi, Easter ended for us. Our round of normal duties resumed, but the respite - brief though it was - had been refreshing and strengthening.

The evening before Good Friday had seen the beginning of yet another battle but, this time, it was the battle that was to bring to an end to the campaign in Tunisia.

General Anderson, the Commander of the British First Army, gave orders for the American Forces to go all out to capture Bizerte, while the British Forces were to go all out to capture Tunis. Of the three routes into the plain of Tunis, the 78th Division was given the shortest and most direct route. This involved capturing a famous and, to us, notorious landmark: a hill known as 'Longstop'. I had been involved in previous attempts to capture Longstop when I was with the 1st Guards Brigade and so I realised something of the terrible task facing our division.

This new battle for Longstop started on Good Friday eve, on the night of Thursday, 22nd April. Four hundred guns firing at the enemy heralded the start of the battle. While attending the service on Good Friday we had heard the guns firing. We had seen and heard the aircraft flying overhead as they went to support the infantry and attack enemy positions.

It was strange to look up at the aircraft and find that they were ours. For so long in North Africa, the enemy had seemed to dominate the skies that it had become almost second nature to dive for cover whenever we heard the sound of aircraft engines. Now things had changed and the enemy was experiencing air attacks such as we had had to endure for so many months.

By Friday evening, Longstop was ours, but at a terrible cost in men. There were still other mountains and hills to be captured, and the fighting was fierce. We were called upon to carry ammunition, food or petrol wherever it was needed and some of the journeys were hair-raising.

By 26th April, the battles for Longstop and of the Ten Peaks (around Longstop) was over. The 78th Division had suffered a great deal and casualties were very high. As a result, the 78th Division did not take part in the final assault on Tunis - except for its artillery, the Royal West Kents and, of course, most of the transport companies. On 7th May, the First Army and the Eighth Army went into Tunis together. When the tired infantry of the 78th Division entered Tunis on 8th May - given pride of place by the Army Commander - it was six months to the day since their landing in Algeria.

The Scottish Daily Express for Friday 14th May 1943, under the heading 'Well Done, 78th Division' said: 'No Prouder Record', and continued: '"No Division in the North African campaign has been more consistently in the thick of the fighting and none has a prouder record", said an official tribute last night to the 78th Infantry Division. The 78th Division was the first to land in North Africa and the first to enter Tunis.'

When the fighting was drawing to a close, our platoon was moved forward, towards Tunis. We were camped on a ridge on the left hand side of the main road to Tunis, near a place called La Mornaghia. There was a large cemetery just where we turned off the main road into a track that led to our camp position. A newspaper correspondent said there were 250 graves there, each with a swastika cross. They were men of the Herman Goering Jaeger Division. I remember seeing the swastika crosses - very ornate - but I did not count them. In the corner of the cemetery was a knocked-out German tank.

When the fighting ended, it was at La Mornaghia that a very large prisoner-of-war cage was erected. None of us expected to see so many prisoners. They were everywhere: hundreds and hundreds of men, Germans and Italians, walking along the roads towards any unit that would accept them. They tried to hitchhike a ride on our lorries to get to the POW camp, and also travelled in their own lorries and staff cars. They carried packages, suitcases and all kinds of articles. It was like a tremendous column of men going for an outing somewhere. When they asked us where the POW camp was, we just pointed them in the right direction - usually behind us. I saw one British soldier sat on the cab of a German lorry and he was alone among a lorry filled with German soldiers, and the Germans seemed quite content just to be taken back somewhere. Some looked dejected, but others looked very pleased.

In the POW camp, the Germans and Italians were all mixed in together, forming one vast crowd. They sat on the grass as if it was a gigantic picnic, eating British rations and listening to the German band. The band was a full sized military band that had come from Tunis. Its instruments were clean and shining. The bandsmen's uniforms were clean. It seemed strange to see these men, who had been fighting us for so long, now lounging contentedly, eating and listening to the band. Near the camp was an immense car and lorry park, where the enemy transport was parked. It must have been a tremendous job feeding and transporting such a large number of men.

During the closing stages of the battle for Tunis, units moved quickly and often at a moment's notice. This resulted in equipment, stores and, often, cases of food being left behind. We were told to collect any stuff we found and return it to a food depot. Of course,

not all items reached the depots. We fed very well during those days. Tins of fruit and spam were very popular and, of course, any extra - and free - tea, sugar and tins of milk were given a home.

One evening, I invited Bill Aish and Nick to come to my tent for a chat. At that time I was using a German four-man tent as my tent. This tent was one of the things that I had 'rescued' in my travels. I made good use of the tent until I was ordered to get rid of it because

● George Barnett in Tunis, 1943.

it was enemy equipment. It was pyramidal in shape. Each German soldier had one side of the tent, triangular in shape and a quarter of the centre pole. The sides were buttoned together to form the pyramid and the four sections of the pole were fitted together - one end being placed in the apex of the tent and the other resting on the ground. This provided shelter for four men. I had this tent all to myself and, so, lived in luxury. One side was left open during the daytime to allow for access and light, and then buttoned closed for the night.

When Bill and Nick arrived, I left one side of the tent open. We sat outside the tent, enjoying the cool of the evening, watching a gloriously colourful sunset. Because Bill and Nick were batmen/drivers, they were at Company HQ and had no chance to get any 'extras' or souvenirs. This meant that they missed out on the extra, free rations that most of us were finding and enjoying.

Bill and Nick had brought their mess tins with them, as I had suggested. I provided them with liberal helpings of spam and Army biscuits, followed by large helpings of tinned pears. It was an ideal supper after a hot and tiring day. As we enjoyed our meal, we also enjoyed the scenic glory depicted in the sky. The sunsets at La Mornaghia were especially colourful and the cloud formations could reflect all the colours of the rainbow. Just to watch the sunsets there was a delight and uplift to the soul.

On 14th May, we were given permission to mention in our letters home where we were and recent events. I told my parents that Tunis was captured on 7th May and that I was in the town on 9th May. I remember how the people of Tunis cheered us and threw flowers at us. The first time a woman threw flowers at me I ducked: I was not sure what she was throwing. The scenes in Tunis were like a great carnival, but many of the people asked us for food. I was in Tunis again on 11th and 13th May but, on those days, I was on duty.

In my letter to my parents I wrote: 'Since we took Tunis, last Friday, there has been a never-ending stream of prisoners. They travel in their own lorries, in British lorries, civilian cars and lorries. It is not unusual to see a lorry full of prisoners without an escort driving along the road. One such lorry stopped and the driver asked a British military policeman the way. The military policeman just said: "Straight on down the road."

'From that point it was 20 miles to the POW Camp. There must be thousands of prisoners, German and Italian, and the stream never seems to end. Some of the prisoners seem glad to be out of the war. There is Axis equipment everywhere abandoned by the prisoners. I saw a large number of men from the Herman Goering Division, and they all looked so very young. We were told that no member of that division is allowed to be married, but we don't know if that is true. One of the boys I saw was only fourteen and a half years old.'

In a letter dated Sunday 23rd May, I wrote: 'This is a day I shall always remember. I was one of four men chosen to represent No.1 Platoon at the First Army Thanksgiving Service held at the Amphitheatre, Carthage. There were representatives from every company in the First Army, so you can guess the crowd present. We had a regimental band and a choir of servicemen. I would very much have liked to have been in that choir, but I didn't know about it.

'We sat in the Amphitheatre where some of the early Christians were martyred. The

● Carthage.

The Canvas Chapel

band, choir and chaplains faced the congregation. They were on a raised dais of stone. Lt-Col Pike, whom Bill and I met at Ain Draham, offered prayers. I don't know the name of the other chaplain. General Anderson, commander of the First Army, read the lesson and did it very well. Most officers are nervous when reading the lesson in a service, but he was not. We heard an interesting address. The whole proceedings were recorded by the BBC, and the film people took a lot of photographs, etc.'

In a letter dated 30th May, I told my parents that I was enclosing a sermon outline I had written, and then told them how I came to write it: 'You will remember Longstop Hill and the fierce battle we had in order to take it. Well, this sermon outline came because of that battle. I am not going to write of that battle. You have read it in the newspapers, but I can now say I helped a bit in it. On the particular occasion to which I want to refer, I had to take ammunition to the guns (Royal Artillery) just before the battle began. It was never pleasant at any time to be in that area and, when Jerry learned we were in the area -probably by the sound of the lorry engines - it became worse. If ever I wanted to get away, it was then.

'Upon thinking over the experience, these two verses came to my mind: "O for the wings of a dove, that I might fly away", and "They that wait upon the Lord shall renew their strength, they shall mount up with wings as eagles...etc". I just sat down and wrote these notes. Perhaps one day I can use them, but they helped me at that time. Whenever I read or hear either of these verses I shall think of Longstop Hill.'

The sermon that developed from those notes was preached later to the men of my platoon, and a copy of it is in the appendix of this book.

The place where I delivered the ammunition at that time was Chaouach, which we called Charwash. It was high in the hills and was solid rock. When we were there and the German shells exploded, we were showered by shell splinters, shrapnel and pieces of rock. It was a most unpleasant place to be at any time.

In the same letter to my parents I wrote: 'I can now mention the places I have been to, and some of the battles I was in. I met Victor in Bone and that was where your lemons came from. Since then, I have been around a few places, including Le Kef, Tebessa, Thala, and Kasserine. It was at Kasserine that I didn't write any letters for a fortnight, because there was no chance to write with the battle of Kasserine Pass going on. At Tebessa I saw ruins that were 2,000 years old. I know Beja very well, also Oued Zarga. Medjez-el-Bab is also well known to me; so is Massacult where the tank battle was fought before we captured Tunis. As for Tunis, I have been there or through it about 12 or 14 times. I have also been to Carthage. I have been swimming at St Germain four times. Also, I have been in and through the battlefields at Sedjenane. These are places you may have read about.'

After the victory in Tunisia and some cleaning up, we were moved back into Algeria, to a place called Quelma, which is about 40 miles from the Algerian/Tunisian border, and 20 miles from Souk Ahras. Our camp was pitched in a depression in the earth like a very large bowl. Unfortunately for us, it attracted the heat and contained it, so that it was very hot all day.

In a letter dated 11th June, I described to my parents a typical day in our life at Quelma: 'It is 8pm. We have had our supper. It is the best part of the day: cool with a slight breeze, and the sun has dropped behind the hills. The flies, mosquitoes and other evening insects are about: the only flaw. I can stand the evenings. It is not too hot and there is usually a breeze. The flies, mosquitoes and other insects can be avoided by going inside the mosquito net.

'Our usual day is something like this. We are called at 6am; so get up, wash, shave, fold blankets and mosquito net. Then we are on parade for PT at 6.45am until 7.15am. Then we prepare for parade, before breakfast, which is at 7.30am. After breakfast, we finish cleaning up, etc. We are on parade at 8.25am until 8.45am. Then, it is on with whatever jobs we are given. It gradually gets warmer from 6.30am but, until then, it is chilly. By 8.30am it is quite hot, and getting hotter. By 1pm it is too hot for work and we find a cool place - some shade if possible - somewhere where there is a breeze.

'It is still scorching hot at 4.30pm, when we think of having our tea meal, which is usually a cooked meal at about 5pm. At 6pm, it begins to cool and we continue our work. The sun slowly sinks towards the mountain top. The beautiful blue sky changes to a light grey and then to yellow and orange. The clouds turn from white to pink, red and orange. I often think of them as the flags of God, the banners of the heavenly host, the company of martyrs marching with flags and banners waving. The colours of the clouds and sky deepen as the sun sinks lower behind the mountain top, until all turns purple; the valley flooding with dark purple and the hills become black shapes. Then comes the very short twilight followed by darkness. Slowly the stars appear, like diamonds twinkling on a black velvet cushion. It is cooler now, almost chilly. Beds are made down, mosquito nets adjusted, and kit placed around the bed. The bed consists of a waterproof groundsheet with two blankets, and these rest on the ground.

'We lie on the bed reading, perhaps writing, until the light fades. Sometimes we sit or lie on our beds just talking. Our topics vary from politics to work, lorries and men, the war, Civvy Street, memories of days before the war, hopes and plans for after the war ends. Sometimes religion is discussed, or some point is raised about a verse of scripture. Music is also a popular subject, and poetry, with reference to my copy of Palgrave's "Golden Treasury".'

My parents had sent me a copy of 'Palgrave's' at my request.

From the same letter: 'Out here, it is all heat, blazing sun, dust, parched sun-baked earth, dry and dusty looking plants and trees. Very little shade, rocks, no hedges, and even the breeze is warm. The water in our water bottles becomes warm before we can drink it. A tin of water left in the sun for two hours is almost boiling, and is hot enough to wash clothes. This is useful for having a hot bath, if you have a petrol tin washbowl.'

It was in this letter that I asked if something could be done for men who were teetotallers, that is, who did not drink alcohol in any form. I pointed out that the free beer issue suited most men but non-drinkers lost the 'free' part of the issue and no other drinks were offered to them. I said many men began drinking beer because there was nothing else for them to drink. Our drinking water was treated with a chlorinating agent for purifying it. It made the water taste awful. Sometimes the water tasted and smelt of sulphur, or salt, or other local minerals.

My father took my letter to a meeting of the Monmouthshire English Baptist Association and the matter was taken up by the Association and passed to higher authorities. In the meantime, I asked our platoon officer, Lt Douglas, if it was possible to obtain soft drinks for teetotallers. He told me that one bottle of limejuice was issued as one bottle per ten men. I told him the bottles were kept in the officers' mess and the sergeants' mess and never reached the men who would appreciate them. I mentioned that the officers and sergeants also had access to beer and wine, in addition to the limejuice. He was very annoyed with me, but I said that I would raise the matter at home and ask the members of parliament to look into it. A few days later he gave me a bottle of limejuice with the words: "Here you are. Hope you are satisfied."

I shared the bottle with several other teetotallers in the platoon.

After that incident, I occasionally received a bottle of limejuice either from the officer or from the sergeant. The outcome of my letter to my father was that several authorities in England raised the same matter and Members of Parliament were approached, with the result that limejuice became more plentiful for men in the ranks.

While at Quelma, I was sent on a job to Cap Bon, which was beyond Tunis, and was the last place the German Army reached before defeat in Tunisia. I had two lorries with me, one of which I drove, and we spent the first night on the seashore at Tunis. The next morning, we continued our journey to Cap Bon. The purpose of the journey was to bring back 300 Bren guns with hundreds of magazines, which had been collected and stored at Cap Bon.

On the return journey, we stopped near a group of trees, intending to spend the night there. After a while, some Arabs came near - which they always did if an Army lorry stopped. I told the man with me to watch the Arabs, because it was the Arabs' usual practice to steal anything they could get their hands on - particularly anything from an Army lorry. I did not want the Arabs to get any of the Bren guns and magazines. Also, they were keen to obtain petrol cans containing petrol, or the cans of engine oil that we carried for use on the lorries. Some of the Arabs began to come towards the lorries, and a few young men tried to get to the oil and petrol cans on the lorry, but we chased them away.

After a while, two middle-aged Arabs came to me, and the rest of the Arabs moved away. One of the Arabs held out his hand to shake hands, and I shook hands with him. He began to speak in Arabic and French and I tried to reply in what poor French I could remember. We both indulged in plenty of mime and hand waving. Eventually, I discovered he was the local sheik and was also the local magistrate and Chief of Police. He then invited my companion and me to sit with him beneath the shade of some nearby trees. The sheik and his companion sat with us, all of us sitting cross-legged, while a group of Arabs stood in a semicircle facing us. We continued our mime and actions plus words for a while; then the sheik said something to a young boy. The boy immediately hurried away, and I wondered what this was likely to mean for us. I think that my companion was also apprehensive at the departure of the boy.

It was with some relief that we saw the boy return without an escort, but carrying a large, polished, brass, circular tray. On the tray were several cups and saucers, along with a coffee pot. When he came to the sheik, the boy poured coffee into each cup. I looked carefully at the articles on the tray. The cups were small and made of very thin delicate china, with saucers to match. There were hand-painted flowers on the cups and saucers - most delicately done. There was a very dainty sugar bowl and the coffee pot was like a small dainty teapot.

It was all so different from what I had expected.

When the boy poured the coffee he asked me: "How much sugar?"

Seeing it was black coffee and I was not sure of the taste, I asked for two spoonfuls. I remembered reading that Arabs considered it rude to take food or drinks with the right hand so I took my cup and saucer in my left hand and told my companion to follow my example. The coffee tasted lovely. We accepted a second cup because it is considered good manners to have two cups - a compliment to the host, but very bad manners to have three cups or to have only one. I was glad that I had remembered this.

We stayed talking to the sheik and his companion for some time and, when the Arabs left us, we climbed into the cabs of our lorries and tried to get some sleep. I felt much safer now because I felt that, after sharing a meal with the sheik, we came under his protection. This seemed to be so because we were not troubled during the night, nor in the morning before we left the area.

The Bren guns and their magazines were delivered to an Ordinance Store and we made our way back to Quelma. Before we reached Quelma we were stopped by the military police and told to take a different route because the roads had been sealed off because of the visit of a VIP who was coming. We drove the lorries into a side street and waited to see the VIP. We were very surprised to see King George VI standing up in a car coming towards us. He didn't notice us: he was busy looking around at the sights.

A few days after returning to Quelma, after my trip to Cap Bon, I suffered an attack of malaria. This was probably due to mosquito bites I had received while sleeping in the cab of a lorry at the seashore at Tunis on the way to Cap Bon. I had not been told we would be away overnight and so we had not taken our mosquito nets and, besides, I had not thought that mosquitoes would breed in seawater. I was very ill for a week.

The man who shared a tent with me at that time, Cliff Read, had also contracted malaria. In fact, a large number of men were suffering from malaria at this time. If Cliff woke up and saw me without blankets and greatcoat over me, he would pull the blankets around me, and I would do the same for him. When the malaria subsided, we felt very weak. It was then that I contracted dysentery, which lasted for a week. I was really ill and had no energy.

Quelma was supposed to be a rest area where troops went to recuperate, but the heat and the flies resulted in most of the men being ill while they were there. We were not sorry to leave the area and return to Tunisia. We eventually camped near a village called Turkie, which was fairly near Sousse. One evening, just before sunset, I was lying in my pyramidal, German tent, with one side thrown open. My head was towards the opening and I was talking with one of our fellows, who was squatting down facing me. Suddenly I saw something move towards us, and shouted: "Look out! A snake!"

As I spoke, the snake came between this man's feet and straight towards me. I leapt up and ran out of the tent, the other man fell over but quickly scrambled upright and ran away.

The men around the tent wondered what was happening and I told them that a snake was in my tent. The men quickly formed a circle around the tent and I went to the tent's opening and shone a torch into the tent, while holding a pickaxe handle in my right hand. The snake was coiled up on my pillow, with its head erect and watching me closely. I warned the men outside that I was about to attack the snake, and swinging the pickaxe handle I advanced towards it. With great speed, the snake ducked its head and wriggled under the side of the tent and out among the other men. Immediately, there were shouts of surprise; then the sound of blows.

Eventually, the snake lay dead. One of the men picked up the snake by its tail, but holding it as far as possible from his body. The snake looked about four feet long. The young man holding the snake carried it towards a small fire as if to drop it into the fire. As he held the snake over the fire the snake raised its head and everyone shouted: "Look out!"

The man holding the snake threw it as far as he could, but it must have been the last conscious effort of the dying snake, for it never moved again.

I did not fancy sleeping in my tent that night, for fear the snake had a mate who would come looking for it. I slept in the back of a lorry that night.

CHAPTER TEN

Base details

Fairly soon after this incident, our style of life began to alter. We realised that we were beginning to prepare for another invasion. This could only be an invasion of Sicily or Italy. One day, I was told that I was being posted to 78th Division Base Details, together with some other men. I was told to report to a Lt Percy Cope, an officer in the RASC.

When we arrived where we were to report to Lt Cope, we found men from other RASC companies of the 78th Division and, with them, we formed the RASC contingent. Later, we found in the same area, men from various infantry and other units from the 78th Division. We discovered that 'base details' consisted of men who were to be first reserves, that is, replacements for men killed in the invasion and subsequent battles. It was estimated that the casualties in the invasion of Sicily would be very heavy and so a reserve of men was needed.

When the troops involved in the invasion moved off to their assembly points, men of the units in base details were used to clear up the staging area now vacated by the combat troops. All equipment and stores that had been left behind were gathered together.

The RASC contingent, under the command of Lt Cope, was used for transport. We had an assortment of vehicles and a rich assortment of men. There was one other NCO in the RASC platoon, but Lt Cope made me senior NCO, so I became acting sergeant - but I never wore the three stripes, nor received sergeant's pay.

I rather enjoyed the job. Lt Cope and I became very good friends and enjoyed some interesting and exciting adventures together.

Our work on Base Details was not hard, and there was plenty of time for swimming in the sea at Hammerliff or at a beach near Sousse - and a trip to the seashore could always be arranged. I discovered a small village near the shore where we could buy the best ice cream I had tasted for a long time. So I often took some of the men with me to visit the ice cream seller. I also used the time to teach some of the non-drivers among us how to drive Army lorries. The driver training route nearly always passed through the street where the ice cream seller had his shop!

While at Hammerliff, I noticed that one of the lorries seemed to be using an excessive amount of petrol in relation to the number of journeys I authorised. Upon closer investigation, I discovered that this same lorry often disappeared from the vehicle park at sunset. When questioned, the driver of the lorry denied any knowledge of the lorry's disappearance in the evenings. So, I kept watch and saw this driver take the lorry out of camp each evening.

I reported my findings to Lt Cope and suggested that I find the man some duty each evening to show we knew what he was doing - being absent without leave, the unauthorised use of an Army lorry and misuse of Government property (for example, petrol).

Lt Cope had a better idea.

We went to this driver's lorry while he was away swimming, and made a simple adjustment. The lorry was a six-wheel Austin, with a normal gearbox and a booster gearbox. There were two gear levers and also another lever that enabled the driver to change from one gearbox to the other. Lt Cope showed me how to put both gearboxes in neutral so that neither were effective. We left the lorry with both its gearboxes in neutral.

We waited for sunset, and watched this particular driver walk to his lorry. He looked around to make sure he was not observed; then quickly climbed into the cab. He started up the engine and put the gear lever into first position and revved up the engine, but the lorry remained motionless. After some time of making vain attempts to get the lorry moving, the driver climbed down from the cab, looking very worried. He stayed in camp that night.

The next morning I told him to move his lorry to another spot and to get ready to go out on a journey. He went to his lorry and started the engine, and tried to put the engine in gear, but nothing happened. Lt Cope and I watched him for a while and then we went over to him and asked if there was anything wrong. He explained that the gearbox was no good. He couldn't put the engine into gear. Lt Cope looked very concerned, and told me to try.

I climbed into the cab and, making sure the driver could not see what I was doing, I adjusted the lever and put both gearboxes back into action. I started up the engine, put the engine into gear and drove off. The driver's face was a picture to behold. I quietly suggested to him that the trouble was due to the lorry being used for unauthorised journeys in the night air by someone who left the camp at sunset. The driver never took his lorry out at night after that and no official action was taken against him, so his Army record remained unblemished.

CHAPTER ELEVEN

The Canvas Chapel

The contents of this chapter are taken from an account of the events written just after they occurred, with very few amendments, because the account seems to capture not only the events but also the spirit of the occasion.

The North African campaign was over and the new campaign in Sicily had begun. To some of the men who had fought in North Africa, it was a grim reality but, to others, it was campaign just across the water. While their comrades were fighting in Sicily, they had been ordered to remain behind as a rear party and reserve troops to replace casualties. This story concerns the rear party of the 78th Division.

The story really begins in Sousse, where two Salvation Army officers had opened a 'red shield canteen'. Religious services were held in one of the rooms set aside as a chapel. Sundays at 10.30am, a Salvation Army-type service was held. In the evening, at 6pm, a Church of England service was held, but attendance was voluntary. Usually about 40 to 50 men gathered for worship at this service. On Wednesdays at 6pm, a short mid-week service was held, which was begun at the request of the men who attended the Sunday evening service.

While attending these services, I met Sergeant Fred Udall of the London Irish Rifles. This casual acquaintance showed no prospect then of the future work for God that we would do together.

After a short time of happy Christian fellowship at Sousse, the rear party, known as the 78th Division Base Details, was moved to Bizerte on 25th September 1943. The campsite was a field, with no shade and no buildings: just a bare expanse of dried mud. The field was several miles from Bizerte and the prospects of visiting the town were nil. We pitched our tents and began settling-in, in a mood bordering on gloom.

On Thursday 30th September, I met Fred Udall again and we discovered that our tents were fairly near each other's. As we talked, we said how much we missed the meetings in the red shield canteen in Sousse, and expressed our wish that some form of religious service could be held in or near the camp. Fred said: "If only there was a church near here, or a tent, we could ask a Padre to conduct a service for us on Sunday."

I replied: "If only we had a tent or a building to use as a chapel, we could conduct a service ourselves. I am quite willing to conduct it, if we can find a tent we can use. I know of one or two fellows who would join us."

We discussed the idea, but always came back to the phrase, 'If only we had a tent.'

We each resolved to pray earnestly about the idea and the need.

We realised it would need courage to make this stand and hold a religious service in the camp. It would also take courage to ask others to join us in open Christian witness and worship. We thought that we could count on four others to join us, but had no idea if there were any more who would be interested in our venture.

Fred Udall had been a choirboy and had attended church regularly; yet it was not until he was in hospital at the close of the North African campaign that he was converted to Christianity. While in hospital, he met a Christian who was a member of the Plymouth Brethren, and this man was in the next bed to Fred. This man spoke to Fred about his need to know Jesus Christ as his personal Saviour, and helped Fred to make the decision to become a follower of Jesus Christ.

When Fred talked about his conversion experience he would say: "Why did no one tell me about Jesus, that he died for me? Why was I never told about salvation? Why did no one tell me that I had a soul to be saved?"

After he became a Christian, Fred was anxious to tell others about his Saviour. He was so filled with joy and peace he wanted others to share in these privileges, and to know for themselves the loving Saviour who died for them

Fred and I were very much aware of our limitations, of our own weaknesses and failings, but we were also conscious of a great and urgent need to spread the Gospel of Christ and to try to help others to know God and to trust in Jesus Christ. There were only two of us and we felt inadequate for this task, but we felt that we could not ignore this challenge; so we prayed about it and expected God to help us.

Friday 1st October dawned. To most people, it was just another day, with brilliant sunshine, a clear blue sky: a day untouched, but it was a day filled with possibilities. Fred Udall soon found me and greeted me with the words: "I've found one piece of canvas and nothing can stop us now."

The way was opened. All that was left was for us to follow along.

In the space of two hours, we had found enough spare canvas, poles, string and wire to build, not a tent, but a structure. All the material we found had been abandoned by previous occupiers of this barren field and so was honestly found.

We set to and began to erect some form of shelter. It was not a thing of beauty. There were no lines of grace or attractiveness. It was only a thing of utility. The structure consisted of three sides of a square, measuring some 20 feet square. The roof was almost flat and was some ten feet from the ground. One side was missing - partly because of lack of material and partly because it was the only way that we could have some light inside. It took no time to furnish it because there was no furniture to put in it: no seats, no table, no pulpit. It was filled with God's sunlight. We had left open the side that faced west to be able to obtain light at eventide. Fred and I had been very glad of the help of volunteers, who wanted to know what we were doing.

By lunchtime, the meeting place was as complete as we could make it. We decided to hold our first meeting at 6pm and began to spread the word, inviting men to attend the meeting.

At 6pm, the sun was nearing the rim of the mountain and peace was settling over the countryside, as 16 men gathered in the makeshift tent. They sat on the floor around the walls of the tent. Since we had no hymnbooks or musical instrument, we sang hymns from memory. Fred read the lesson and I conducted the service, giving a talk on the words in First Letter of Peter, chapter five and verse seven, 'Casting all your care upon Him; for He careth for you.'

At the close of the service, many of those present expressed the hope that there would be other services. Some expressed their gratitude for the service held and for the help received.

Fred and I were greatly encouraged by the attendance and by the two men who offered to help organise the services and other activities. Frank Utley, from Weymouth, was a member of the Church of England. He gave valuable assistance and acted as secretary. Joe Colley was a member of the Salvation Army, and he proved a real pillar of strength to our group. On the Saturday evening, several men met together in the tent for a discussion evening.

On Sunday 3rd October, we planned to hold two services and the invitation to attend these voluntary services was spread around the camp. At 10.30am, 18 men attended the service, which I conducted. I spoke from the words in Galatians chapter six, verses seven and eight, 'Be not deceived, God is not mocked; for what a man soweth that shall he also reap.'

Once again the hymns were sung from memory. By the time we met for the service at 3pm, Frank Utley and Joe Colley had written out by hand eight copies of four hymns, and so there appeared, 'Base Details Hymn Sheet'. We used them at the 3pm service when I was, again, the speaker. I gave an address on Matthew chapter two, verse ten, 'When they saw the star they rejoiced with exceeding great joy.'

Twelve men attended this service and, at its close, there were numerous requests for a service to be held at 6pm.

By 6pm, the 'Base Details Hymn Sheet' contained eight hymns, but there were only eight copies. It was an agreeable surprise to find 12 men present. I was asked to introduce a subject for Bible Study. I spoke briefly on 'The Love of Christ', and then invited those present to say a few words on this theme. We all felt it had been a profitable time.

At the close of the discussion, a man, who had remained silent all through the discussion, said: "I am a Jew, and have always been taught that this Jesus you worship is an imposter. You believe he is the Son of God but I know nothing about him. What does he teach?"

The meeting continued as we told him about Jesus Christ and our faith in him. At the end of this additional Bible Study, the man asked permission to attend our services and to be allowed to ask questions, saying he had become interested in Jesus Christ. We later learned that four other men had been greatly impressed by this Sunday evening Bible Study.

We decided to hold some form of meeting every evening at 6pm, with a variety of activities. Services would be held on Sunday and Wednesday evenings. On the other evenings we would hold discussions on a variety of subjects, or a singsong, or whatever the men, who were present, chose on that evening. The attendance varied in number but there was always a meeting, discussion group or service for those who were interested. This venture caused a great deal of discussion among the men in the camp, and also aroused some caustic comments.

The meeting place was now called 'The Canvas Chapel'. The congregation was made up of men from many denominations: Church of England, Methodists, Presbyterians, Baptists, the Brethren, Salvation Army, and one Jew, with some of no previous church affiliation. All denominational differences were forgotten. We were united in our worship and in our witness for Jesus Christ. There were many denominations, but only one Gospel.

Those who did not attend the meetings passed many comments, but the influence of those who attended was felt throughout the camp.

Lt Cope told me that in the Officers' Mess, when the sound of our hymn singing reached them, the officers became quiet and listened. Some of the officers said they would like to attend the services but felt it was wiser to leave us on our own. Lt Cope said the influence of the Canvas Chapel services and meetings was definitely felt in the Officers' Mess.

The Canvas Chapel was twice blown down by the wind. Each time, it was rebuilt.

I approached Lt Cope and Captain Eason (of the Royal West Kents) and asked if it was possible to obtain a real tent that was suitable for use as a chapel. There was a severe shortage of tents at that time, but they promised to do what they could.

The daily meeting, at 6pm, rapidly became a firm favourite. Just before 6pm, the faithful few could be seen making their way through the tent lines, often the targets of sarcastic remarks, as they made their way to the Canvas Chapel.

The sight of the Chapel was a challenge, comfort, help and a constant reminder, not only of Christian fellowship, but also of the things we professed as Christians. One of the men said: "I look forward to 6pm all through the day. It is a mark to which I aim. It is a peg upon which to centre my thoughts, and it helps me to live a Christian life when taunted and tempted."

The Chapel became a place of peace where anyone could pray in silence; read the Bible, or just sit quietly. It was open to all the men in the camp and was used by some who never attended any of the services or meetings. Some went there every evening to say their prayers. It was not unusual to see men in there during the day reading their Bible or bowed in prayer.

Months later, in Italy, I met men who spoke with affection, longing and, even, respect for the Canvas Chapel. Many of these men had never attended the services, but they remembered the influence they felt it had had on them and, indeed, the whole camp.

On Sunday 10th October, three services were held and, because no one else would do it, I gave the talk at each service. The other members of our group would read the lesson, offer prayer, and some would sing solos, but they were all reluctant to lead the Bible Study and give the talk. The following evening was a social evening. Tuesday 12th October was a musical evening because we found a piano-accordion player in the camp who agreed to play for us - and we all enjoyed a singsong.

On the morning of Wednesday 13th October, we received a tent to use as a chapel.

We soon erected it. In the evening, we were loaned a battery from a lorry and soon had electric light installed. We also obtained two forms for seating, and a table. Somehow, Fred Udall went into Bizerte and found a chaplain and persuaded him to lend us some copies of a hymnbook. This sudden affluence excited us, because we had previously decided to make the Wednesday evening service a special service.

We had been praying that, as a result of this service, someone would come to trust in Jesus Christ, and a few of us had been praying that it would be Jim Wyatt. Jim was a communist, but had attended a few meetings at the Canvas Chapel after much encouragement by Joe Colley and myself. To make sure he was present, I asked him to read the lesson at the service and he agreed to do so.

Joe Colley had agreed to conduct the service and give the talk. As the service began we could hear men outside the tent singing their type of songs hoping to disturb us. Joe continued leading the service. Jim Wyatt read the first lesson and Frank Utley read the second lesson. Fred Udall and I each sang a solo; then Joe stood up to begin his talk. As Joe began to speak the disruptive singing outside ceased.

In his talk, Joe linked up all the talks I had given and showed how they all led to a climax that he saw in the parable of the prodigal son. At the end of his talk, Joe invited anyone who wished to follow Jesus Christ to come to the front and confess Christ as Saviour.

Reg Tarrant came forward and Fred went to him and knelt with him and prayed for him. Joe again invited anyone to come forward who wished to accept Jesus Christ as Saviour and Jim Wyatt walked to the front. Joe and I went to Jim and talked with him about the way of salvation, and we prayed with him. We had prayed for one convert, but God gave us two.

The meeting began at 6pm, and was followed by a social time when mugs of tea were served to all present. They were still there at 10pm, talking and singing and enjoying the fellowship. At 9.30pm, I had received a message to report immediately to Lt Cope. He told me to get everything ready for the RASC platoon to move off at 5am when we would proceed to Phillipville. I returned to the tent and told the men of the RASC to return to their tents and prepare to move at 5am.

Many of the men present were deeply disappointed at the thought of the breaking up of the fellowship we had formed. I reminded them this was the 13th meeting that we had held and, as this special meeting was completed, two men had found the Saviour through the meeting. So God had enabled us to do his will before the Army moved us on again. When the RASC platoon left Bizerte, those who remained continued meeting together until, eventually, they were all moved out.

Many months later, in Italy, I learned that two men of the Royal West Kents, who had attended the meetings and services in the Canvas Chapel, had been greatly influenced by those meetings. One of them, aged about 20, told his friend when they left for Italy: "I don't want to die, but I am now prepared to die because of what we heard and found at the Canvas Chapel in Bizerte."

Unfortunately, he was killed in his first time in action against the enemy in Italy, and his friend was badly wounded. His friend sent me the message.

The RASC platoon left Bizerte on Thursday 14th October and made the journey to Phillipville. After a brief stay there, we embarked on infantry landing craft (ILC), leaving our vehicles at Phillipville.

The landing craft were not built with any thought to the comfort of any passengers they may carry. Each craft was flat bottomed and, as it moved forward, would rise above the waves and then fall down on to the sea with a resounding crash that shook all on board. Also, the fuel tanks were between the flat-bottomed hull and the deck on which we sat, so that we could hear the diesel oil swishing and slapping about all the time. The hold in which we 'lived' had a low ceiling so that we had to walk in a crouching position. The living quarters were filled with rows of seats. They were very square in shape and formed of wooden slats and arm rests. All we could do was to sit in these chairs with our kit around us.

We were allowed on deck in the daytime, but there was very little room for movement and the deck seemed very narrow. Toilet facilities were primitive in the extreme, and consisted of a garden seat for four jutting out over the stern. Three or four of the slats forming the seat had been removed to allow a necessary opening. It was wise not to look down because we could see the propellers were slightly in front of our sitting position, virtually directly under our feet. Being at the extreme end of the stern, and almost in the water, the lurching and wallowing of the craft did not encourage anyone to linger in this precarious position. Miraculously, no accidents or incidents were reported from this stern end!

At meal times, we slowly moved in a line towards the centre of the craft. We were told it was 'amidships'. There, the cooks ladled out whatever was on the menu for that meal. There was barely room to walk between the various fittings and equipment on one side and the flimsy retaining rail or chain on the seaward side. Successfully negotiating this narrow passageway on a lurching ship, trying to maintain our balance and, at the same time, trying to retain the food in our 'dixies' demanded a high degree of skill.

After two days at sea we landed in Sicily, but stayed in port only two days. Then we sailed on to Italy, landing at Taranto on 24th October 1943. We were glad to leave the ILC and to walk on a surface that did not move violently up and down.

● In the desert.

The Canvas Chapel

CHAPTER TWELVE

Arrival in Italy

The crossing from Sicily to Italy in the ILC was uneventful, but we were glad to leave the landing craft when we arrived at Taranto on 24th October 1943. We were billeted in a partially constructed hospital. We had barely found places to put our kit and claim a bed-space when other members of the base details in other units made their presence known. Those who had attended the Canvas Chapel in Bizerte took it for granted that a service of some sorts would be held that evening.

I spoke to the company sergeant major (CSM), who was a member of the Transit Camp staff, and asked if it would be possible for us to have the use of a room in which to hold a religious service. I think he was surprised by my request and said accommodation was scarce and no room was available. I explained about the Canvas Chapel and that many men had requested a Christian worship service be held. He hesitated a moment then said: "You can use my office after 6pm. There is no electric light but I'll try to find you some candles, and a blanket to cover the window for blackout."

The news that there would be a service in the CSM's office quickly spread and, at 6pm, some 20 men turned up at the office.

There had been no time for me to prepare a talk, so we began with singing a hymn. Someone read a lesson. Then we sang another hymn; someone offered a prayer, and then Fred Udall sang a solo. While the service was proceeding, I had spent time in prayer for guidance and tried to gather my thoughts together and place them in some sort of order.

It came my turn to speak and I reminded the hearers of our recent crossing from North Africa to Italy and compared it to our voyage through life. I said our trust had been in the skipper of the ILC and he had brought us safely to port. I spoke of God as the Divine Skipper in whom we ought to trust if we wanted to make a successful voyage through life. Some of the men expressed the opinion that was one of the best talks I had given. It was so topical that it made a special appeal.

After this we stayed together, singing hymns and choruses from memory. I sang 'The Holy City', which was always a great favourite with the lads. I had heard of one platoon of Bren carriers who sang it together before going into action on one occasion during the North African Campaign.

This service in the Taranto Transit Camp was the final service for the base details men because, within a few days, we were all scattered to various units.

The RASC detachment of base details stayed together, and we moved further inland. The weather began to get colder and snow could be seen on the tops of some of the mountains. One cause of great joy was the arrival of mail. Because we were on detached duties from our own companies, the arrival of mail was rare.

The first week in November, a large sack of mail arrived and, for some men, these were the first letters from home that they had received for almost six months. I was more fortunate. It was the first mail that I had received for seven weeks. The arrival of letters from home lifted the morale a great deal.

On Wednesday, 10th November, Lt Percy Cope, officer in charge of base details, asked me if I would conduct a service on 11th November. I readily agreed to do so. We gathered together beneath the spreading branches and leaves of a large fig tree, which formed a graceful canopy over us. I had a number of copies of the Army Prayer Book that also contained a selection of hymns, so we were able to sing hymns.

Joe Colley offered prayer. Jim Wyatt read the lesson: Psalm 27. I spoke on 'Remembrance':

* Remember past mistakes and past blessings, past protection and guidance.
* Remember these things after the war is over.
* Remember the cause for which we are fighting and strive to prevent future wars.
* Remember our ideals and plans for the post-war years.
* Remember that a nation can only be changed if the individuals in it are changed. Jesus Christ is our Hope, the answer to our problems and the source of power able to change us all.

Many of the men, and the officers present expressed appreciation for the service.

Base details was disbanded on 15th November and the men returned to their units. We had been together for five months and had shared some happy and useful experiences.

I rejoined my own unit - 237 Company, RASC - near the Sangro River. I found that there had been several promotions while I had been away, so I had missed my chance of promotion. There were also a number of new faces among the men in my platoon. It was soon back to the usual routine for we were involved in the preparations for what became the Battle of the River Sangro.

One evening, just as it was becoming dark, I was detailed to go with other men on a troop lift, that is, transporting troops from one place to another. This time we were to take infantry troops into the front line, almost on the banks of the river Sangro. I had been given an Austin six-wheel truck, one of the trucks we had had on base details. With its double gearbox and double set of wheels at the back, it was considered suitable to act as the platoon breakdown truck. The only trouble was that this vehicle was the worst of the six we had had in base details because it had a warped cylinder head, due to being driven with little or no water in the cooling system during the North African campaign. It was necessary to carry a five gallon drum of engine oil to be able to carry out frequent topping up of the engine oil level. Despite this, it was a powerful vehicle and ideal for a breakdown truck.

At the infantry regiment's location, the men climbed aboard the trucks and the officers sat in the cab with the driver. The officer who sat with me - Lt Phillips - I had met in North Africa, when he was a sergeant. During one of the battles he had been awarded the Military Medal and, during another battle, he had been 'promoted on the field' to second lieutenant and he was now a first lieutenant. He was one of the battalion of The Welch Regiment which had been divided among the three Irish regiments in the 38th Irish Brigade in North Africa as replacements for casualties suffered. That was when I first met him.

As we slowly moved away from the location, I discovered that Lt Phillips was from the Rhondda valley. As we talked, our conversation turned to Wales and the things of home.

I cannot remember how it happened but we began singing hymns to Welsh tunes, especially 'In heavenly love abiding' to the tune Penlan. At times we could hear the men in the back of the lorry joining in the singing. Eventually we arrived at the point where the men were to take up their positions, and the men climbed down out of the lorry, and Lt Phillips led them away into the darkness. Before he left me he shook hands as I said: "God be with you."

I am glad to say he survived the battle and the war.

The journey to the front line did not involve too much excitement. We took the troops in front of the line of guns and we were told there were at least 400 in position ready to open fire at 9pm. We all hoped we would be able to get away before this massive barrage opened up. The troops left us and made their way forward and we began the complicated business of getting the convoy of trucks turned around. Somehow, something went wrong and we were just in front of the guns at 9pm. When the guns fired at the same time it was deafening and blinding. We found ourselves looking almost down the muzzles of the guns - which, to say the least, was a frightening experience.

I had been in a similar position before, but it was still frightening as the shells screamed overhead. One young driver had never been in the front line before and he ran around screaming in fear. I managed to grab him and tried to calm him, but my efforts were in vain until I slapped his face. He stopped screaming and began to cry. I took him back to his lorry and told him to turn it around and pointed to the way out.

In the furious activity to get the lorries away, one driver - Bill Finch - attempted to get his lorry to climb a small bank of earth. It was a Bedford three ton truck and the bank was too steep. Whether he hit something or whether it was the angle of the bank was to steep we could not be sure, but the engine fan blades ripped the radiator to pieces and the cooling system was wrecked. He could not drive the lorry any further. This accident happened near one of the few exits from the area we could use, so that added to the confusion.

Sergeant Ted Cake, of Hamworthy, Poole, directed the other lorries around the disabled truck, but stopped me and told me to wait until all the other lorries had left and then tow Bill Finch and his lorry back to our location. Once again, I was to act as the platoon breakdown waggon. We had to wait for what seemed a very long time, just in front of the guns knowing that, at any moment, the enemy would start shelling the area and the gun positions.

It became a very lively time and was getting worse by the time I was able to get the breakdown truck into a position where I could fasten a tow chain to the broken-down truck. By this time, between the gun flashes and noise of the explosions, and the crash of incoming shells bursting among us, with the flash of the burst and the over-powering breath-catching smell of cordite, it was not a place to linger. I hitched the tow-chain onto the Bedford truck, warned Bill Finch where I was going to drive and slowly began to haul the truck out of its perilous position.

It was a pitch-black night, and it was raining heavily. Trying to remember the landmarks I had noted on our way into the line, I gradually progressed pass the gun-lines. Away from the flash of the guns and of the bursting shells my night vision returned and I found the track leading from the front line.

Suddenly, a battery of 25 pounder guns, hidden behind a hedge on the left-hand side of the track I was following, fired together. The flashes from the gun muzzle of the first gun seemed to be at the end of the lorry radiator and seemed to envelop the cab. Momentarily blinded, I drove by instinct but, as soon as my eyes adjusted again, I went as fast as I could before the next batch of shells arrived or the guns fired again. I felt sorry for Bill Finch in the lorry being towed. He had no choice but to sit there and take it all and follow me.

We arrived back at our camp about 11pm. There were no hot drinks, no meal, and no one to say, 'Glad you made it back'.

We parked the lorries and waded through the mud to our respective tents, with the rain pouring down on us. There was a faint hope that we might be able to get a few hours sleep before the next job in the morning. I made my way to the place where I normally slept, a large tarpaulin stretched over the iron framework taken from the back of a lorry.

There were no lights. I stumbled to my 'bed'. I undressed and dropped into bed and immediately leapt out again. My bed was full of water. The canvas tarpaulin had sprung a leak immediately over my bed. I dressed, put on my greatcoat, spread my groundsheet on the mud and lay down and slept until 6am.

After the battle for the Sangro and the follow-through, the 78th Division was brought out of the front line for a rest.

The division had been in almost constant action since November 1942. During this time, the losses had been heavy and the replacement of men had been many. Morale was still good, but the whole division was now tired; so the powers that be decided to give the division a month's rest for reorganisation, retraining and refitting.

The rest and retraining was carried out near Campobasso, which had been a holiday resort and a market town in peacetime. Now, it became a leave centre for the Eighth Army. There were three cinemas, an ENSA theatre, together with clubs for officers and for NCOs, with canteens for everyone.

For some units of the 78th Division, this rest period was very short - for some were sent back into the line - but, for most of the men in the division, it meant Christmas being spent out of the front line. Christmas dinner for most of the men in the division included turkey, roast pork, plum pudding and mince pies. There was also beer available and some said that there was also whisky in some units, plus supplies of the local wines.

Perhaps one of the best parts of this Christmas for most of us was that we were billeted in a house or farm. Consequently, we were dry and warm - which was a rare treat. Our clothes were dry. So were our boots and socks, and we could wash in warm water. There were even chocolates and cigarettes, and I was able to exchange my beer and cigarette rations for chocolate and sweets, which suited me better. Added to this, instead of being called at 6.30am - or earlier - with breakfast at 7.30am, our normal routine was breakfast at 9am. Another relief was the absence of regimental duties. Indeed, we had few other duties.

It was a real time off work.

We decorated the large room, that we used as our mess hall, with paper trimmings, branches of mistletoe. We even had paper tablecloths on the table. The cooks worked miracles and were loudly cheered by all. This Christmas did a great deal to lift the morale of the troops.

After Christmas we moved to Isernia, in the middle sector of Italy, and took up our normal work of transport. Winter had really set in and two of our men were isolated in the mountains when they ran into a 20 feet deep snowdrift. At times, I drove up into the mountain region and found the roads there to be narrow and, often, only ledges on the side of the mountain - with very deep drops on the side.

While we were at Isernia, a British Chapel was 'founded'. In this building, religious services were held, along with community singing evenings, discussion groups and lectures. At these activities I met many friends I had known at various times, including some who had attended the meetings in the Canvas Chapel.

I was appointed the NCO in charge of the Army cinema. This was the local cinema taken over by the Army. I had to deal with the allocation and booking of seats by the various units in the area. The appointment greatly amused me because my first job had been as a cinema projectionist, coupled with trainee electrician, stagehand, and spotlight operator for live shows. Now I was 'almost a manager', co-operating with the Army projectionist.

My next job was attachment to a mobile bath unit for transport duties. This was one of my fortunate attachments because the Bath Unit was stationed in the town of Campobasso. It was a good, dry and warm billet. The duties were few and I had plenty of time to look around the town, visit the NAAFI, the clubs and cinemas. One of the clubs had a scheme whereby, for five shillings, a parcel of foodstuff from South Africa could be sent to a family in England. One parcel per family was the rule. I sent a parcel to my parents, and also sent a parcel to the parents of my friend Bill Aish. Bill was surprised a few weeks later to receive a letter from his mother thanking him for a wonderful parcel.

One of the jobs I had was to collect the daily ration issue for the bath unit, and hand them over to the cook.

One day the cook came to me in a very bad mood. He complained about the quality of the cocoa I had brought. He had tried to make cocoa but the cocoa refused to dissolve, despite much stirring. I went with him to the cookhouse to examine the cocoa. The cook opened the sandbag containing the substance. It was the custom for dry rations to be put in clean sandbags, items such as flour, sugar, salt, lentils and the like, for transport to the units. I looked at the contents of the open sandbag and said: "You'll never make cocoa with that stuff. It's dehydrated meat."

He had never seen dehydrated meat before. I explained the meat was in very small granules and were brown in colour, and needed to be soaked in water for several hours before being used.

Campobaso was the lull before the storm.

The mobile bath unit moved to some place near Caserta. It was a journey that took the convoy from 8.30am until 5pm on 16th February 1944. We arrived in the dark and had to put up tents, and the weather was very cold. I remained there ten days before receiving orders to rejoin my own unit.

I eventually found my platoon, near Capua, billeted in a cemetery. It was then the custom in Italy for coffins to be placed end on in long narrow recesses in the cemetery wall. Some of these long horizontal recesses were empty and provided dry sleeping quarters - and they were not too draughty.

The mortuary was used as the cookhouse, and we quickly became accustomed to seeing the cooks using the slab as the service bench on which they put the various cooking pots containing the food they were to serve to us.

On arrival at the cemetery, one of the men decided to have a look around the place. He examined the chapel and then found his way down into the crypt.

It was also the custom for the zinc coffin to be taken from its resting place in the cemetery wall ten years after interment. The bones were then removed and placed in the crypt. The man discovered this mountain of bones and rushed up into the chapel and said: "Don't let the cooks go down there or we will have bone soup for ever!"

CHAPTER THIRTEEN

Introduction to Cassino

We moved from the cemetery and found ourselves much nearer to Cassino. On our way to our new location we drove along one of the main roads to Cassino. At one point, we came to a slight rise in the ground, and the road made a wide curve to the left. As we came almost to the top of the rise there was a military cemetery on the left, enclosed partly by the curve. In it were what seemed to be hundreds of wooden crosses and each one bore the silver fern on a black background: the sign of the New Zealand Division.

We had heard that the New Zealanders and the Americans had suffered very heavy casualties in the first battle of Cassino and the number of crosses testified to the truth of the report. The New Zealand troops suffered heavy casualties, especially in the area of the railway station in Cassino.

It was a place I was destined to visit in the near future.

The first battle for Cassino took place between 12th January and 12th February 1944. General Alexander's orders to General Mark Clark of the 5th Army were 'to make as strong a thrust as possible towards Cassino and Frosinone (on the road to Rome) shortly before the Anzio assault landing, to draw in enemy reserves which might be employed against the landing forces and then create a break in the enemy front through which every opportunity will be taken to link up rapidly with the sea-borne operation.'

The second battle began on the night of 14th/15th February, with General Freyberg in command, and using the 4th Indian Division, the 2nd New Zealand Division and some British units.

The third battle was planned to begin on 24th February, and was to be launched with an aerial attack on the town of Cassino, but it had to be postponed for three weeks because of bad weather conditions.

The fourth battle opened on 11th May 1944 at 11pm, when 1,600 guns opened fire.

At the time, few people, except those engaged in the battles for Cassino, realised the tremendous loss of life, or the suffering and horror of Cassino. It is reported that General Freyberg, commanding the New Zealand forces, who, when reviewing the scene at Cassino on both sides of the Rapido river, saw the shell-holes and bomb craters full of water, said it reminded him of Passchendaele in the First World War - which had cost over 400,000 casualties.

Some people believe that Cassino, between January and May 1944, is 'the Stalingrad of the Italian campaign'. It was also reported that Hitler said of Cassino, that it was the equivalent of the battle of the Somme in the First World War. After the battles of Cassino, Lieutenant General Anders, Commander of the Polish Corps, himself a veteran of World War I, said that Cassino was the only battlefield of the Second World War that resembled those of the First World War.

After the final battle was over, I went back to Cassino with some comrades who had been there with me. We visited some of the places I had been in the darkness of night, but now I saw them in broad daylight. I was horrified and wondered how we had even been able to drive jeeps into such places and in such devastation. I had seen devastation of towns, villages and countryside, but I had seen nothing like this. It reminded me of photographs of the battlefields in the First World War. I was not surprised, after the war, that Cassino was linked with Stalingrad and a few other of the worst battlefields, as being reminiscent of the horrific battlefields of World War 1.

From newspaper reports that reached us during the battles for Cassino, and immediately afterwards, it seemed that the people at home did not realise the horror and suffering and devastation of Cassino. This may have been due to censorship. Then, as the fighting moved up the Liri valley and reached Rome, the D-Day landings eclipsed the Italian Campaign. The troops in Italy felt that their efforts and suffering were quickly forgotten or ignored and that the people thought the real war was now confined to France.

The conditions under which front line troops existed in Cassino were dreadful in the extreme. Dead bodies could not be buried. The terrain was so rocky it was impossible to dig neither graves nor slit-trenches. To afford some kind of protection, 'sangers' were made by arranging lumps of rock to form a wall and, if possible, some form of roof was improvised. The true extent of what men suffered there seems now not to be sufficiently appreciated. The suffering and sacrifice and discomfort of the ordinary infantrymen, who bore the brunt of the battles, seems now largely forgotten.

When the infantry, or any other soldier going into the forward area, passed the artillery gun-lines, there seemed to be a change of atmosphere and of personal feelings.

This was not just my impression. Others have testified to the same sort of experience. It is difficult to describe it, but it was real and we all felt it. At that point, it seemed that we moved forward into another kind of world detached from the world behind the guns. It was some other kind of existence. This was the exclusive world of the infantry, which only the infantry and those who worked closely with them know. This was the world of horror and hardship, of suffering and fear, a place of mental and physical discomfort. Yet, strangely, it was also the world of a special brand of comradeship and compassion.

All who served in the battles of Cassino said the same thing: their abiding memory is of the great white stone Benedictine Monastery perched on top of Monte Cassino. To us, it was like a malevolent thing watching every move. To see the monastery was to be in constant danger.

There has been a great controversy as to whether the Germans ever occupied the monastery. We, who were there, were sure that they had. David Nahmad, of Bath, served with the London Scottish at Cassino. He was one of a machine-gun crew who occupied a house at Monastery Hill in Cassino. He has gone on record as saying that, for him and his comrades, it was common knowledge that the monastery was occupied by German troops. From their machine-gun post they had a clear view of the monastery.

John Deans, of Swansea, served with the 132nd (Welsh) Field Regiment, in the 78th (Battleaxe) Division. He said that his regiment took part in the four battles for Cassino. He spent two weeks with the Lancashire Fusiliers and the West Surrey's in 'The Bowl', which was less than a quarter of a mile from the monastery. One night, he went out to lay a telephone wire to a forward observation post and, when about 150 yards from the monastery, came under very accurate machine-gun fire from the monastery. He says that he can vouch for the fact that the Germans did use the monastery in a military sense.

Monte Cassino was the key position so far as the road to Rome was concerned. As we faced the opening to the Liri valley, Monte Cassino was on our right and San Angelo on our left. The enemy occupied both positions and, effectively, they blocked the entry into the Liri valley and so closed the road to Rome. Only when Cassino was cleared of Germans and Monte Cassino and San Angelo were captured could the Allies advance on Rome.

With increasing command of the air, General Alexander was able to bring heavy bombers to attack Cassino and the monastery. These were eventually reduced to rubble. I remember watching the first wave of bombers attacking the monastery. Earlier, we had watched heavy shells bursting against the walls of the monastery. The immediate result of the bombardment was disappointing. The devastation in the town of Cassino hampered the attacking Allied forces because it had provided the defending enemy with very effective cover for pockets of resistance. Also, the huge bomb craters became filled with stinking water from which a large multitude of frogs kept up an incessant croaking chorus.

The battle of Cassino became an expensive stalemate. But, out of this, there were some advantages. Because of Cassino it was reported that 20 elite German Divisions had been kept in Italy for many months. Also, the Foggia airfield system gave the Allied Strategic Air Force both a valuable base from which to support ground troops in Italy and from which to operate against targets in southern France and central Europe.

During all this time, from January to May, the painful and costly fighting in Cassino continued. Then, in the final battle, Polish troops captured the monastery and its surrounding military positions. The Allied troops fought their way through Cassino and into the Liri valley, and on to Rome. In the space of about three weeks, Cassino had been stormed, the Gustav Line had been broken and the Anzio beachhead relieved. Allied troops entered Rome on 4th June.

It was against this background that we became involved in the battles of Cassino. It all began with a training programme. The 78th Division went into training that, for the infantry, included river-crossing exercises, street fighting and co-operation with tanks. This intensive training lasted for three weeks. But, for our company, transport work continued as normal.

My own introduction to Cassino did not involve any new training. One of the jobs given to our platoon was the transport of ballast from the railway track to forward areas to help make a road, ready for use in the next attack. Those on 'ballast transport' began their journey in the afternoon and went to a certain spot on the railway track and, with the help of the Royal Engineers, loaded each lorry with about three tons of these cobblestones. At about 5.30pm, as the darkness of evening began to fall, the lorries moved forward, sheltered between two high embankments. As the darkness deepened, about 6pm, the lorries cautiously moved forward, slowly making their way towards Cassino. The nearer the lorries got to the battle area the more intense was the enemy action.

Upon reaching a certain point, the lorry driver would be told where he was to unload the ballast. Sometimes, this would mean going through the front line and into no-man's-land. This usually provoked enemy action towards us while we were unloading. This was a task that could not be done quietly. The lorries were made of steel and the moving of three tons of stones by means of a shovel scraping along the steel floor and sides, created a noise that carried for long distances. Enemy mortar bombs would soon begin to arrive, and sometimes an enemy machine-gun would add to our discomfort and, frequently, enemy flares would light up the scene, causing everyone to fall to the ground and hug the earth.

One of the places for unloading was on the edge of what remained of a wood, and, in the starlight, pale moonlight, or in the glare of a flare, the trees seemed to move and this increased the tension. Several times an enemy patrol came out to investigate. When this happened, the drivers were told to continue the unloading and leave the German patrol to the infantry. All these activities acted as a tremendous spur to perform the unloading in very quick time.

One evening, as an engineer and I were hurrying to unload the ballast, we became the object of concentrated hate from the German mortar platoon. We worked hurriedly as long as we could, but things became too hot for us so we dived for cover, which was a ditch near the side of the lorry. As we hit the ditch a vehicle known as an 'Ark' came towards us, and stopped nearby. The Ark was an armoured vehicle like a scout car that could travel at very good speeds - forward or reverse - but the floor of the Ark was only 18 inches from the ground.

Suddenly, the top of the Ark opened and an officer climbed out. Just as he put his feet to the ground a concentrated volley of mortar bombs arrived, accompanied by some accurate machine-gun fire. The officer hit the ground and tried to crawl under the Ark. He succeeded in getting his head and shoulders under cover but was still on his knees, so that his posterior was pointing to the sky. I said to the engineer with me: "He's got his tin hat on the wrong end."

The reply came: "If you don't keep your so-and-so head down, you won't need your tin hat."

He had no sense of humour!

One night, one of the drivers inadvertently drove his lorry into a shell-hole and, despite our best efforts, we could not get it out. Our efforts attracted the attention of the enemy and we had to withdraw, leaving the lorry in the shell-hole. The next evening, I was told to take the driver of that lorry and recover it, if it was still there. I left the driver at the front line and cautiously advanced in what I thought was the right direction, to find the lorry. Somehow I took the wrong direction and I was alone in no-man's-land without a clue which way to turn.

As I anxiously looked around for some sort of landmark, I noticed a movement and quickly dropped to the ground. The figure of a man approached me, and as he came closer I recognised a British uniform. Very slowly I rose to my feet and softly called to the man, identifying myself. The figure approached me very warily. He was an infantry officer who had been having a look around. I asked him if he had seen a three-ton Bedford lorry in a shell-hole. He told me where it was, only 20 or 30 yards to my left.

I returned to the front line to bring the other driver and another lorry to collect the stranded vehicle. Suddenly, a sentry whom I could not see, challenged me.

I realised I had not been told the latest password. The password was frequently changed to prevent enemy soldiers using one they may have heard. I turned to where I thought the infantry officer was and called softly to him: "What is the password for tonight?"

There was a pause and it seemed a very long pause to me. Then: "Oh. Ahhhhh. Hmm. Ah. Try 'pipe'."

As I turned to give the password I heard a Bren gun being cocked ready for firing. I quickly said: "Pipe."

A voice answered: "Tobacco."

Then came those beautiful words: "Pass, friend."

I moved forward and was abruptly halted by that voice again, saying: "Watch out. Don't walk on me."

The sentry was in a hole near a pile of bricks and I could not see him. I told him I would soon be back again with a three-ton Bedford lorry and would then be towing another three ton Bedford away. All he said was: "Well, do it quietly."

We recovered the lorry without further incident.

CHAPTER FOURTEEN

The Jeep Platoon

The 78th Division Jeep Platoon was formed from men drawn from the four RASC companies in the 78th Division. None of us were volunteers. The men began arriving at the very primitive billets assigned to the Jeep Platoon at Mignano.

Mignano was about ten miles from Cassino and, as usual, was set among the hills. It was a very busy place where all sorts of military supplies were stacked or stored. It was the end of the fuel pipeline and, at this point, the fuel was transferred to four gallon jerricans, ready for transport to forward positions. This hive of activity was really the springboard for the front line positions.

When I arrived at the location of the Jeep Platoon with Jock Berry from my own company, there were a number of men already assembled, including men I came to know very well: Jim Farrell, Bobby Hewitt, Jack Morphet, Ted Roberts, Bert Jones, Billows from Bristol, Dickinson, and several others. Over the next few days, other men arrived, plus a few NCOs, and also Captain Sharman.

The Jeep Platoon officially came into existence on 12th March 1944, with the usual chaos. No one seemed to know where we were to go, or if we were to stay in our present location, or what we were supposed to do.

Eventually the confusion was partly sorted out and we were taken to a field overlooked by a railway embankment. By the time we arrived at this location it was dark. We were issued with small two-man tents, which we erected by the light of the gun flashes.

On the other side of the embankment, on the rising ground, was a battery of very large guns of the American Army. When these guns were fired the ground shook and the sides of a small two-man canvas tents vibrated violently.

The rising ground occupied by the American artillery was called 'Million Dollar Hill'. The Americans told us that the name referred to the cost of the ammunition and shells used to capture the site - and also because of the large number of American casualties suffered in capturing it.

One of these huge guns was named 'Belching Bertha'. One evening when 'Belching Bertha' was fired, there was a premature burst in the breechblock, and the explosion shattered the gun and several Americans were wounded. Large chunks of metal flew in all directions and for considerable distances. Some pieces fell on the Jeep Platoon's location.

Two days later, we collected our jeeps and learned a bit more about the job we were to do. Because of the roughness of the terrain, and the steepness of the mountains, getting supplies to the front line presented terrible problems. In many of the forward positions it was impracticable or impossible for ordinary Army transport lorries to operate.

Mules were used, but their load carrying capacity was limited and their progress was slow. The mules and the muleteers were marvellous. They did a tremendous job and earned the admiration of all who saw them, worked with them, or had to depend on them for supplies. The muleteers were Indians and, since we later worked alongside them, our only means of communication was through Italian words we knew and which they understood, plus much sign language.

To try to increase the quantity of supplies to the front line in the mountains, and in Cassino itself, the commander of the 78th Division, General Keightley, decided to form a jeep platoon. That was where we came in.

While awaiting orders to begin active operations, we learned how to handle our new vehicles. The jeep had three gear levers. One was the normal gear lever for operating the three forward and one reverse gears. The second lever was to engage the four-wheel drive - a very present help in trouble. The third lever was to put the gearbox into booster, which proved to be a most useful lever in our active operations.

The jeep had no sides or doors, only open gaps. The windscreen was covered in a canvas envelop and was permanently secured, lying flat on the engine cover or bonnet, to prevent it reflecting the moonlight, starlight, Verey lights or gun flashes. There was no hood or roof because that would make to jeep a bigger target to be seen. There were two seats in front, for the driver and a passenger. The two seats at the back were designed for dwarfs, because there was very little legroom, and the available space was narrower than the width of the jeep because the rear wheels' covers occupied some of the seat space. Protection from the weather and the enemy was non-existent.

Each jeep had a two-wheeled trailer, and the top of the sides were splayed outwards. The trailer was roughly as long and as wide as the jeep, but was not very deep. It was obvious that the jeep and trailer were functionally designed. They were designed to operate over rough and hilly terrain and also to carry a fair-sized load. The jeep's ability to climb steep gradients and cover very rough country and so be able to maintain supplies to forward areas made them ideal transport for the Cassino area. They were marvellous vehicles.

While getting to know our new vehicles we also began to get to know our new comrades. This familiarisation is recorded by Jim Farrell in his book, 'My War' (page 58), where he writes: 'By this time, I was getting to know some of the other drivers either by name or accent. It was the usual mix with London, Bristol, Glasgow, Manchester, the North East and South Wales all represented.

'The odd one out was the South Wales man. He didn't swear, but that did not stop him talking! He was, in fact, very articulate. He could sing and did, sometimes, in the evening before we went out. It was an interest I shared with him, but not on the same level. With his fine tenor voice, he was much better than me. Besides, he knew all the words. He wrote them down for me: "Lover come back to me", "Call, call, Vienna mine", "I'll walk beside you" - and I still have them in faded writing in my old 1944 diary. His name was Bryn Little. He was popular, a lance corporal and inclined to be religious. That's what made him different.'

The day after we collected our jeeps, the attack on Cassino began.

General Keightley came to see us and told us quite bluntly what he expected from the jeep platoon. He warned us that the going would be very tough. I cannot now recall all that he said, but I remember his closing words. He said: "You are in for a dreadful time, and not all of you will live through it. But those who do live through it, will get a week's survivors leave."

General Keightley did not underestimate our task in any way, and he kept his word. Those of us who lived through it were given a week's leave in Bari.

We were reminded of the tough prospects ahead when a squad of Royal Irish Fusiliers joined us to be our protection on our journeys into forward areas. They were to ride in the front passenger seat of the jeep to defend the driver and his load. The men hated the job and said they were in danger sitting in a jeep, which was an easy target for the enemy. They were used to digging in and taking cover in slit trenches or buildings. They felt too exposed in a jeep and kept saying that they would not have our job at any price.

Just after the Royal Irish Fusiliers joined us, one of them came to me and said: "Are you the medical orderly?"

I thought some of the men from my own platoon had been talking, so I said I was. Dropping his trousers, he said: "Take a look at this."

One look was sufficient, and a slightly longer visual examination confirmed my diagnosis.

"Have I got a packet?" he asked meaning, 'Have I got a dose of venereal disease?'

I said: "Yes, get your small kit and report to the Field Dressing Station."

His only comment was: "Good, that gets me out of Cassino."

That says a lot about what the infantry thought of being in Cassino. Venereal disease was preferable to being in the horror and danger that was Cassino.

When St Patrick's Day arrived, the members of the Royal Irish Fusiliers asked permission to return to their unit to join in the celebrations. They never returned to the jeep platoon, and I wonder what tales they told their comrades of life with the jeeps.

In the morning of Wednesday 15th March, we watched wave after wave of Allied bombers flying over us and bombing the town of Cassino and the monastery. After about three hours, the aerial attack ended and the artillery began shelling the same targets. The main purpose of the combined attack failed, but the resulting ruins and rubble prevented the use of tanks and also prevented the infantry attack because the ruins and rubble had greatly improved the defensive positions of the enemy. Then it rained and filled the shellholes and bomb craters with water, turning them into miniature lakes.

Despite all the attacks, the monastery was still there, staring down on all the Allied movements like a malevolent monster.

In this brief lull before the storm, I had registered as an ordination candidate. That is, I had notified the appropriate body that I wished to apply for entry into a theological college to train for the Baptist ministry as soon as I was demobbed. This involved certain studies and the submitting of a written sermon at regular intervals to the Ordination Candidates' Secretary for Middle East Forces.

One evening, under the shelter of the railway embankment, I began preparing a sermon. The candle was balanced on top of my tin hat, which was perched on top of my upright kitbag. By this feeble glimmer I wrote my notes. At least, I did while the candle was alight but, about every ten minutes, one of the huge American guns fired and the shock-wave made the kitbag shake and wobble. This caused my tin hat to fall to the ground, and the candle ceased to glimmer. The whole edifice had to be re-constructed and the candle re-lit and concentration re-focused. It was exasperating, but it helped to teach me patience and endurance.

Two days after the bombing of the monastery, the jeep platoon went into action. Sections of jeeps were assigned to help various infantry units, and moved along 'Speedy Highway' in the direction of Cassino.

The first action in which I was involved began about 5pm, when I was told to take five jeeps and trailers, with drivers, and report to the Royal West Kent Regiment location. On arrival, the company sergeant major (CSM) instructed us to load up with cookhouse equipment, food, and various other items, plus ammunition. We also had to make room for a number of infantrymen who were going forward as replacement for casualties. Our destination was the railway station in Cassino. A guide would show us the way. By the time we had loaded everything it was dark, and we moved off, hoping that the guide knew the way.

The track we followed was fairly good until we turned left and we realised we were going towards the gun flashes and shell-bursts. This track was very rough and littered with shell-holes. Then we came to the inevitable white tapes denoting the safe lane through a mine-field. There were a few exciting moments and then the guide said: "Stop here."

I looked for the railway station, but all I saw was a heap of rubble, with debris every-where. We knew we were now in the world of the infantry.

Firing seemed to come from all quarters. We could hear rifle fire, tommy guns and mortars but, when I heard pistol shots and remembered that their range was only about 40 yards, I became a bit worried. Then we came under fire, so we quickly unloaded the jeeps and trailers, and the replacements. These infantrymen made their way further forward. Our guide disappeared.

Before we could turn the jeeps and trailers around, ready to leave, the CSM came to me and said: "Some of the men you brought up have been wounded. Can you take them back?"

We loaded the wounded into two of the jeeps and trailers. I called Driver Mattheson and told him that we were putting a very badly wounded man in his trailer. The man was wounded in the back and had spinal injuries, and I asked Mattheson to drive carefully and avoid shell-holes if he could. We carefully laid the wounded man on the floor of the trail-er, and Mattheson drove off.

While all this activity was taking place, Jim Farrell and others in the second section arrived and began unloading.

The guide did not re-appear and we were ready to leave, so I went to look for him. As I crawled to the heap of rubble, which was the largest remains of the station, I came under enemy fire. I crawled around to the other side of the rubble and again came under fire. Eventually I managed to get past the rubble and went towards the front line. Suddenly a Verey light exploded in the sky and burst into blinding brilliance. Someone shouted: "Stand still."

I froze and hoped to be mistaken for a tree or post or something. As the Verey light died away I dropped flat, just as an enemy machine gun swept the place where I had been standing.

I changed direction and began to make my way back to the station. Just before I reached the heap of rubble, a shell burst very near me. I was blinded by the flash and lay still. A voice called me. It was Jim Farrell's voice. I ran towards the sound of his voice. I was nearly at Jim's position when another shell burst alongside me and I felt the heat of the explosion and smelled the cordite. By the light of another bursting shell I saw a Bren gun carrier and Jim called: "Over here."

I ran; then rolled under the front of the carrier and Jim pulled me to safety as another shell burst close by.

I decided not to wait for the guide and told the men to make their way back to our location. I saw them all leave then climbed into the jeep driven by Driver Hebson. We were the last to leave the station. Jim Farrell was in the lead of the last three jeeps, followed by Bobby Hewitt. Then came Hebson and me. We had not gone far along the track, threading our way between shell-holes, when a shell burst alongside us. Bobby's jeep stopped, I told Hebson to stop and got out and ran to Bobby, but he was unhurt. The shell had thrown up a lot of evil smelling mud and Bobby had received a generous helping in his face and eyes. We cleaned his eyes so that he could see, and continued on our way.

We had not travelled very far when we came under shell-fire again, and this time Hebson said: "I've been hit."

He stopped the jeep and I got out and ran around to his side of the jeep, asking where he had been hit, and was told it was in the calf of the left leg. The starlight was not sufficient to see by, so I quickly felt his leg. I could not feel a wound or blood, but found a hole in his trouser leg. A piece of shrapnel had passed in front of my legs, hit the outer casing of the steering column and passed through his trouser leg and had burned a line on the calf of his leg. We confirmed this when we reached our location.

Hebson was a rather quiet man. He rarely made any fuss and was a good, conscientious driver, and a very brave man. He had already had a lorry blown up under him when it hit a mine, which made him naturally nervous of mines and minefields. Now he had had this experience. All the time he was with the jeep platoon he showed courage and endurance and was most dependable. Some months after the jeep platoon was disbanded, Hebson reported to the medical officer (MO) with stomach pains. The MO didn't know Hebson and thought he was malingering; so gave him some aspirins. A few weeks later Hebson died of a burst duodenal ulcer. This was a needless death of a very brave 21 year old man.

The location of the jeep platoon was moved several times - each time a little nearer to Cassino - until we found ourselves a few miles from the village of San Michele. Our location was at a place that was called 'Clapham Junction' because it was the meeting place of several tracks and the place where supplies of all kinds were brought ready for distribution to forward units. It was a place sheltered by trees, and also overlooked the roads leading to Cassino. It was the meeting place for all troops moving up to Cassino. It was an important junction and a very busy area. During this time of moving locations, Captain Sharman left us and was replaced by Captain Smith.

It was slightly forward of this junction that the jeep platoon camped and dug our dugouts and slit-trenches, just behind the highest ridge in the slightly forward position. We were warned not to crawl above the ridge's top because we would then be seen by the German observation posts on Mount Cairo and would attract enemy shellfire. We crawled to the top of the ridge and peeped over, keeping very low, and saw the monastery staring back at us. Normally we kept well below the ridge, and listened to the enemy shells whistling over us on their way to some target behind us.

In a straight line, the monastery was about three miles from our dugouts but we discovered that our journey to positions behind and above the monastery was about eight miles. This was due to the twisting roads and winding tracks and various diversions. During our nightly journey along this route we were under almost continuous enemy fire, including shellfire, mortars, and machine guns. It also included the 'Mad Mile' and torturous mountain tracks.

Rations and water were brought up to the jeep platoon daily and, with the rations, came the mail. One day, the mail arrived just as heavy shelling began and so I lay in my dugout, which I shared with Sergeant Ware, and read a letter from my mother. As the bombardment continued I read my mother's comments: 'Don't be silly and go where it is dangerous.'

As if I had any choice!

The water for the jeep platoon was brought to us in a water wagon, which was a small tanker. This was driven by a man who had been an undertaker's assistant in Civvy Street, and was always called 'Coffin'. He was a tall, thin man with a very serious face, but he had a very dry sense of humour. One day he came with the water tanker and we hurried to fill our water bottles and other containers. The previous day we had had a replacement for a casualty and as the 'new boy' began to fill his water bottle, Coffin looked at him and then began to measure him with a ruler. The new boy looked at him in amazement and asked: "What's going on?"

Coffin, with a very serious look on his face said: "Yes. I've got one to fit you."

"You've got what to fit me?" asked the young man.

"A coffin," came the reply.

The new boy looked very worried and turned pale, until the rest of the men burst out laughing and told him to take no notice of Coffin.

The jeep platoon began to settle down to regular routine. There were now three sections and each section was allocated to serve certain units in each of the brigades in the 78th Division. Each section had its own routes and areas. Sergeant Ware's section, in which I served with Jim Farell, Ted Roberts, Bert Jones, Bobby Hewitt, Hebson, Billows and others, were assigned to the 38th Irish Brigade and the support group, the Kensington Regiment.

One of our regular trips - a nightly trip - was to the Enniskillen Fusiliers and the Kensington Regiment. Others served the London Irish Rifles and the Royal Irish Fusiliers. My own association was with the Enniskillen Fusiliers and Kensington Regiment and I came to know many of the men and NCOs and warrant officers. The Enniskillens' position was behind the monastery and slightly above it. The nightly trip to this position was always hazardous and often exciting.

I always led my section on our trip to the line. So I was first in the front line position and always the last to leave so that I could look after casualties or stragglers. On arrival at the unloading point, in a slight depression in the ground and just behind the actual front line, RSM Slatterly would ask me what we had brought, and then told us where to stack it. While the drivers were doing this, he would tell me how many dead bodies there were to be taken back and show me where they were.

The ground was so very rocky that it was impossible to dig holes in the ground, so the dead could not be buried. The dead of both sides were still lying in some places because it was impossible to recover them. We did not like the job of carrying the bodies back to the field dressing station where there was a cemetery, but it had to be done and we soon became used to it. The bodies were sewn up in blankets, according to Army Regulations, so there was nothing unpleasant in handling them, and we soon became used to it.

Men who were given leave from the line for a few days would often ask us to take them back. One night, a sergeant asked me if he could travel back with us and I said he could. When I checked everyone present before telling them to move off I couldn't find the sergeant. Eventually I found him lying in a trailer, and invited him to sit in the jeep. He replied that he was alright where he was in the trailer in the rolls of blankets. When I said they were bodies, he quickly scrambled out of the trailer and refused to travel in the jeep or trailer. I put him in another jeep.

The journey to forward positions had to be made every evening. Our evening meal was about 5pm to 5.30pm. At 6pm, the jeeps were taken to Clapham Junction and loaded with supplies for the various units. Usually, the loads consisted of ammunition for rifles, mortars, machine-guns, and also grenades. To these were added a great variety of articles, according to the needs of the forward units, plus food and the very precious item: mail.

There were also teams of mules helping to take supplies forward. The mules were usually docile, but could also be stubborn at times and would kick out with the back legs when annoyed, or try to bite anyone near them if they were aroused. But they were marvellous animals, carrying heavy loads over uneven ground and climbing very steep gradients - enduring enemy fire for most of the journey. Some nights there were casualties among the mules and we were always sorry to see the bodies of mules that had been killed. The Indian muleteers were a remarkable group of men and seemed to take all the discomforts and dangers in their stride and, often, showed great bravery.

The mule teams started some time before the jeeps and trailers left Clapham Junction, and they travelled by a different route, but we often met them at part of the forward area. If a jeep came too close to a mule as both made a precarious descent down the mountain track, the mule would lash out with both hind legs, and several jeeps bore the marks of mule hooves on the radiator grill. One thing we quickly learned was to watch the mules ahead. If they stopped and refused to move forward we always stopped and waited, because it usually meant that the road ahead of us was about to be shelled or heavily mortared. How they knew we never discovered but the mules' sixth sense saved our lives many times. We came to have an affection for these stubborn, awkward but brave animals.

One evening at the Enniskillen Fusiliers' forward position, the mule team arrived after we had unloaded the jeeps and trailers. Each mule team was given a protection party of infantrymen, and I asked the sergeant of the protection party how they had made the trip. In a very pronounced Irish brogue he replied: "Sure, and all me mules are through, bar one, and that's a 'hoss."

I suppressed a chuckle and congratulated him on his good trip.

The route taken by our section of jeeps began at Clapham Junction and the road dropped down a fairly steep hill into a large, round area at the bottom of the valley. This was called 'the Inferno' because it was an area that received a lot of enemy shelling. However, some called it 'the Bowl'.

We always raced down into the Bowl and up the other side. As we came out of the Bowl, we passed a battery of 25 pounder guns. They were usually busy when we passed them. About half a mile past the 25 pounders, the road turned left and that was the beginning of 'the Mad Mile', so-called because it was under almost constant enemy fire. No one stopped on that part of the road. Every driver increased speed to get through it as quickly as possible.

At the end of the Mad Mile, the road continued on towards Cassino and the railway station, but we always took a turning to the right into a narrow road that went over a stone-built, humped-back bridge over the river Rapido. The turning to the right was known as 'Hell-fire Corner' because there was an almost continuous barrage of airbursts, that is, shells set to burst in the air just above this road junction. These airbursts were a great incentive for the driver to speed on. The stone bridge also received attention from the enemy so that any driver approaching the bridge often wondered if there would be enough bridge left for him to cross in safety.

Once over the bridge, the road continued in a straight line to another road junction. This was another exciting spot. The jeep section had to turn sharply to the right at this point, and a military policeman in a slit trench with a reinforced roof, with a longitudinal opening on the side nearest the road, through which this unfortunate man thrust an arm to wave on the vehicle hurtling past him. I never knew the waving hand to signal stop - and I doubt if anyone would have obeyed such a signal if it had.

Behind the military policeman's outpost and on the other side of the road that turned left at the junction were the remains of what had once been an Italian police station. The present occupants were members of the German Army in an outpost on the edge of Cassino town. Their machine guns covered a wide area and certainly pointed towards the road junction and its immediate area. They must have heard the traffic coming over the bridge because they usually gave us a very warm welcome as they heard us approaching.

Once safely around this road junction, it was a race to an open track on the left-hand side of the road and, once in that track, the tension eased somewhat. There were hills on either side of this track and enemy fire could not be directed on us at this part of the route. Some distance along this track was a semi-circular, flat patch of land. This was the mule and jeep unloading point for the Northampton Regiment and certain other units in that brigade. Those destined for the Irish Brigade units drove straight on to yet another junction in the track, which was named 'Dannet Wire Corner' because, at the beginning of the battle, a large quantity of rolls of barbed wire were stacked there.

At Dannet Wire Corner, things usually became exciting and interesting. Sometimes we turned left here and, passing the ruins of a barn, turned sharply right, following another track to a farmhouse. This farmhouse was the Kensington Regiment's counter mortar battery platoon headquarters, where Captain Silk was in command. There will be more of Captain Silk and his farmhouse later.

If, at Dannet Wire Corner, we continued straight on, we began a steady and steep climb up the side of the mountain. This track had been cut into the side of the mountain and was only about two feet wider than the jeep. As the climb continued, the drop over the side on the left-hand side grew greater until, at Mortar Corner, there was a very sharp left-hand bend. It was said to be a 1,000 feet drop to the valley below. At one stage, a tank had been taken up this track, and found Mortar Corner too sharp a turn and went over the side, rolling down to the bottom.

Mortar Corner was not the end of the journey, for jeeps and trailers had to negotiate a steep rise to another sharp bend, named after the first soldier to be killed there: Wright's Corner. Once around this bend, the ground became less steep and eventually became almost flat, except for a small bank of earth, which had to be climbed by the jeep and trailer using bottom booster gear. Above this last obstacle was a flat area, with the ground rising between this spot and the monastery. It was not a large rise, but it was just enough for the jeeps to shelter behind while unloading.

At this unloading point, RSM Slatterly of the Enniskillen Fusiliers met me and asked what loads we had brought, and told me of any items to be taken back, or any men to be taken back, and also how many bodies we were ready to be transported back. All conversations were conducted in whispers because the sound travelled so easily and the enemy was quite near. When all the transactions were completed, the jeeps began their journey back to Clapham Junction and, if all went well, we hoped to be back in camp by about 1am or, perhaps, 2am. If things did not go well, we were fortunate to be back by 5am.

One night, I took a replacement driver with me, allowing him to drive the jeep and hoping that he would remember the route. He was a quiet lad, aged about 19. We called him Tubby, and he seemed unflappable. When we arrived at the unloading point, the RSM invited me to have a cup of tea. I told Tubby to stay with the jeep and not to wander away from it and keep his head and voice low. The RSM and I ran towards the cookhouse, which was buried underground like a large dugout. A German machine-gun crew must have heard us and began firing, but luckily the shots were falling behind me as I followed the RSM. I think we must have broken all records for the 200 yards dash.

Suddenly the RSM dived down into a hole and I followed him. This was the entrance to the cookhouse. We passed through two sets of blankets covering the 'doorway'. The cook handed me a mug of tea, and I held it to my lips.

I smelt it and said: "Is there rum in this?"

"Yes," replied the cook.

I said: "Sorry, but I don't drink rum."

The RSM grabbed the mug and said: "I do."

He drained the mug and the cook gave me another mug of unlaced tea and it tasted fine.

After drinking the tea and exchanging news with the cook and his helpers, telling them what was happening in our little world outside the cookhouse, the RSM and I emerged from this large dugout. The German machine-gunners must have been waiting for us because, as we started our short journey back to the unloading point, the machine-gun opened up again and, once more, the shots fell just behind me, urging us to speed on.

On arrival at the jeep loading point, I found the jeeps and trailers loaded and ready to depart. I went to the jeep where I had left Tubby and found him sitting on the bumper bar of the jeep, with his back resting against the radiator, and his head leaning forward with his chin on his chest. I spoke to him, but there was no reply. I quickly went to him and grabbed his arm, calling him by name. Slowly his eyes opened and I asked if he was alright, and he said he was alright. I asked him: "Have you been to sleep?"

He admitted he had dozed off, but the mosquitoes had kept waking him up. I told him that there were no mosquitoes at this time of the year in this area, nor at this height. Tubby insisted that they had been flying over his head most of the time. Just then the 'mosquitoes' buzzed over our heads, but they were enemy machine-gun bullets. It was a very good thing that Tubby had not stood up to deal with his 'mosquitoes'.

Not all our casualties were due to enemy action.

On a trip to the Enniskillen Fusiliers' position, we came under a very heavy and sustained mortar fire attack as we reached Wright's Corner. I halted the section in a fairly sheltered position between Mortar Corner and Wright's Corner. When the worst of the attack slackened, the front jeep moved forward. One of the drivers near Mortar Corner forgot to release his handbrake on the jeep, and putting the jeep into bottom booster began to climb the slope. The handbrake was a webbing band around a kind of flywheel on the prop shaft, and as the prop shaft revolved the webbing band tightly gripped the flywheel. The resulting friction caused the webbing band to catch fire. The driver jumped out and peered under the jeep to see what was happening. At the same moment, another driver aimed the contents of a fire extinguisher at the seat of the fire. Unfortunately, some of the fluid hit the jeep driver between the eyes and he staggered back with hands to eyes. I ran to him and quickly wiped the liquid from his eyes and face and sent him back to the advanced dressing station. We never saw him again but, later, we heard that his sight had been saved, although it had been damaged. I took over the damaged jeep and continued with the job.

On another occasion, a replacement driver, aged about 19 years, came with me on his first ever trip into the front line. As we got nearer the front line he became more and more agitated. When we reached Mortar Corner, we came under mortar fire. There was not very much, but there was enough to cause this poor lad to lose his nerve. He broke down and cried and screamed, which attracted the enemy's attention and made the attack more severe. I grabbed the lad and tried to calm him, but this was impossible. So there was only one thing to do: slap his face very hard, which stopped his screaming. I sent him back on the first jeep returning to our location and then took his jeep and completed the job. The next morning I reported the incident to Captain Smith and asked for the lad to be sent back to his unit. This, of course, meant another raw replacement.

One evening, one of the platoon sergeants was told to come with me to learn our route. I had known him as a lance corporal in England and, when we were warned we were going overseas, he went sick for a hernia operation. But he was still sent to North Africa later, and now he arrived at the jeep platoon. Until this moment he had avoided ever going near the fighting area or front line positions. To bolster his courage he had drunk more than a few rum rations and also brought a tomato ketchup bottle full of rum with him, which he sampled at frequent intervals. I warned him to take it easy because he would need all his wits the further on we went.

When we reached the Enniskillen Fusiliers' loading point, he got out of the jeep and began shouting all sorts of weird orders and then just shouting. This attracted the enemy machine gunners and mortar sections. By his behaviour he was endangering all our lives. I suggested that he return to the jeep location since he was attracting unwelcome enemy attention, he was not accustomed to the way we worked in forward areas, and he was obstructing us in our job. I persuaded him to leave but he refused to be driven by one of the drivers and jumped into a jeep and drove off. He negotiated the first hairpin bend at Wright's Corner but failed to keep to the track as he rounded Mortar Corner, and the jeep went over the side. I was informed and hurried to the spot. Fortunately, the jeep hit a small tree as it rolled down and had become lodged there. I went down to find the sergeant and found him crawling towards the track. I discovered he had broken his arm. I put him into another jeep, this time with a driver, who took him to the field dressing station, while I went back to my section and continued unloading the jeeps.

The next evening, I took Captain Smith, Sergeant Janzen and Taffy Morgan, our mechanic, to recover the jeep. We waited until the jeep section had reached the unloading point for the Enniskillens; then we began our recovery task. Sergeant Janzen and I went down to the jeep and fastened skid chins together to make a towing cable. Then Sergeant Janzen brought our jeep to the edge of the track and we attached the towing chains. I stayed with the jeep that had gone over the side. Slowly, we drew the crashed jeep to the track, and found it was not badly damaged and would still work. Taffy Morgan took the towing chains off and threw one set into the jeep, which made a dreadful noise. I told him to do it quietly because he would attract enemy action upon us. He then proceeded to lift the chains and set them down very quietly, one link at a time. Despite this we came under heavy fire. We made our way back to our location without mishap.

A replacement sergeant appeared in a few days time. He was Sergeant Ware, and I had the task of showing him the routes we used on our nocturnal activities. I had found chewing gum a great relieving agent for tensions during moments of excitement on our journeys. The new sergeant strongly objected to me chewing gum, and made a few choice expressions so that I would know of his disapproval.

When we arrived at the Enniskillen loading point, I explained our procedure, and the layout. In particular, I told him about the Canadian tank.

One tank had gone over the side at Mortar Corner but one had made it to the top and was now on the left-hand side of the Enniskillens' position, and was being used as a 'pill-box'. I showed him the track leading to the tank, should he ever need to go there. He decided he would go then. As he set off, a thought came to me. I warned him to go to the first tank, but not the second, because the second one was a German tank. Since it was very dark, I warned him to be very careful. The sergeant suddenly changed his mind about visiting the tank, and we retraced our footsteps towards the jeeps. As we arrived we came under very heavy enemy fire, and we were pinned down for some time. The sergeant whispered to me: "Got any spare chewing gum, for me?"

It was the custom for the jeep drivers to bring back from the front line any man given a few days leave from the front line positions, or who had to report to battalion headquarters. One evening, a sergeant of the Enniskillens asked me if he could travel back with us. I agreed, but advised him to take cover under an over-hanging part of the bank until we were ready to leave. When we were ready to leave I went to look for the sergeant. Just as I found him, we came under fire from an enemy mortar section.

The Germans were very methodical in their fire orders, so that both artillery and mortar shells usually came in threes or fives. This often enabled us to judge when to move, and when to take cover. As I crouched by the sergeant we heard the mortars coming over, and then one stick of mortars sounded different, they were coming towards us. I said: "If there are three in this lot we are safe, but if there are five, we've had it."

We counted them as they exploded: two, three... four.,

"This is it," I said, and we braced ourselves.

The fifth mortar shell landed on the ledge immediately above our heads, we heard the thump as it landed and waited for the crash and shrapnel. Nothing happened, it was a dud. We both breathed a sigh of relief and I recorded yet another 'near miss'.

One night it was both very foggy and very dark and it had taken us longer than usual to reach the Enniskillen Fusiliers' unloading point. When we had completed our tasks there we prepared to descend the mountain track but we found it even more difficult and dangerous than our climb to the unloading point. The driver of the jeep proceeded very slowly, while he and I strained our eyes to see the track. On our right was a 1,000 feet drop that, on this occasion, seemed more threatening than ever. An infantryman travelling with us volunteered to sit on the bumper bar of the jeep and drag his right foot on the ground slightly to the right of the front wheel. If his foot went into space he called, 'Left hand down a bit' and the driver moved the jeep away from the edge of the track. Travelling very slowly we arrived at the bottom of the mountain and drove through the village of Caira - sometimes called 'Cairo' - and arrived safely back to Clapham Junction.

There was a Lieutenant De Piniere in the Kensington Regiment who was well-known among the men of his company as a very brave and remarkable man. Since it was said that I knew the forward areas better than most men in the jeep platoon, Lt De Piniere would come to me and say: "Can you get a spare jeep for tonight? I have a special job and would like you to come with me."

This usually resulted in an exciting expedition. Sometimes he would come to me just as we were about to leave for the forward areas, and I would tell one of the drivers to go back to his dug-out and have a free night, while I took his jeep and trailer up the line for him. I never had a refusal of that offer.

It was about 6pm when Lt De Piniere came to me one evening and asked if I could get a spare jeep for a special job. When I reported to him under the trees at Clapham Junction, he indicated a major standing by him and said: "He wants a grand tour of the forward area. Shall we go?"

The major sat in the front passenger seat of the jeep and Lt De Piniere sat in the back seat. The major did not speak.

The jeep sections had all left the loading areas in Clapham Common. The mules had also left and we had a clear run down into the Bowl. As we approached the beginning of the Mad Mile, I suggested to the major that it would be wise to wear his tin hat. I was told in no uncertain terms in an 'icy' voice that he would not be wearing his tin hat. The lieutenant leaned forward and said, quietly: "If Corporal Little thinks it wise to wear a tin hat, then it would be wise to do so. I'm wearing mine."

The major reluctantly placed his battle bowler on his head.

As we neared the beginning of the Mad Mile, I warned the major: "Hold on tightly when we go around the next bend to the left and enter the Mad Mile because, if you fall out, I shall not stop for you."

There was another icy comment and a glare. As we entered the Mad Mile, the usual shell bursts came over us and we sped to the pace of the airbursts. I warned the major of this and of the sharp turn to the right while travelling at speed, and also mentioned the humpback bridge around the corner. As we approached the former police station, I warned him to keep low because of the machine-gun fire, and to hold tightly as we turned right. There was no reply.

When we reached the comparative safety of the track between the hills, the major asked: "How often do you make this journey?"

I replied: "At least once every night."

There was no comment.

I pointed out the jeep and mule unloading point for the Northampton Regiment and then went on to the Northampton Regimental HQ where I stopped. The major and lieutenant disappeared down a track to the HQ position, and I waited by the jeep.

Slowly, I became aware of a group of men approaching along the track we had just travelled. Gratefully, I recognised English voices. The group stopped and an officer hurried down the tract to the HQ. The men began chattering quite loudly. I walked towards them and said: "Keep your voices down."

There was instant silence. I asked who they were, and discovered they were replacements for the Northamptons. I suggested they rubbed mud or dirt on the brasses of their equipment because the buckle on the webbing belt, together with the brass hooks for the big pack on the front straps, made a perfect triangle - thus presenting the enemy with a clear target. One man said: "Put mud on them when we will have to clean them for parade in the morning?"

My reply was: "If you don't put mud on them now, you may not see the morning. Besides, there are no parades up here."

Then a quiet voice said: "Where are we?"

Pointing to the skyline I gave them a brief outline of the forward positions of their brigade. It was dark, but the outline of the mountains and hills could just be seen. I told them where the plateau was, which looked like a dark smudge; where the Northamptons' positions were; the direction of Cassino, and finally, the position of the monastery. When I had finished speaking, a voice said, very quietly: "Is that the monastery? I was watching that on Movietone News in the cinema last week when I was on leave."

These men had landed a few days previously and had been brought almost immediately into the forward area. They had no idea where they were. I told them to speak quietly because sound travelled a very long way in this area and enabled the enemy to make a good guess as to where we were and so could fire at us fairly accurately. I need not have mentioned it, because no one seemed to have anything to say. A little while later, the officer reappeared and led the men across the open countryside towards the Northamptons' positions.

Some time later, Lieutenant De Piniere and the major re-appeared and we continued our tour of inspection. At Dannet Wire Corner, I pointed out the track to the Kensington Counter Mortar Platoon HQ. As we climbed the mountain track toward the Enniskillens' position I pointed out the location of the Kensington 4.2 inch mortars' position. We moved on to the Kensingtons' forward HQ. I was invited to go inside the battered building, which offered a little more protection than lying down outside. In the course of the officers' conversation I heard my name mentioned, as they spoke to the Lt-Colonel commanding the Kensington Regiment. The Lt-Colonel came over to me. He said that he had heard of me, and of the work of the jeep platoon. He paid tributes to the way we worked and the risks we took. He than added: "If you and your men fail to get through, or the jeep platoon is unable to keep going, we shall not be able to hold out for very long. You are our life-line."

That was the first time that I had heard any expression of appreciation of the work of the jeep platoon.

When we left the Kensingtons' HQ, I warned the major that we would be returning by a different way, because it was a one way traffic circuit. I explained that we would be entering a 'stonk' area - that is, an area under constant heavy and concentrated shellfire. I mentioned that the area was usually saturated by enemy shelling. I said that, once through the stonk area, I would stop just before we entered the village of Caira and wait for the shelling of the village and of road we would travel to allow the enemy shells to follow the usual pattern. The shells came in threes or fives and there was just time after the fifth shell burst to move through the village and on into a minefield. We would turn a sharp right turn into the village and then a sharp left turn into the minefield and speed towards a Bailey bridge, before the next salvo arrived.

We had worked this out to a fine art and used this routine every night. I stopped near the first house on the corner, counted the shell-bursts, and as the fifth shell burst pushed the jeep forward at speed, around the corner of what remained of the house, down the road and turned into the safe lane in minefield. As we entered the safe lane the first shell of the next salvo burst behind us. The major's comment was: "Good timing."

When we arrived back at Clapham Junction, the major shook hands with me and thanked me for a very interesting tour, and for bringing us all back safely. Then he said: "I would not like your job, but it is essential."

One evening, as we loaded the jeeps and trailers at Clapham Junction, Lt De Piniere said to me: "Very special job tonight. Which jeep is going to Counter Mortar HQ? Send the jeep driver back and take his place."

When I had completed the loading, Lt De Piniere came to the trailer and said: "Keep this flat and make sure it doesn't move or become tilted."

He carefully handed me a flat oval object, about two inches thick. I immediately thought of some kind of sensitive mine or a booby trap and I handled it with great care as I wedged it in a position where it could not move.

We allowed the other jeeps to pull away and, when the road was clear, I began the journey to Dannet Wire Corner. There, I turned right along the path to the Counter Mortar position, and stopped as close to the wall of the building as I could. I followed Lt De Piniere inside the ruins and spoke with Captain Silk and the sergeant there. After a while, the lieutenant whispered to me: "Get the special parcel from the trailer."

Aloud, he said: "Bring in the tart."

The sergeant looked up startled and exclaimed: "A tart. Oh, I could just do with her. Bring her in."

He looked very disappointed when I brought in a fruit tart in the camp kettle lid.

One evening, I asked for two volunteers to help me recover a jeep that had overturned in the stonk area on the edge of the village of Caira. Louis Gateri, said: "You don't need to ask for volunteers. Me and Tichie will come with you."

So that was settled. Louis was an Italian born in England, but his family came from Cassino area, and his grandparents lived in Cassino. He hated Germans with a fierce hatred. This hatred was increased by what he had seen in Italy of the Germans' actions, and by what he found in Cassino. Tich Brahms was a Jew and we - and Tich - knew what would happen to him if he was captured. He knew the danger he was in but he never shirked frontline duties or dangerous jobs. They were both very fine and brave men.

It was about 8pm when Louis, Tich and I left San Michele. We had waited for both the jeep convoy and mule teams to have cleared the roads on which we would travel. Tichie drove the jeep, and he really did speed along the Mad Mile and as he skirted the Italian Barracks. We went on to Dannet Wire Corner and down to the stonk area, where the enemy greeted us with the usual warm welcome. Tich stopped the jeep near the overturned jeep we had come to collect. We began to work on the jeep to be able to set it upright. We spoke in whispers.

Suddenly Tich whispered: "Hold it."

We froze. Tich whispered: "Over there, by the road."

Slowly, Louis and I turned and looked. Shadows moved; then merged into the darkness; then reappeared. They were figures of men cautiously moving up the bank toward the front line. I think the three of us whispered together: "Jerries."

There were six or seven men in this German patrol, and they were moving away from us up the hillside. Louis grabbed his tommy gun and growled: "Let me go and get them."

I explained that we were not there to fight Germans but to recover the jeep. Louis was not convinced and Tich and I had great difficulty in restraining him from going after the Germans. He kept saying: "I could have got them all. I could have paid them back for what they have done to my family."

I don't think Louis ever forgave me for refusing to allow him to fight that German patrol.

We put the jeep back on its wheels. I told Tich and Louis to wait there and I went to the edge of the road, replaced the white tapes showing the safe lane in the minefield. The German patrol had moved them so that vehicles would be directed into the minefield. I returned to my two companions. They had already fastened a tow-chain between the jeeps and we set off back to San Michele, judging the right time between the salvoes of German shells. It was just another job for the jeep platoon.

There were many exciting moments and hazardous missions for all members of the 78th Division's jeep platoon, and every man had his stories to tell. There were many acts of heroism witnessed but not recorded; some were performed in isolation and under cover of darkness. Many of the dangerous jobs performed were done willingly and without fuss, as part of the normal work of the platoon. The comradeship was wonderful. When it was necessary for me to ask for volunteers for a dangerous job, there were always more volunteers than were required. It is still a regret to me that the bravery of so many of these men was not acknowledged.

Every soldier has certain dates, particular places, or exciting events that, to him, have a special significance. Among the many exciting events in my wartime experiences, two days stand apart from all the others: 17th and 18th April 1944, while I was serving with the 78th Division's jeep platoon. There were gallant comrades, who shared in some way or other in these events, and each will have his version of the story to tell, but my story must be personal, and it is vivid to me, even now.

The 17th April was a Monday. It promised to be just an ordinary day for members of the jeep platoon. About 6.30pm, the jeep section serving the Enniskillens went to Clapham Junction to load up with supplies. When the loading was completed, I led the convoy out from under the sheltering trees and down through the Bowl, along the Mad Mile and on to Dannet Wire Corner. Enemy action had been about normal until we came to Dannet Wire Corner. Then the action intensified. Slowly, we began our climb up the narrow and rough mountain track. We had just passed the Kensington heavy machine gun position and rounded a bend in the track when a salvo of shells began bursting on the track ahead. An ammunition dump was set alight.

Not wishing to expose the men to unnecessary danger, I stopped the convoy and walked ahead to ascertain the chances of getting through. Suddenly, I was aware of someone running after me. It was one of our drivers, named Billows. He said: "It's not safe for you to go alone, I'll come with you."

Slowly, we walked for about 30 to 40 yards. I told Billows to wait while I went a little further along the track. After looking at the track and the blazing ammunition dump, I rejoined Billows and we returned to the rest of the jeeps. I told the drivers that we could make it if they kept as close to the bank as possible, and leave 50 yards between jeeps.

I got into the passenger seat of the first jeep, driven by Ted Roberts.

"OK, Ted. Let's go," I said.

As we approached the blazing dump, the glare was blinding. I asked Ted: "Can you see?"

I leaned forward to get a better view and, at that moment, a shell burst just in front of the jeep, on the edge of the track, on our left hand side, my side. We felt the heat of the shell burst. Ted quickly moved the jeep onwards and we continued to Mortar Corner, glad to get away from the exploding ammunition dump.

When we arrived at Mortar Corner, we found a group of men pinned down by enemy fire. One man was wounded, and I made sure he was receiving first aid treatment. The glare from the blazing dump and the flashes of the bursting mortars and shells made the place look like daylight, and attracted more enemy fire. The remainder of the jeeps arrived and I organised the ferrying of loads up to the forward points and unloading area. We could not use the trailers because of the enemy fire and the steepness of the track we had to use. I told the driver of the first jeep to tell the RSM what was happening and that there was a badly wounded man who needed medical attention and transport to the advanced medical dressing station.

Ferrying the loads to the unloading point was an operation that took longer than usual because the trailer loads had to be transferred to the jeeps and drivers had to make two journeys from Mortar Corner to the unloading point. I helped to transfer the loads. When all the loads had been ferried forward, I went up with the last jeep and spoke to the RSM and to the medical officer about the wounded man, and was assured that action had been taken. I then organised the jeeps for the return journey and left in the last jeep. The dumps were still blazing and exploding as we continued our return journey under very heavy enemy fire. Thankfully, all jeeps and drivers returned safely to San Michele.

The next morning, Ted Roberts called me to look at his jeep, showing me the back of the seat I had occupied the previous evening. Embedded in the centre of the back of the seat was a lump of shrapnel, an inch cube in size, with one side split and jagged. As I had asked Ted if he could see, I had leaned forward as a shell burst near us. The shrapnel was from that shell and would have pierced my chest and heart if I had not leaned forward. It was yet another near miss to go on record.

That evening I was due to have a night in the dugout: my 'rest night'. I saw the jeep convoy move off for loading at about 6.30pm. I watched them as they returned and passed the jeep location on their way to the front line. The platoon sergeant had taken my place, and I was looking forward to a restful evening. I was standing some distance from my dugout at about 7.30pm when a shell burst near me. The explosion blew me up and over, and I landed on my back, but I could not breathe. I had been 'winded'. The cordite fumes had also filled my lungs and I was choking. I rolled over onto my tummy and put my face on the ground to escape the cordite fumes. I thumped my side and at last gasped a mouthful of air and coughed up the cordite fumes. I gasped and spluttered, and tried to examine myself and decided I was not wounded. This took only a few minutes.

I jumped up and ran towards the place where the first shell had landed. More shells were coming into the area at a fairly rapid rate. I saw Corporal Cherry come out of a small tent, with blood streaming down his face. I had a quick look at him and saw shrapnel had partly severed the lower part of his nose from his upper lip. He said he was going for an ambulance jeep because two men in the tent were badly wounded. The two-man tent had been placed over a large hole, in which these two men lived.

I went into the tent and realised that both men were very badly wounded and that one of them - Dickinson from Manchester - was mortally wounded. I did what I could for him; then looked at Jock Berry from Glasgow. I realised that he had a spinal injury. When the ambulance jeep arrived, Jim Farrell and Ted Roberts put the two wounded men on board, while I went to another wounded man who was injured in the forearm. I did what I could for him. I looked around for further casualties and found Billows, my brave comrade from the previous night. He was very badly wounded and I realised he was dying. There was nothing anyone could do for him, and he died just after I found him. Dickinson also died and Jock Berry was invalided out of the Army because of his injuries.

About four weeks after these incidents, I was informed I had been granted the immediate award of the Military Medal. RSM Slatterly of the Enniskillens had recommended me for the Military Medal for my actions on the Monday night. My own Lt-Colonel, who had visited the jeep location just after the shelling had stopped on the Tuesday evening, had asked me what had happened and had spoken to other men present, had also recommended me for the Military Medal. So, instead of being given two decorations, I was given the immediate award. A copy of the official citation appears in Appendix II.

On the Tuesday evening someone counted the shells that burst among us and said there were 28 in less than 15 minutes. No wonder the shrapnel was falling like hailstones. I was too busy to count them. I learned afterwards that John Ray, one of our drivers, had run after me towards the spot where the first shell had burst, though I was unaware of it at the time. He told me a shell burst behind us, and he was badly wounded in the back. In his letter from hospital he told me he had saved me from being wounded by taking the shrapnel in his back. He eventually recovered. There were several near misses recorded that evening.

When I surveyed the damage to our location, I realised a new location was advisable. I looked around and found a better place and moved the jeep platoon to a new site, among some olive trees.

That was not the end of the exciting times with the jeep platoon; nor at San Michele. A few days after the shelling of the jeep platoon location, I stood with Sergeant Ware, a colour-sergeant, the regimental quartermaster and RSM of the Kensington Regiment, and we stood under some olive trees at San Michele. Suddenly a shell burst very near us and the shrapnel whistled around us.

I had been standing by the colour-sergeant, my left elbow almost touching his right elbow. As the shrapnel whistled past, the colour-sergeant looked down at his right arm. Shrapnel had ripped off his stripes, but neither he nor I were touched. He looked down with surprise and said: "Look at that, busted and I didn't know."

'Busted' was the term for being reduced to the ranks.

One day, Sergeant Ware and I were running side by side, during a period of enemy shelling, and a shell burst a little way in front of us. The shrapnel whistled over and around us and, when I looked at the sergeant, I burst out laughing. A piece of shrapnel had hit the centre stud in the top of his tin hat - the stud that held the outer metal bowl to the inner lining. The stud had been taken out, so that the metal bowl of his hat had been knocked off and he was left wearing only the inner lining, a round ring with crossed supports at the top. It looked at as if he was wearing a crown and I said: "You look like the Queen of the May!"

When the shelling ceased and we assessed the damage, Sergeant Ware was extremely annoyed to discover a piece of shrapnel had gone through his big pack in his tent. It had punched a hole through his spare shirts and underclothes. But what really annoyed him was that the shrapnel had ruined a large quantity of his 'surplus stock' of airmail letterforms. The damage to his spare clothing did not annoy him, but the loss of the airmail letterforms was a major tragedy. These forms were so scarce that we valued them like gold dust. His language was very colourful when he discovered his loss.

It began as a rumour, but it grew in strength.

How we fervently hoped it was true. The 78th Division was to come out of the line. Then came a whisper: 'The Poles are taking over from us.'

Rumours are often wrong, but when Polish troops began to appear, the rumour grew in strength and so did the hope that, at last, we would be taken out of the line and away from Cassino.

A Polish officer appeared at the jeep platoon location and, despite being warned not to show himself on the crest of the ridge, did so. He said he was not afraid to die and he wanted to see the countryside between the ridge and Cassino. He was again warned that, if he went on the ridge the Germans would see him and the shells would soon arrive. He repeated that he was not afraid, and we watched him climb to the crest of the ridge and along the top, looking carefully at the surrounding countryside through his binoculars. He came down and left the area. About ten minutes later the shells began to arrive, and that was when the jeep platoon lost men killed and wounded. The day was Tuesday 18th April 1944. The Polish officer did not die, but my comrades did because he would not listen to our warning.

From the day of the Polish officer's visit to the jeep location, other Polish officers and soldiers were seen in the division's area. The desire to move out immediately grew stronger in every man's mind. Having survived so far, no one wanted anything to happen to them now when the chance of leaving Cassino seemed most likely. It was with immense relief that we heard the date of our withdrawal.

The evening before we were to leave, it was business as usual. I led a section into the line and, when the jobs were done, the drivers set off back to San Michele, but I remained with the jeep driver, Jim Fletcher. One jeep was to remain at counter mortar HQ and bring out Captain Silk, a sergeant (the one who was disappointed with the tart), and a private soldier. They were to remain until the last section of the Kensington Regiment had withdrawn from the line. The last section was told to come down from their positions and check in to Captain Silk.

As the dawn broke, Captain Silk said we could not wait any longer. I reminded him that no one was allowed to move in daylight in that area because of revealing the positions to enemy observers and so attracting shellfire. The reply I received was to the effect we would have to chance it. We loaded the jeep and trailer with equipment. The sergeant lay on the equipment in the trailer, Captain Silk and the private soldier sat in the rear seat of the jeep. Jim Fletcher had only been with the jeep platoon a few days and had no experience of the stonk area or of the route through the village of Caira and the minefields, so I drove the jeep.

As we left the farmhouse that had served as HQ, we came under enemy observation and, as we entered the stonk area, we came under severe fire. We were obviously clear targets. We came through the stonk area and I stopped in a shallow depression in the track and counted the shell bursts. When I heard the fourth shell of that salvo burst I shouted: "Hold tight."

As the fifth shell burst, I jabbed my toe hard down on the accelerator and the jeep darted forward. A touch on the brake as I swung the jeep around the corner of the ruins of the corner house, a jab at the accelerator and we were speeding down the ruins of the street. We made a sudden swing to the left and through the minefield; then over the Bailey bridge as the first shell of the next salvo burst behind us. We raced along the track and joined the Mad Mile and made it to the turning for the Bowl and Clapham Junction. As we turned off the Mad Mile we breathed easily. It was the first time in several months that I had actually seen the road we had travelled.

As we climbed out of the depression that we called the Bowl, we saw infantrymen slowly walking in front of us. They were formed in three ranks but the men could not keep in line. As we drew level with them we recognised them as Indian troops, and they had put up a terrific fight in Castle Hill in the centre of Cassino. They had walked the very dangerous road to the Bowl.

They had been in a terrible battle for weeks or months and had suffered appalling casualties. We had heard stories of these soldiers' bravery and sufferings. The evidence of all this was written plainly in their faces and the utter weariness of their bodies. They staggered along, leaning forward as they slowly put one foot in front of the other. They were exhausted but continued to lurch forward up the hill. When a man stopped, unable to put one foot in front of the other, the company sergeant major went to the man and gently gave him a slight push, just enough to get him moving again. I had seen soldiers utterly battle weary in North Africa but I had never seen men so utterly exhausted, so battle weary, and yet struggle to keep going forward. These were very brave men.

We soon left these struggling Indian soldiers behind and made our way to the Kensingtons' location near Clapham Junction. There we discovered that the missing section, for whom we had waited in vain, had missed the track in the dark and had come down the mountain another way, and were safely back.

I returned to the jeep platoon location to be greeted with the words: "We thought you were dead. Someone saw a jeep with a body in it and thought it was you. There was no head on the body to check if it was you. You have been reported missing, believed killed."

I quickly dashed to the jeep platoon officer, Captain Smith, to prove that I was alive and to prevent the message being sent to company HQ.

Some months after the end of the battles for Cassino, a site was selected for the Cassino War Cemetery. It is situated in the valley of the River Liri, about 87 miles south-east of Rome. The rebuilt Abbey of Monte Cassino overlooks it. The River Rapido flows to the east of the cemetery, and the rebuilt town of Cassino is about a mile away. The cemetery is a reminder of the cost of the battles for Cassino because it contains 4,264 burials. There are 2,450 from the United Kingdom, 855 Canadians, 13 Australians, 464 New Zealanders, 47 South Africans, and 431 Indians.

In the centre of the Cemetery, on marble pillars, stands the Cassino Memorial, which commemorates 4,068 men and women of the Commonwealth Land Forces who died in Sicily and Italy but have no known graves. Added to these figures must be those who were wounded during the battles, and also those who suffered mental injuries.

The German dead and wounded reached large figures and must also be counted in the total cost.

CHAPTER FIFTEEN

The breakthrough

Just after these incidents, the 78th Division was taken out of the front line and the Polish Division took our place. We pulled back for a well-deserved rest. The jeep platoon was based in a field near the 328 Divisional Troops Company RASC. We had been there for a few days when I suggested to Captain Smith, the jeep platoon officer, that I thought the men would appreciate a church service and, since no chaplain was available, I was willing to conduct the service. He agreed to this and borrowed some Army prayer books with hymns, from a chaplain. He announced that the service would be held for anyone who cared to attend, but attendance was strictly voluntary.

The platoon cooks asked if the service could be held near the cookhouse so that they could share in it. Several Roman Catholic men in the platoon came to me and said: "Since you are not a priest, but one of us, we would like to attend the service, if you are willing."

I invited them to attend. They said that they would attend but would have to stand a little way apart from the others. That way, they could tell the priest that they did not attend a Protestant service, but were only near it. They attended the service, as did the officers of the platoon. In fact, every member of the platoon was present, even though it was a voluntary church service.

In a letter to my parents, dated 3rd May 1944 I wrote: "Last Friday, I conducted a service for the detachment. The officer borrowed hymnbooks from a padre. There were about 40 men present, plus the two officers. I spoke on the text 1 Kings chapter 19, verse 7, 'Arise and eat; because the journey is too great for thee.' I mentioned that the prophet Elijah was suffering from the after-effects of the contest on Mount Carmel, but now he was weary and depressed and in need of help.'

I continued, 'we also were suffering the after-effects of our recent experiences. Like Elijah, we needed refreshment - not only physical and mental, but also spiritual. This, God would provide. It was for us to partake of it, but we had to arise and eat.'

I quoted some of the comments made after the service, showing how God had guided me to offer to conduct the service and also how God had spoken to these men through me. Afterwards, several men thanked me. Some said that it was the best service they had been to since joining the Army. One man said: "I feel real wicked since I heard you preach."

Another said: "That was the best service I have attended. There were hymns we knew and the sermon led somewhere and was not rambling."

The men had chosen the hymns we sang. They were: 'Eternal Father, strong to save', 'The King of love my Shepherd is', and 'Abide with me'.

The officers also expressed their appreciation.

As I reflected on this service and on the experiences in Cassino, I felt that God had a purpose for my life. This strengthened my sense of God's call to me to enter the Christian ministry.

A few days after the church service, the members of the jeep platoon who had served the Kensington Regiment were invited to a 'survivors party', by the regimental sergeant major and the regimental quartermaster. Sergeant Ware and I had become friendly with the RSM and the RQMS; so we took with us about 14 members of the jeep platoon. We obtained the loan of a three ton Bedford lorry for our transport.

When we arrived at the Kensingtons' location, we found two large lorries, placed back to back, to form a fair sized party area. At the front end of one lorry was an array of drinks - amazing in their quantity and in variety. I had never seen such a selection, and our men were amazed. We sat on the floor of the lorries, around the sides.

The RSM began by coming to me saying: "Bryn, I know you are a teetotaller, so I have brought this for you."

He gave me a one gallon jar, filled with orange juice, ready for drinking.

A little while later, the RQMS - Dickie - came to me and said: "Bryn, I know you don't drink alcohol, so I have brought this for you.

He gave me a one gallon jar full of ready-to-drink lemon squash. I sat there with these jars either side of me and had to endure the good-natured teasing of the other fellows although, later in the evening, some of them asked for a drink from one or other of the jars.

As the evening progressed and the drinks flowed freely, the drinks began to take effect, a man would 'pass out' and I would carry him outside and lay him on the grassy bank alongside the lorry. By this time, some of the men felt they had had enough alcoholic drink and asked if they could share my non-alcoholic drink and I was always glad to agree.

Dickie asked me who was the man who kept sending up his mug and requesting whisky every time. I pointed him out and Dickie said: "Let me know when his mug comes up again."

I did so, and the man's mug was passed back to him. He looked at Dickie and raised his mug and then took a drink. Almost immediately, he passed out. I asked Dickie: "Did you slip him a Mickey Finn?"

With a very innocent look on his face, Dickie replied: "Not at all. It was plain water, and plain water on top of a large quantity of whisky will knock out most drinkers."

So, I learned something new to me.

Eventually, about ten men were laid out in a row outside the lorry. I suggested it was time for us to leave. With the help of those who could walk, or stagger, I loaded the ten unconscious men into our lorry; bolted the tailboard into position and then climbed into the cab. I started up the engine and was about to move away when someone tapped the cab window. I lowered the window and a slurred voice asked who was driving. When I replied that I was driving, the man said: "That's alright. You are sober."

With that, he climbed back into the lorry. That was long before we heard the slogan, 'Don't drink and drive'. Muddled as he was, that man knew that a sober person was needed to drive the lorry. When we arrived back in our location I carried all the insensible men to their tents, put them to bed and saw they were alright.

The following day - Monday, 1st May - the 78th Division jeep platoon went on leave, to a rest camp in Bari, on the Adriatic coast. At the formation of the jeep platoon, the divisional commander, General Keightley, had told us that we were already written off because the nature of the work we would have to do. He also promised we would have a dreadful time, but those who lived through it would be given a week's leave. He was quite right about our experiences and kept his promise about leave.

We went by train to Bari, travelling through the night. We arrived at the rest camp in Bari at 6.30am on Tuesday morning. This camp was sheer luxury to us. It had huts to live in; beds to sleep in; free laundry; a theatre, and a cinema with frequent changes of pro-

● At Bari, on survivors' leave.

grammes. Imagine our delight when, for our first evening meal, we had - and greatly enjoyed - salmon, lettuce and spring onions with salad cream. This was followed by a large piece of tart and a cup of tea. All this cost one shilling and three pence, which is about eight new pence.

After such a sumptuous meal, Ted Roberts, Albert Jones, Jim Farrell and I wandered down to the beach on the edge of the camp. We sat there in silence, listening to the waves lapping on the shore, watching the sunset and enjoying the peace. After the noises of battle, this was sheer bliss: peace and quiet. Its soothing influence calmed our spirits and probably settled our nerves. None of us spoke for a long while. We just soaked up the peace and quietness. This was one of the memorable moments of this leave.

The jeep platoon left the rest camp at Bari on Monday 8th May and arrived back in our location on Tuesday. Cleaning and maintenance of the jeeps was the order of the day, but there was an air of relaxation. One evening we saw, in the distance, the screen of a mobile cinema. An Army mobile cinema unit would suddenly appear, set up a screen against a wall, or hang the screen between two trees. The 'patrons' would sit on the ground - if dry - or stand, or sit on any vehicles nearby or anything else available, determined to enjoy the open-air cinema.

We walked along tracks, over fields, through hedges and ditches, through creepy looking ravines, over weird bridges, and still the silvery screen seemed as far away as ever. Eventually we staggered up a rise in the ground and found the screen was not far away. With renewed zeal we hurried up the hillside, through a camp, falling over tent ropes, wires, petrol cans and slipping into holes, all unseen in the darkness. We joined the crowd watching the film. It was a film we had not seen - but it was a Hindu film and the speech

was in Hindustani! All our efforts had been in vain, and we turned and made our weary way back to our camp.

While we had been on leave in Bari, the rest of the division had also been on leave in various places, including Sorrento. When this leave period ended, we went back to training for the infantry. This was intensive training with special attention to crossing rivers. The Rapido and Liri rivers had posed very serious problems to all previous attempts to breakthrough into the Liri valley and in the attacks on

● With Jim Farrell and (seated) Ted Roberts.

Cassino.

The period of relaxation and intensive training came to an end as the division began to take up its position ready for the battle. At 11pm on Thursday 11th May, the Allied Forces mounted an intensive barrage against enemy positions. This was the start of a major offensive and 78th Division was back in the line. On Sunday May 14th, 30 jeeps and trailers were fully loaded with mortar shells and small arms ammunition, along with various other supplies. We made our way forward and most of the jeep platoon sheltered behind Mount Trocchio, a large humped-back shaped mountain at the entrance to the Liri valley. We waited for the battle to begin.

The 78th Division was assigned to advance up the Liri valley, with the Germans on the monastery heights and the heights of San Angelo, either side of the Trocchio and guarding the gateway to the Liri valley. The battle began and we were told to move forward. Fighting was furious and, in places, groups of German soldiers fought furiously, though isolated from their units. In one place, I led my section of jeeps along a sunken track with walls on either side. The ground beyond the walls was level with the top of the walls. We soon discovered that the Germans were on one side of the track and the British on the other, and they were firing across the top of the walls. We all bent low over the jeeps and sped through as quickly as we could, and were fortunate not to suffer any casualties.

The advance along the Liri valley had many moments of danger and excitement, but nothing like the experiences we had endured in Cassino and in the mountains around Cassino. It seemed very strange to look back at Mount Caira and Monte Cassino and realise that they were no longer a threat to us. Now the Gustav Line was our objective. For the jeep platoon, the going was not quite so arduous, although it was often dangerous.

It came as a shock to realise it was Whitsun.

I conducted a service on the evening of Whit Sunday and reported it to my parents in this way: 'We gathered together in the cool of the evening, beneath the branches of a spreading tree. Around us were lime trees and vines, with tall grasses and wild mint. We sang four hymns chosen by the men, "Lead us, heavenly Father, lead us", "Jesu, lover of my soul", "When I survey the wondrous cross", and "Abide with me". All were sung from memory and without the help of a musical instrument, which meant I had to lead the singing. The platoon officer read the lesson - Luke chapter six, verses 37 to 49. I spoke on 1 Corinthians chapter three, verse eleven.

'The theme was the need of the only true foundation for national and individual life. We must rebuild our own lives before we can rebuild Britain. There were about 20 men present, plus the officer. A Canadian soldier heard the singing and joined us, staying with us after the service for about an hour. The platoon officer told me, afterwards, that men in other platoons nearby said that they would have joined us, had they known that it was a simple service and that one of the men, rather than by a padre, was conducting it.'

The advance along the Liri valley was comparatively swift. We moved forward to a new location every few days There were some exciting moments but, thankfully, few casualties.

As we moved up to the river Rapido one night, I was driving a jeep along a well-rutted track. It was almost like being on railway lines or on tramlines. Suddenly I heard the rumble and squealing of a tank, and at the same moment I saw the turret of a tank appear over the rise of the track. I couldn't turn the jeep out of the track and saw the tank heading straight for me. The driver of the tank must have seen the jeep as he levelled off after the climb. The tank was within a few feet of the jeep when it swung to the side into a field, passed the jeep and then swung back into the track and continued on its way.

On another occasion, I found myself heading into a tank battle, due to a young officer's lack of experience. I pointed out that we were heading into a tank battle and explained what was happening in front of us. Thankfully, he listened to me and we managed to turn away and avoid the action.

As we advanced, we found ourselves in all kinds of locations. One of them was a real beauty spot. It was in a small ravine, thickly wooded on either side, with a river running through the bottom of the ravine. It was green, shaded, pleasant and quiet. We had barely settled in when a man came to me and said quietly: "There is a German SP on the ridge."

'German SP' meant a German self-propelled gun, which was like a tank with a gun mounted on a platform instead of a large turret. The gunners sat and worked from a box-like structure placed just above the tracks.

I told the man to take me to see this self-propelled gun. We made our way through the trees and saw the gun on the ridge above our location. There seemed no one about, except for one man who was sat on the firing platform. I went ahead and before reaching the gun I realised the German soldier was dead. A large hole was in the armour plating just in front of him. When I climbed on to the tracks and looked into the box-like structure, I saw the armour piercing shell had blown off both his legs at the knees. Also something had sliced off the top of his head. The look on his face was peaceful, so he had felt nothing. He looked about 20 years of age. I returned to my comrade and told him the news and we returned to our location.

The weather was more like summer and we were in hot pursuit of the enemy. New names of towns appeared so quickly we hardly had time to memorise them: Aquino, Arce and Ceprano. On 2nd June 1944, we were at Frosinone and we drove on through the night.

At 6.30am the next morning we entered Rome, but only to drive through the suburbs and on after the enemy, passing through Viterbo, Montelone and on to Lake Trasimeno. It was not a straightforward tour, because the Germans were fighting a fierce rearguard action, blowing bridges and doing everything to delay our advance.

As we passed through the outskirts of Rome, it was just after dawn, and everything looked peaceful. We had no time to admire the beauty of Rome and its buildings because we sped on, trying to catch up with the steadily advancing infantry. As we advanced, the jeep platoon was not used so much, and life became easier for us. The battle for Lake Trasimeno was to be the last battle for the 78th Division before being taken out of the line for its promised rest. Some of us in the jeep platoon watched this battle from a cliff top overlooking the plain below, the battlefield. We were glad that we were not involved in it.

At Pianiccle, on 5th July, the 78th Division jeep platoon was disbanded. After handing over our jeeps to a vehicle park, the men of the jeep platoon were sent back to their respective units. I had been away from my parent company (237 Company, RASC) for four months and, during that time, I had made many good friends. Some of those friendships lasted over 50 years.

I was very sorry that Jim Farrell and Ted Roberts did not receive the recognition they deserved for their work with the jeeps, but I was told they had each been recommended for the Military Medal. They deserved it, and should, at least, have received a mention in despatches. But all the members of the jeep platoon deserved recognition. They were a grand group of men.

As I looked back on my time with the jeep platoon, I realised how God had used me to help others.

I had been a medical orderly looking after the sick and wounded, and ministering to the dying.

I had been acting as chaplain, conducting a number of 'church' services, and trying to give spiritual guidance and comfort to men living in dangerous and stressful conditions.

I had also tried to keep up morale by arranging singsongs, and singing solos as requested.

Of course, other men had also contributed to the welfare of the platoon.

I had not always found it easy to carry out these 'extra' duties, but God had given me the strength and guidance necessary to do so. God had wonderfully preserved me from harm and death. This is no reflection on those who were killed or wounded. They were good men - and brave - and, usually, they had a wife, sweetheart, a mother and family. I cannot say why they were allowed to suffer or die while I was kept safe, but I had a growing conviction that I was being spared for a special purpose.

While I was in the jeep platoon, I had some exciting and some frightening experiences. I was very fortunate - for many men had far worse experiences than I had, especially those who were in the infantry. In all those experiences, except one, I felt that God was with me, guarding me, because I had so many remarkable escapes from death.

The one exception was when I was alone in no-man's-land and came under very heavy and concentrated fire from several machine guns and mortars. I was pinned down, unable to move as the soil around me was churned up. I just hugged the earth and hoped the firing would stop. I have no idea how long I lay there, but it was probably not very long. As I hugged the earth, I remember saying: "Where is God is all this?"

I felt more than alone. It was not just human fellowship I was missing but, somehow, I felt that God had forsaken me. For the first time in my life, I really felt God-forsaken, outside the love and care of God, outside his protection and his concern. I had never felt anything like that before and have never felt it since.

I eventually made my way back to our own lines and to the men who were with me. I couldn't tell them how I felt, but in the days that followed I realised that hell is real. It is to be God forsaken; to be outside his love and care and mercy. I remembered Christ's words on the cross: 'My God, why have You forsaken me?'

I cannot understand what Christ suffered in the dark moments of physical, mental and spiritual agony as he bore the sins of the world, but I know something, albeit only a fraction, of what it feels like to be God-forsaken.

I realised afterwards that I was not really God-forsaken, because he still had me in his care and brought me safely through a dreadful experience. But that was how I felt at the time, and it felt very real. For several days afterwards, I felt unable to pray or to read the Bible, and I was troubled with many doubts. Gradually, I worked my way through the doubts and began to pray again. I had to examine my faith and, gradually, built up my faith again. This took time, but a more mature faith emerged.

I have since realised why God allowed me to have such an experience. It was so that I would be better able to speak from my own experience to those who felt that God did not care about them, or whose experiences of life had shattered their Christian faith. I thought that God had let go of me, but he was still holding me and preparing me for the work that he had planned for me. This frightening experience was part of my spiritual pilgrimage through the war years.

CHAPTER SIXTEEN

Egyptian interlude

The whole of the 78th Division was out of the front line by 4th July 1944, and the pursuit of the enemy was handed over to the British 6th Armoured Division. The first halt for the 78th Division, as it withdrew from forward areas, was at Tivoli, in the Sabine Hills, a few miles east of Rome. The men rested, cleaned everything, and were allowed to visit Rome. For those who wished to do so, audiences with the Pope were arranged, and it was reported about 4,000 men took advantage of this special offer.

The next move was from the Tivoli area to Taranto in goods trucks. These were dry, although somewhat draughty. The countryside looked different when viewed through the open sliding doors. The journey took us through some of the scenes of hard fought victories.

Cassino looked so different in daylight, but haunting in its appearance of desolation and ruin. The monastery, which had seemed so majestic perched on top of the mountain, was now a ruin. I was reminded of the moment I saw the first shells burst on its walls. Castle Hill was easily recognised with its ruins like a gaunt finger pointing to the sky. Nearby, was Hangman's Hill, the scene of bravery by friend and foe.

As I looked at Castle Hill, I was reminded of the story told

● Bill Aish and George Barnett in Rome.

me by the Rev Harry Lannigan, a chaplain with whom I was very friendly. He told me that, during the bitter fighting in the castle, the British troops were one side of the courtyard and the Germans on the other. After one very fierce engagement, a German medical officer appeared, holding a white flag. He asked if the British troops would lend him some stretchers because they had none left. Several stretchers were passed to him and he disappeared. The next day, the white flag appeared with the same German medical officer, and the stretchers were returned, all scrubbed clean. When the return of stretchers was complete and the German officer thanked the British for their kindness, he disappeared and the fighting began again.

● With Frank Davis and Bill Aish in Rome, 1944.

Cassino railway station was just a scattering of stones and mounds of rubble, and I recalled my first visit there with the Royal West Kents. All that seemed a lifetime ago.

Then, it was on to Taranto. The sea voyage to Egypt was all too short. We left Taranto on 18th July and arrived at Port Said on 22nd July. Those few days on the sparkling blue Mediterranean brought their own kind of relaxation. The evening of the second day on board, a group of men were standing on deck, most of them looking over the rail. The conversation ranged over many subjects. Then, as darkness deepened, someone asked me to sing. I sang several solos, and was then asked to sing 'The Holy City', which I did. It seemed quite natural after that to sing hymns, and sentimental songs as a reflective mood spread over the group. There was a pause in the singing; then someone began to sing a popular song of that time, 'When day is done, I think of you'. That song was very popular and was often sung at eventide as men thought of their wife or girlfriend. I knew a man in North Africa who never turned in at night without singing this song and thinking of his wife.

The evening of the third day of our short sea voyage, I was alone, standing by the ship's rail watching the waves curling up and away as the bow-wave formed. The sun began to set and it seemed so peaceful. In the deepening shadows, the phosphorous glowed in the bubbling bow-wave. The stars looked like diamonds on a black velvet cushion. In the solitude, I began to think of recent experiences, and my thoughts returned to when I felt God-forsaken. Slowly, I began to feel a sense of peace stealing over me and then came the realisation that God had never deserted me; that he had been with me all the time and was now bringing me back to a clear sense of his nearness and to a fellowship with himself. I spent time in meditation before spending time in prayer.

At that moment, I realised more clearly that God had been guiding me through all the experiences I had had since joining the Army, and that he would continue to guide me throughout the remainder of the time in the Forces. I could not describe, nor explain, the peace and joy and relief I felt in that time alone with God, but its effect was real and lasting. It was another milestone on my spiritual pilgrimage.

We disembarked at Port Said, and quickly moved to new quarters at Qassasin. This was a rest camp about 70 miles from Cairo and 20 miles from Ismalia. It was in the middle of the desert, and, as we soon discovered, the temperature rarely dropped below 100 degrees Fahrenheit - and that was in the shade. Wherever we looked, there were endless rows of white tents and, in them, we lay on beds during the day, with the walls of the tent rolled up, and waited for the cool of the evening. Some afternoons we played cricket on coconut matting laid on concrete pitches.

I often spent most of an afternoon standing under a shower of tepid water. The showers were a very popular way of keeping cool in the heat of the afternoon.

Despite the heat and the sand, it was a rest camp with running water, shower baths and

● Rome, July 1944.

NAAFI canteens with more goods for sale than we had seen for a long while. There were also clubs and cinemas.

The cinemas were not the most luxurious, but we frequented them. The seats were planks of wood fastened to short wooden posts sunk into the sand. Before entering the cinema, it was wise to buy a large bottle of mineral water, take off your tunic and bring several handkerchiefs. Despite the slightly cooler temperature of the evening, it was still very hot in this open-roofed cinema. The usual routine was: sit down, take a drink of mineral water, and a few minutes later begin mopping up the perspiration - and, all the time, refuse to allow these operations to interfere with your enjoyment of watching the film.

One evening, Frank Davis and I went to the cinema to see the film, 'The Mummy's Tomb', which was set, of course, in Egypt. It dealt with the usual curse on anyone opening a tomb. As Frank and I walked back to our tent, slowing plodding along on the soft sand, and looking at the stars in a navy blue sky, I suddenly felt something wet and cold in my left hand. I said to Frank: "See if anything is walking behind us?"

He glanced over his shoulder and replied, "Of course not. Why?"

I said: "Well, something wet and cold is in my hand and keeping pace with us."

We stopped and looked around - and found a large Alsatian dog alongside me. He had wanted company and was telling me he was there.

During our stay in Qassasin, every man and officer had five days leave in Cairo, Alexandria or Ismalia. I went with others from our platoon to Cairo for leave, although I also visited Ismalia.

While at Qassasin I met several men who had attended the meetings in the Canvas Chapel. Some of these men were in tents near mine, so we often met together for social activities or for Bible study and prayer. I also met a Church of England chaplain who was a great help to me, giving me advice and guidance about entry into the Christian ministry. He discussed with me preparation for ministerial training, suggesting subjects that I should study, and greatly encouraged me. During this time, I was able to give more time to Bible study. A chaplain, who was the secretary for Baptist Ministerial Candidates in the Mediterranean area, also contacted me. For him, I completed questionnaires and submitted written sermon notes for criticism.

Qassasin was more than a rest camp for me. It was a time of spiritual renewal.

One day I was told that, if I wished, I could be transferred to an RASC company in the Middle East so that I could attend a moral leadership course in Jerusalem. If I accepted the offer I could not return to 237 Company, RASC.

● Cairo, 1944.

Very reluctantly, I declined the offer. I would very much have liked to have accepted and gone to Jerusalem and studied on the course, but I wanted to stay with my friends. Many of us had been together since April 1940. Later events confirmed to me that I had taken the right decision, but it was a most tempting offer.

Much later, we learned that when the 78th Division came out of the front line at Tivoli, the intention was for the division to go to Egypt for a rest and refit, and then move to Palestine for further training for a couple of months. Events in Italy caused a change of plans. On 7th September 1944, the division left Egypt and sailed for Italy - not for England, as many of the troops had hoped and some believed. Rumours had been rife that the division was to return to England on its way to France to strengthen British forces there.

I wondered what was happening because, before we left Qassasin, I had been told to give a series of lectures on first aid to men of 237 Company. I did so, using, as illustrations, some of the casualties I had treated in North Africa and Italy. While we were in England I had given many lectures on first aid every time there was a new training programme for the company; so I was quite used to the task. In this, I was following in my father's footsteps because he was the lecturer in charge for the annual series of lectures for St. John's Ambulance Brigade in the place where he lived, a position he held for about 30 years. It was from him that I began learning about first aid and, later, from St. John's Ambulance Brigade. This training stood me in good stead throughout my service in the Forces, and enabled me to help those in need.

While we were in Egypt, there was a change in the command of 237 Company RASC. Major J S Dorling, who had joined the original 4 GHQ Company as a second lieutenant in April 1940, and had risen in rank to command the revised 4 GHQ Company, which became 237 Company, was promoted to Lt-Colonel. He was posted to Malta and became the deputy director of supplies and transport for Malta. His place in 237 Company was taken by Major Carpenter.

Our Egyptian interlude had come to an end and we returned to Italy to take up the struggle again. We were not sorry to leave Egypt with its heat, myriads of flies and smells.

So, we endured another short sea voyage.

CHAPTER SEVENTEEN

Return to the struggle

The 78th Division arrived back in Italy on 11th September 1944. It was quickly moved up, through the country, towards the battle area. The only settling-in period was the two weeks it took to re-equip the division with vehicles of various kinds, and with the equipment and stores needed to enable the division to become, once more, a mobile fighting unit. The journey northwards began on 25th September. The weather was much colder than in Egypt and the exchange of khaki drill uniforms for battledress was welcomed by the troops.

On the afternoon of 24th September, along with other drivers and their lorries, I reported to the Royal Irish Fusiliers' company sergeant major, for the purpose of troop transport. The next morning, reveille was at 3am. During the day, we travelled 162 miles and arrived at the campsite at 6pm. The next morning, reveille was at 3.30am and we covered 145 miles, arriving at a campsite at 5.30pm. On the morning of 27th September, the reveille was at 3.30am and the journey was only 110 miles, which brought us to the location where the Irish Fusiliers were to stay, at least for a while.

We, who had transported the troops, now returned to our own unit. During those three days of travel we had passed through familiar places, and the scenes of some the battles in which our division had fought. In some places, attempts had been made to repair the damage caused by war. In other places, very little repair work had been attempted. Cortona and Ancona were much worse than any of the other places we saw. Pescara did not appear to be in such a bad condition. As we went northwards, there were improvements in the scenery, in living conditions and housing. There seemed to be plenty of fruit growing: grapes, apples, pears, nuts, figs, pomegranates, tomatoes, ripe peaches and green oranges. The journey took the division over former battlefields: Termoli, the Trigno and the Sangro.

Before the division reached Rimini on the Adriatic coast, it was transferred to the command of the British XIII Corps, occupying the right sector of the Fifth Army (American). So we returned to more troop transporting duties.

On 3rd October, I was attached to the Royal West Kent Regiment for troop carrying. As soon as I reached the unit, preparations for the move began. The journey started in the evening and continued through the night. The route involved climbing up and crossing a mountain range that, with heavily laden lorries, took some time.

About midnight, we reached the top of the mountain road and, as the road levelled out, we halted for a brief rest. I walked to the edge of the road and leaned on the rails forming a protective fence. I looked at the mountains towering above us. There was bright moonlight from a full moon and, by this light, the pale grey colour of the mountain's rugged walls could be clearly seen. Slowly, my gaze travelled upwards towards the towering peaks. The grey rocks began to look like silver, rising in majestic grandeur. It was awe-inspiring and, as I gazed upon this scene, peace came to my mind. I thought of the mighty God who had created all this. I thought of his majesty and power, and I bowed my head and worshipped him.

All too soon came the command to resume our journey, but that scene lives on in my memory and often comes back to me to help me to worship God. The words of the Psalmist took on a new meaning. 'I will lift up mine eyes unto the hills' is always a reminder to me of the midnight hour when I saw the majestic mountains that inspired worship.

The following morning, we halted at a place near Assisi. We stayed there until 12.30pm before continuing our journey. Travelling through the night, we arrived at a staging area at 11.30pm. These night movements were usually to reduce publicity on troop movements and so prevent the enemy knowing about troops being moved. This time, that aim was achieved. The Germans had no idea what had happened.

We stayed in the staging area that night and left the next morning, when I returned to my own unit. At 3pm that afternoon, I was sent to another unit for more troop transport. We were allowed to rest that night and transported troops from 9am until 6pm. This was the last of the troop transport for a while, and the division settled into positions in the centre sector of the line. It was there that autumn found us and winter came upon us.

The rainy season in Tunisia had been bad, but October and November 1944 was equally bad in our area. In an eight week period, there were only eight days without rainfall. The three months from the middle of October were to prove to be, for us, a horrible winter. Most of the troops lived in the open, under canvas or in ruined buildings. The damp and cold seemed to enter into everyone's bones. The weary troops were ordered to consolidate their positions. The main supply routes to the division's forward areas became too difficult for the British built lorries with only two-wheel drive, and so American transport, with four-wheeled drive, were loaned to the division.

As October ended and November began, the rain turned everywhere into a sea of mud. On 19th October, in the early hours of the morning, the river bordering the field in which we were camped in tents, overflowed its banks and flooded the field. It all happened so quickly that the first my tent-mate and I knew of it was when the water flowed into our tent.

My tin hat was floating away when I managed to grab it. Everything was soaking wet: blankets, our kit and the clothes we wore. The waterlogged and bedraggled men salvaged their blankets and kit and spent the rest of the night wringing out the dirty water from them. Then we looked for empty lorries in which to spend the remainder of the night. The next morning, those not engaged in transport details tried to salvage tents and equipment from the mud - and re-pitched their tents on slightly higher ground.

The field in which we were camped had become a sea of deep mud, and the lorries constantly moving into the field wore deep grooves in the mud. These eventually became so deep that the back axles of the vehicles scraped along on the surfaces between the wheels. These ruts became extended trenches and were used by the men as safe walkways from one part of the camp to another. The disadvantage was that one had to go where the track went, unless one was brave enough to step out of the rut and sink knee-deep into mud.

The bivouac tents in which we lived, usually called a 'bivvy', were low pitched tents, about a yard high at the apex and about four feet wide at the base. To provide extra room, it was customary to dig down into the earth for about two feet, and place the excavated earth around the outside of the base of the tent and provide a small wall for extra protection while allowing openings for drainage. There was not much room inside the tent for two men and all their kit.

In the continuous wet weather, living in a bivvy was very frustrating. Most men made a bed frame from pieces of wood. They nailed sandbags across the wooden frame and then put blocks of wood under the frame to keep it off the ground.

Before retiring for the night, you scraped your boots clean of mud, wrung out your socks and then hung them on a piece of string fastened between to the two tent poles. The next morning, you put on your socks and boots. Invariably, they were still wet. In addition, at night, you removed your trousers and scraped off the mud that had collected on the legs. Then you laid the trousers on top of your greatcoat, or overcoat. This acted as your top blanket.

Laundry was a real problem. If you could wash clothes, there was nowhere to dry them because of the continuous rain. Any garment that was washed took a very long time to dry. Before wearing such a garment, I placed it between the blankets on top of me in the hope that the heat from my body would 'air' it before I wore it.

One day, I washed a pair of socks. Three days later they were dry. When I looked for them they were missing, and I discovered Cliff Read, with whom I shared the tent, had washed them thinking that they were his socks. A little later I noticed that my dry socks had a hole in them, so I darned them and wore them. Later in the day, Cliff Read asked if I had seen his sock with a hole in it. He did, at least, thank me for repairing his sock.

During November, the rain turned to snow. Then the snow and mud became frozen. At least it was drier to walk about and it only took three or four days to dry the clothes that had been washed. The cold was intense at times and the metal skid-chains on the wheels of the lorries sometimes snapped in the cold. When this happened, the driver would tie the chain links together with wire. This was usually telephone wire that we found on the side of the road. This had come from broken telephone lines, or had been left behind by repair wiremen.

It was rather frightening to be driving a lorry down a steep hill, or slowly descending a mountain road with ice covered surfaces, to hear a loud report as the links snapped and the broken ends slapped against the mudguards or sides of the lorry. The driver would slow down as soon as possible, but with care, because it was unwise to apply the brakes too suddenly or too severely. This would have induced a skid that could take the vehicle and driver over the edge of the mountain road. When the vehicle stopped, the driver would use old telephone wire - which most drivers carried for use in emergencies - to tie up the links and continue slowly on his journey, in the hope that he would be able to get the skid-chains repaired when he reached camp.

During this period, our platoon did a great deal of work with the Royal Engineers of the 78th Division. The tasks were of a very varied nature. Some of these involved journeys into forward areas, and some of them were very exciting.

One of our tasks was to transport tree trunks of a certain diameter and length to what was known as the Appolinare Track. The roads in that area were insufficient for the volume of traffic required, so a new track had to be built as quickly as possible from Cuviolo to San Appolinare, where two brigades had their headquarters and where the divisional tactical headquarters were also situated. Such was the urgency of the task that all troops who could be made available were brought in to help cut down the trees and to help to lay the track.

The track was being made up the side of a mountain. It was really a rough track cut into the mountainside - although, in some places, 'scraped out' would be a better description. Chestnut palings were fastened to the banks on either side of the track to prevent earth falling onto the track. Tree trunks were laid, side-by-side, across the track and securely fastened into position to form a rough road. The track led to the top of a ridge, which was the front line, held at the point above us by the Welsh Guards. While delivering a load of tree trunks to the foremost point on the track, I met my cousin who was serving in the Welsh Guards. This was our first meeting in Italy.

One day, when the snow lay deep upon the countryside, I delivered a load of tree trunks to the Appolinare Track. There was a delay until the trunks could be unloaded, so I began to walk about to keep warm. There were members of the Bechuanaland Regiment working on the track and I spoke to one of them. After chatting for a few minutes this man said to me: "I'm a Christian. Are you?"

I was surprised, but quickly took my New Testament from my top pocket of my battle-dress blouse, and answered: "Yes, I am."

He then took out his New Testament, and we began reading the same chapter and verse, he in his language and I in English.

This man's courage in declaring his faith in Jesus Christ greatly impressed me, and challenged me to witness more openly and readily to my own faith. He was not afraid to witness to his Lord; nor did he hesitate to speak a word for Jesus Christ. Here was the product of some mission station in Bechuanaland being a missionary in Italy.

It was mid-November when we moved forward to a new location, near San Clemente. Our camp was reached by following a track immediately in front of a battery of 25 pounder guns of the Royal Artillery. The muzzles of the guns were very near the track and we always hoped the guns would not fire as we passed. When they did, the flash of flame went just over the top of the lorry and the noise was deafening. The track led to the bank of the river and, since there was no bridge, each vehicle had to 'ford' the river. We soon learned which was the shallowest and safest part of the river at which to cross.

On the opposite bank was a fairly level patch of ground, but we pitched our tents on the hillside, taking care to keep the hillside between the enemy and us. The in-coming shells either hit the hillside on the enemy's side, or went over the top of us. We dug in and used the excavated earth to make a protecting wall around the bivvy. During the night, the water seeped into the dugout, became frozen and, each morning, we threw out a thick sheet of ice that had formed on the dugout's floor.

A thorny bush, outside the entrance to the bivvy, was excellent for hanging our washing on to dry out, and the washing usually dried in three to four days. Each evening, you crumbled the garment in order to break out the ice and so reduce the moisture content, allowing the sun the next day to continue the process of drying.

One day, I had to go to Castel del Rio, which was away from the front line. This meant going in front of the guns and turning left at the main track leading back down the line towards base. It was a very foggy day. Visibility was down to five or six feet; so it was a slow crawl. After what seemed a long time, I came to a clear patch in the fog and suddenly I saw a German soldier on the side of the road. My immediate reaction was to think that I had turned the wrong way as I came out on to the main track and had gone through the front line and into the German lines.

Second thoughts were that it was useless to grab my rifle and try to fight my way out because I would be outnumbered. My thoughts raced on and I wondered if I turned the steering wheel quickly I could knock the German down and try to turn the lorry and make a run for it. I was about to turn the steering wheel when I saw a British soldier behind the German, and the British soldier had a rifle and fixed bayonet pointed at the German's back. With relief, I realised that the German was a prisoner being taken to Divisional Headquarters for questioning. He will never know how near he was to being hit with a Bedford three ton lorry.

One of the tasks performed by our platoon was for several lorries to go back down the line towards base, to a town called Borgo San Lorenzo. There the drivers stayed overnight in the house of a friendly Italian family. This family were given army rations to feed us, with sufficient to feed themselves.

Next morning, the drivers proceeded south, to the woods in the old Gothic Line. Here troops on 'rest leave' from the forward positions cut down trees, trimmed the branches off and cut the trunks to a certain length. Some of these trees showed scars where bullets and shrapnel had hit them. Sometimes, the bullets and shrapnel were still embedded in the trees.

These trunks were then moved to our platoon location near San Clemente. Usually, they arrived late in the afternoon. The lorry drivers would then have a meal and, about 6pm, would take the lorries in front of the 25 pounder guns and turn right onto the main track. They would drive through the front line and out into no-man's-land. On arrival at the designated spot, men of the Royal Engineers met the lorries on the site at the end of the 'road' they were making. The drivers and the Engineers would unload the tree trunks and place them in position. Sometimes work would be interrupted as warnings were received that enemy patrols were in the vicinity. Then everyone would 'stand-to', looking for the patrol and preparing for battle. When the all-clear was given, the work resumed.

CHAPTER EIGHTEEN

Christmas at San Clemente

The appropriate carol would have been, 'See, amid the winter snow', because the countryside was covered with snow, varying in depth from one to ten feet. The work of transport had to continue and there were many stories told of hair-raising experiences on the roads, as well as of excitement in the forward areas.

Our chaplain at that time, the Rev E Emrys Hughes, kept in touch with me. He was a good friend who gave me good advice. He told me that he would not be able to visit our platoon over the Christmas period, so I asked our platoon officer for permission to conduct a short service on Christmas morning. He agreed.

I told the chaplain and asked for his permission to conduct the service in his absence. He also agreed and promised me his support in all my efforts. He wrote to the commanding officer of 237 Company RASC, explaining his inability to visit the company, but adding that I would be conducting the service in his stead. This was the first time I had been the official 'stand-in' for a chaplain in my own company, with the official recognition from both the chaplain and commanding officer. The chaplain asked me to send him a report of each service I conducted, so that he could include it in his monthly report to the deputy chaplain general.

On Christmas Eve, I was guard commander, beginning at 6pm and ending on Christmas Day at 6am. Just before midnight on Christmas Eve, we heard the usual sounds of gunfire, artillery and machine-guns. Then there was a lull in the firing.

A few minutes before midnight, we heard the German machineguns firing short bursts, which we recognised as 'daa-da-da-daa'. After a slight pause, the British machine guns completed the call with 'daa-daa'. This was a common signal for many things in the Forces. It seemed that both sides were 'signing off' for the night, because there was no more firing from either side for 24 hours. There was no artillery; no machine-gun fire. It was an unofficial truce just for Christmas Day.

The Christmas Day Service began at 10.30am and was held in two tents, joined end to end. The ground was frozen mud. There were no seats and no musical instruments. Company HQ had supplied some hymn sheets, containing the words of carols.

It was very cold with strong winds. There was nothing to attract the men to the service; yet 20 men attended. Our platoon was miles away from the rest of the company; so only men from our platoon attended and, of those able to attend, about a third did so. It was a simple service. We sang, 'O come all ye faithful', 'While shepherds watched their flocks', 'Silent Night' and 'Good King Wenceslas'. The lesson was Luke chapter two, verses eight to 20. I spoke on Luke chapter two, verse 19: 'And Mary hid all these things in her heart.'

During Christmas Day, six men came to tell me how much they had enjoyed the service. One man, from the North Country, said: "That was a smashing service. You did champion - better than a parson. Why don't you go in for a parson? You would make a good parson and you could do it alright."

This man had been in the platoon for about three years. I knew him very well and he knew me very well, so his words were really sincere.

That man did not realise how much his encouragement meant to me, because I had been thinking very seriously of my decision to enter the Christian ministry. The conditions under which we lived; the experiences through which we were going; the lack of time for serious study, and the constant insistence - by chaplains and the ordination candidate secretary (OCS) - on the importance of studying and the need to make time for serious study of Greek and English, plus submitting written sermons at regular intervals on texts set by the OCS or some other chaplain, had begun to sow doubts in my mind as to my suitability to do all the preparation. I felt that God was calling me to give my life to his service as a Christian minister, but I was beginning to wonder if I had the ability to achieve the standards set by men for my entrance into theological college.

My ability to talk to men on spiritual matters, and to preach in a way that the men understood had been demonstrated many times, but conditions made serious study very difficult. Time for serious reading was also difficult to fit into our way of life. Necessary books were not easy to come by, except the New Testament. Things seemed to be very discouraging at times - so I greatly appreciated a word of encouragement. I decided to continue to prepare myself for training for the ministry as best I could, witnessing to the men and conducting services as opportunity arose.

On one occasion, I was asked to write a sermon on John chapter eight, verse 32, 'And ye shall know the truth, and the truth shall make you free.' After completing the sermon, I asked Bill Aish and Frank Davis to listen to it, in the hope of receiving constructive criticism and suggestions on how to improve the sermon. When I had finished reading the sermon, Frank Davis said: "I cannot understand how you can think those things and write them down in these conditions."

This encouraged me to keep studying. I obtained a few books with help from chaplains and also from my parents; so I tried to read and study when I could.

This period in the Army was a spiritually testing time for me. I had learned to live one day at a time in the Army because we had realised we had only the moment in which we were living and could not look forward to 'tomorrow' with any confidence. My trouble was that I looked too far ahead concerning the Christian ministry and saw the difficulties as a mass, instead of taking things a bit at a time and leaving the future to God. I eventually came to the decision to leave everything in the hands of God and do my best to study and prepare myself in the hope that the way would open for me to enter college.

About this time, I was greatly encouraged by two letters I received: one from the Rev D W Jones, minister of my home church (Oakdale Baptist Church in Monmouthshire) and a very dear friend to me, and the other from a friend who lived in Southampton. In their letters, they both quoted the same text - which had special significance for me. The text was Revelation chapter three, verse eight, 'I know thy works; behold, I have set before you an open door, and no man can shut it; for thou hast a little strength, and hast kept my word, and hast not denied my name.' Later experience proved the truth of these words.

In January 1945, I was told that I had been chosen as one of five lecturers for 237 Company. The others were the company sergeant major, the company quartermaster sergeant, a sergeant and a corporal. We were to give lectures on any subject we chose, to help to inform and entertain the men in off duty periods. In 1941, I had attended an instructors' course at the Army Gas School and had passed as a first class instructor. I had also given many lectures on first aid, water purification and anti-malarial precautions, and had been allowed to conduct services. Recently, I had been given official sanction to act as a chaplain's assistant. So, perhaps it was not surprising that I was included as one of the company lecturers.

In February 1945, the 78th Division was moved from the San Clemente area and from in front of Bologna, to the Forli area. I was involved in moving units of the Royal Engineers. The first time, it was a five day job and, on the journey, we enjoyed seeing some very nice scenery. On the second 'troop lift', we covered the same ground as the first time. When we stopped for the first night, a corporal in the Royal Engineers, with whom I was friendly, arranged a concert. This corporal had been awarded the George Medal for bravery in the air raids in Liverpool.

The corporal asked me to take part in the concert and I sang 'The Londonderry Air' and, by special request, 'Trees'. I was asked to sing again, and one of the men from my own platoon asked me to perform my burlesque of an opera. This was always very popular with the men of my own company and was often requested. I gave the burlesque and, judging by the reception it received, the men of the Royal Engineers liked it too, and I was treated as a 'star performer'.

Before reaching our destination we spent the night in a block of flats, some of which were occupied by Italian civilians. Most of the men went out in the evening, but a few stayed in and listened to one of the men playing a piano accordion. We sang a few songs and some Italians joined us, listening to our 'music'. It was suggested that I sang a few solos, which I did. The Italians then asked me to sing solos from various operas. I explained that the piano-accordionist could not play music from operas. They said that I could sing without music, and I replied I did not know the Italian words, to which they replied: "Sing in English."

Since I could not escape from the task, I warned the English men not to laugh because I would have to make up the words for the songs. I did my best and the Italians must have enjoyed it because they brought out bottles of wine for everyone to drink. Because I did not drink wine I asked for water, which was brought to me. Nothing I could say could convince the Italians I was not an opera singer. That evening and the next morning the Italians spoke to me, smiled and were very friendly, some of the men even raised their hats to me, which was embarrassing.

When we arrived at our destination, I discovered an opera was being performed that evening in a nearby village. I persuaded one of my companions to come with me and we saw an Italian Opera Company perform 'The Barber of Seville'. It was a musical feast and the bass soloist was magnificent. This visit to the opera at Forlimpopli, is one of my happy memories of Italy.

When the 78th Division completed its move, we found ourselves billeted in the outbuildings of a farm house a few miles from Forlimpopli, which was a few miles from Forli. We lived in a loft of a barn. It was dry, clean and warm. Our cooks provided good food, and we were kept busy but not too busy, and night driving was rare. I arranged with the farmer's wife to do my laundry, for which I paid her. Sometimes I gave her some chocolate and soap and, in return, she occasionally gave me an egg. A mobile NAAFI van visited us most days; so we felt we were highly privileged. This rest period was greatly appreciated.

While at Forlimpopli we had a change of chaplain. Our new padre was the Rev G Solomon, an Anglican. He was a very clever men and a Greek scholar. He read his Greek New Testament and translated it into English as he read it. This proficiency staggered me and made efforts to study Greek look most inadequate. The Rev Solomon was a very humble and friendly man and he helped me with my studies in Greek and also helped me with my other studies. Early in March he asked me if I would care to attend a 'Christian Fellowship Conference' to be held at an Army hospital near Forli. It would be held from 8th to 10th March. The conference was for chaplains and ordination candidates of 78th Division. I accepted the invitation and the chaplain spoke to our commanding officer and arranged for me to attend.

On Thursday 8th March, I packed my blankets and small pack and was taken by lorry to the Army hospital near Forli, arriving in time for the first meal at 5pm. Nine chaplains were present. Seven were from the Church of England; one was from the Presbyterian Church of Scotland, the other was a Methodist. There were also 13 ordination candidates, of whom three were officers and the rest were 'other ranks'. The officers were given two bedrooms between them. The other ranks had one room between them, but were given stretchers for beds, and they were very comfortable. We shared the same dining room, and a chapel was placed at our disposal. A small library of selected books was provided.

The chaplains gave lectures and each lecture was followed by a discussion group. Services - including a communion service - were held. The Rev K L Tyson, a Church of Scotland chaplain, gave a most stimulating series of lectures on an 'Introduction to Bible Study'. The Rev J P Stevenson gave lectures on 'Prayer', which were also stimulating. The ground covered in the lectures and discussion groups was very wide, demanding careful thought and concentration, but they were exceedingly helpful and valuable. The notes I had taken provided food for thought for a very long time.

On the Friday morning, the Rev H C Lannigan MC, a Methodist chaplain, conducted a service and spoke on Mark chapter two, verses 13 to 28. When speaking of verses 21 and 22 - 'putting new wine in old bottles' - he warned his hearers of the danger of trying to fit Christ into our plans, saying Christ was too big for them. I realised that I had been trying to do just that and this was the cause of many of my problems. I now had to fit in with Christ's plans. It was a most uplifting sermon and service, and provided another step forward in my spiritual pilgrimage.

The Conference ended on Friday evening when the Rev Kenneth Tyson conducted a short service, followed by a communion service. The atmosphere of that service greatly impressed us all. The serenity, peace, hope and comfort were very real to us. It was in sharp contrast to the kind of existence we had known for so long. We had found new spiritual hope and strength at that conference.

Another benefit from the conference was that the ordination candidates were able to share their ideas, hopes, fears and difficulties. Though we came from various sections of the Christian church, we found we were all facing similar situations. We all found it very difficult to study under active service conditions. We found we also shared the same frustrations that there was very little time for relaxation and we all had difficulties in concentrating for study - although we acknowledged the need for study and preparation to train the mind. The sense of fellowship among us, along with the realisation that we were not alone in our efforts and hopes was very refreshing, and we were encouraged to continue our efforts to enter the Christian ministry. We also gained an insight into a chaplain's life and work. We found the conference had been a spiritual uplift, with encouragement and guidance.

A few days after returning to my platoon, the senior chaplain for 78th Division, the Rev Ivor Phillips, came to see me. He had arranged the Christian Fellowship Conference. He came to make sure that I knew I was to report to Eighth Army HQ at Cessena on 17th March to meet the Rev M E Aubrey, the General Secretary of the Baptist Union of Great Britain and Ireland. He was visiting Italy to interview ordination candidates applying for entry to Baptist and Congregational Colleges. The Rev Ivor Phillips was most concerned about me attending this interview at Cessena. When he left me, he went to our commanding officer to make arrangements for me to be allowed to go to Cessena and to ensure that transport would be provided for me.

When I arrived at Cessena, I met three Baptist and four Congregationalist ordination candidates. The Rev A G Hill, the ordination candidates' secretary, received us and then gave us a short talk. I was the first to be interviewed by the Rev M E Aubrey and the interviewing board, which consisted of three chaplains. The board would report its findings to the theological colleges and the colleges would make a decision whether or not to invite the candidate for further interviews.

The Rev M E Aubrey seemed to have a great deal of information about my Christian activities during my time overseas, and knew that I had been conducting services. The Rev A G Hill, to whom I had submitted sermons and a record of services I had conducted, had probably supplied this to him. The Rev M E Aubrey also referred to my immediate award of the Military Medal at Cassino.

Many months later I received the news that the Candidates Board had recommended that I be accepted for training at a Baptist Theological College.

CHAPTER NINETEEN

The final phase

It became obvious that the rest period was over. The usual signs appeared: the moving of troops, the leaving of comfortable billets, the stock-piling of ammunition, petrol, diesel and food, plus a wide variety of other stores and equipment. New names of towns were mentioned and, slowly, the 78th Division began to move into the battle area.

Then came the usual order: 'all lorries to be issued with four sandbags, these to be half-filled with fine earth (it used to be sand in North Africa). Two sandbags will be placed under the driver's feet but not obstructing the foot pedals, and two will be placed under the passenger's feet.' This was to minimise injuries should a lorry be driven over a mine.

Then came the order: 'if on detail - that is, transport to the front line area or in an advance - do not stop to attend to the wounded. It is imperative that transport be kept moving and loads delivered as soon as possible.'

This meant that we were about to take part in a 'big push' and could expect a very tough time. Then came the 'Order of the Day' from the supreme commander and we knew we were about to take part in the final advance in Italy.

Our platoon was attached to the Royal Engineers and we moved to a place called Russi, which was a few miles from Ravenna. We lined up in a field and waited for the attack to begin. It was very late in the evening, so we knew it would be night driving without lights. Suddenly, the biggest chandelier flares we had ever seen illuminated the whole area. There were more of them than we had ever imagined. Then the Verey lights began to go up. The battle was joined and we moved forward.

We lost count of the time and, eventually, lost count of the days. There was hardly time to eat and very little time for sleep. We carried all sorts of loads and worked with a variety of units. Amid all the apparent chaos, we continued to advance. We encountered stiff opposition at Argenta, and we heard a lot about the Argenta Gap, and the advance was delayed for a few days. Then we moved forward again; this time towards Ferrara. We heard we were pushing on towards the River Po.

During the advance, we were carrying ammunition and pushed forward as fast as we could. On one of our forward dashes, some infantrymen stopped us and told our platoon officer that we could not go forward. The officer explained we were to deliver ammunition at a particular map reference as soon as possible. He was told it was impossible for him to do this because the infantry had not yet captured the field where we were to unload the ammunition but, if he could wait a few hours, the field would be captured and we could unload the ammunition at the designated spot.

The lorries were taken from their exposed position on this country road, and moved into a field. The order came not to dig slit trenches because we would soon be moving on. Some of us wandered out on to the road and down to a crossroads.

Then, we saw a long column of German soldiers walking toward us. There were hundreds of them, all prisoners of war. The men looked tired. Many were dirty, and some were dazed. Others seemed to be happy to know that they were walking towards a POW Camp and were out of the war. Only a few British infantrymen walked with them, and the military policeman at the crossroads just waved them on their way. We had seen scenes like this in Tunisia as that campaign drew to a close, and we were encouraged to see the same thing repeated in Italy.

Then came the order to dig in because the battle for our unloading point was taking longer than expected. The cooks set up the cookhouse and we had an evening meal. We dug slit trenches, and as the evening deepened into night, we put up our mosquito nets. This we did by sticking short sticks at each corner of the slit trench and draping the mosquito netting over the sticks. The groundsheet was placed on the earth, blankets on the ground sheet, and we settled down for the night. The noise of artillery, mortars and gunfire did not prevent us sleeping.

Just after dawn came the cry from the cookhouse telling us that breakfast was ready. The invitation was couched in these words: "Come and get it before I throw it out to the other pigs."

I raised myself up and, as I did so, I became enveloped in my mosquito net. Every man getting up did the same thing. It looked like a lot of ghosts rising up out of graves. I called to the man in the next slit trench to mine: "Frank, quick, get up. It is resurrection morning and you are going to be late."

He jumped up quickly, became entangled in his mosquito net, saw what was happening, and he was not amused. His language convinced me that it was not resurrection morning.

Later in the morning we proceeded to the newly won field and deposited the ammunition in readiness for the artillery, who were to advance to the spot almost immediately.

On another occasion, we had been driving most of the night and all the next day, and we had to deliver ammunition to an artillery battery in a forward position. We arrived after sunset, unloaded the ammunition and were told to stay until morning. We parked our lorries about 50 yards behind the guns, in the hope of avoiding any incoming shells. Then we lay down on the earth beside our lorries, but keeping the lorries between the artillery and us. The guns fired all night long, but we did not hear them. As soon as we lay down we fell asleep and slept until morning.

The advance continued northwards and we were constantly on the move. We stopped for a day and a night in a large timber yard, with sawmills and other wood cutting machines. In the evening, we saw a group of men approaching and, as they came nearer, we recognised them as British soldiers. They told us that they had been prisoners of war and advancing troops had liberated them, We gave them food and cigarettes and directions to where they could find further help and food. This incident strengthened our belief that the war in Italy was drawing to a close. Yet when the end came, it was an anticlimax.

During this advance we reached the River Po and, where we stopped, on the banks was the remains of a steel bridge over the river. This bridge had been bombed by Allied planes. What remained of the bridge was crowded with German wooden carts, because the Germans had been using horse drawn vehicles for a long time. Among the wreckage we could see bodies - both human and horses. We had seen many dead human beings but it was a shock and very disturbing to see these poor horses lying among the wreckage: innocent animals needlessly sacrificed.

We reached a large town called Pordonone and were billeted in an old Italian cavalry barracks. Late one afternoon, the order came to take ammunition to an artillery unit in a forward position, and the need was urgent. We sped to the large ammunition dump and loaded up, and then delivered the ammunition. As we began our return journey the darkness began to close in on us. We had not travelled far when we saw Verey lights and tracer bullets stabbing the darkness.

● Pontoon bridge over the River Po.

I had been caught between German pockets of resistance before, and had found myself between Germans and British as they fought, and I thought that we had somehow come upon some pockets of resistance. The lorries halted and I walked on alone to try to discover what was happening. Eventually I saw a British soldier and asked what was happening. In a very unemotional voice he said: "It's all over. The war in Italy has ended."

I asked why the firework display and he replied: "The lads are celebrating."

I returned to the lorries and told the men what I had learned. The only response was: "Let's get back and get some food and sleep."

The morning after the Italian Campaign ended, everyone seemed lost, wondering what would happen next. We listened to the radio to hear King George VI speak, and then to hear Winston Churchill. Afterwards, Frank Davis and I decided to walk around the town. The streets were deserted as we strolled in the sunshine. Then we heard the sound of music, and walked towards it. An Italian man suddenly appeared from a house, listened to the music, and shouted to us: "La Gioconda."

We agreed with him. Then he said, in Italian: "The Dance of the Hours."

Again, we agreed with him. Then we strolled back to the barracks. We had celebrated the end of the war in Italy.

In the afternoon, a chaplain held a thanksgiving service in a room in the barracks and many of the men attended.

CHAPTER TWENTY

The Austrian Tyrol

Eventually, we left Italy in a gigantic convoy slowly moving towards the Alps. The scenery changed the nearer we came to the foot of the Alps, and we enjoyed looking at it. The beautiful valleys and unspoilt countryside through which we passed were in such contrast to the devastation we had seen in the Po valley.

Then began the climb up the twisting road, with its innumerable hairpin bends so that, at times, it was possible to look down and see the long twisting convoy far below. Then came the summit of this Alpine road - the Croce Pass - and the view from this vantage point was breathtaking. We looked down into Austria and saw the villages looking so neat and clean, nestling in the green landscape.

Slowly we made our way down the Alps and into Austria. The convoy gradually divided into the various units, each proceeding to its allotted area. 237 Company RASC were billeted in Portschach, but only for a short while. We soon moved on to Arnoldstein. The 78th Division was scattered over Carinthia.

The 38th Irish Brigade, to which 237 Company was attached, was given a task that involved many difficulties. Within its area, and on the fringes of that area, were 'White' Russians who had fought with the Germans. There were also Cossacks and Caucasian divisions and, added to these, were Bulgarians, Slovaks, Croats and Yugoslavs. Keeping the peace among such a collection of units and diverse nationalities was not easy.

The 38th Irish Brigade sorted out the situation and prevented hostilities between these different factions, until they were relieved of the task by the 46th Division. Eventually, all Hungarians in the British Zone were taken to a camp north of Villach, and the Croat troops were handed over to the Yugoslavs.

The fate of the White Russians was a different story, and controversy has surrounded them and their treatment ever since. The evidence points to the fact that they were returned to Russia to be dealt with by the Russian authorities. Some of my comrades were involved in transporting these troops to the Russian Zone. The White Russians were convinced that they would be shot on arrival in the Russian area. They traded their possessions in return for chocolate or cigarettes, because they did not expect to live long and wanted to enjoy a few luxuries while they could.

Just after our arrival in Arnoldstein, a German division surrendered to our troops, and many of us watched as they arrived at the surrender area. At the head of the column came

● The Italian - Austrian border at the Croce Pass.

the German divisional commander, standing erect in his staff car, looking proud and somewhat arrogant. The car slowly entered the field prepared for the reception of the German troops. As the column advanced down the field a British sergeant held up his hand, extended at arm's length, to halt the column. The German general immediately came to attention and smartly gave the Nazi salute, arm extended to the fullest extent. The immediate reaction of the British troops in and around the field was a very loud and long 'raspberry'. The German general's faced turned red and the British infantry sergeant turned the air blue with his comments.

While the German POWs were waiting to be transported to POW camps, we often spent time with them. It was very interesting to hear their stories and learn how the war looked from their point of view, and of the experiences they had had. Many of them were very young: some being only 16 and 17 years of age. One corporal, aged 20, had served on the Russian front for three years, as had a lad of 19. They all expressed great fear of the Russians and of the threat to Germany and other countries posed by the Russians.

These German POWs were surprised at, to them, the very high standard of living enjoyed by British soldiers. They couldn't understand how we always had white bread, which they now enjoyed. In the German army, white bread was reserved for hospitals and for the wounded. Chocolate was almost unknown to them. They said they had received only ten new razor blades in six months, one small piece of soap per month and ten sweets per week.

These disillusioned soldiers threw away their badges and regimental markings, and some even threw away their medal ribbons and medals, including Iron Cross and Russian campaign medals. They were so disgusted with their living conditions.

I met one German soldier who spoke very good English. He had worked in London before the war. I discovered that he had fought against us in North Africa and also at Cassino. We compared our experiences and the places we had been in, and it was interesting to hear things from the other side. He praised the accuracy and efficiency of our artillery and mortar crews.

In May 1945, the Allied Military Forces in Austria printed new money. The rate of exchange was one Austrian schilling to one British sixpence.

Also in May we moved from tents in a field to a school in Arnoldstein. It was while I was in that school that I received a letter from Dr A C Underwood, the Principal of the Baptist Theological College at Rawdon, near Leeds. He said that I had been accepted for training and an application had been made for my release under the Army Class 'B' Release. He said the candidate board had considered the report made by the Rev M E Aubrey, who had interviewed me at the Eighth Army H Q at Cessena.

My sense of call to enter the Christian ministry began when I was a teenager. This was gradually strengthened by the comments of those who heard me give talks at church activities and, also, when I conducted services and preached sermons. My experiences in preaching and speaking while in the Army, especially during the Canvas Chapel period and, again, when appointed chaplain's assistant and conducting services for my own unit, all served to further strengthen my sense of call. Now it was confirmed by the Candidates' Board and by acceptance for training at Rawdon.

The conviction of my call was not always without questions. Some of my experiences in action, especially at Cassino, were unsettling. The sight of wounded and dying men, and horribly injured bodies, plus some traumatic personal experiences, all served to create doubts. It is hard to believe in a God of love while hugging the earth as all hell seems let loose around you.

I had asked God to give me clear guidance concerning the reality of my call to the Christian ministry and the candidates' board's decision was God's answer. So, I had no more doubts and fears. The theological college's business was to train men for the ministry. So let them train me.

Despite the excitement of learning that I could now think of entering college, Army duties continued. Occasionally I went on journeys to Villach, Graz, Klagenfurt, Spittal and, sometimes, to Udine in Italy, which was 70 miles away. We often transported German POWs to Udine. We did not cross the Alps to do so, but went via Tarvisio.

About 50 Germans from a supply column were attached to our platoon to help in the feeding and transport of supplies to German troops in our vicinity. One of these Germans was Henry Viereck, who had worked for a shipping company in Hamburg before the war. He spoke excellent English and was appointed as an interpreter. I was appointed liaison NCO between our platoon officer and the German POW group. This meant that I worked very closely with Henry, and we became friends. After demob, we continued to correspond until he died in 1993.

Eventually things became sorted out. The prospects of leave in England - and even demobilisation - were being discussed.

One day, the senior chaplain for 78th Division, the Rev Ivor Phillips MC, came to see me. He said that the prospect of early demobilisation for some of the older chaplains was being considered, and this would leave the division short of chaplains. Would I consider being appointed a chaplain's assistant and officially allowed to carry out some of the chaplain's duties, including conducting regular services for my own company? I readily agreed to do so, and it was arranged. Until now, I had been accepted as an unofficial chaplain's assistant. Now, however, my position was to be made official.

On 4th June, I went on leave to Venice with my friend Frank Davis. We were called at 5am and travelled in an Army truck, arriving in Venice at 2pm. From St. Mark's Square, we travelled by an Army Dwck (amphibious vehicle) across the lagoon to The Lido, and found that we were billeted in the luxurious hotel, 'The Excelsior'. In peacetime, this had been the haunt of the rich and famous, including the then Prince of Wales.

This was my first leave since I had spent four days in Cairo in July 1944.
'The Excelsior' was sheer luxury. The private beach came to the steps of the hotel terrace, and the sea was 50 yards away. Professional waiters served us our tea meal - sandwiches and cakes - on the terrace. An orchestra played for our enjoyment. Frank and I shared a room with twin beds. They were real spring beds - and there was a constant supply of hot and cold water in the room. It was unheard of luxury. About 7.30am the next morning, we were very surprised when a maid brought us our early morning cup of tea to awaken us. It was sheer bliss.

● In Venice, with Frank Davis, 1945.

The day after our arrival, we returned to Venice to do some shopping and also some sight seeing. Frank wanted to buy his wife a set of silk underwear, so we entered an appropriate shop. My knowledge of such garments was nil, but Frank insisted on asking my opinion of some of the garments he examined. I declined to comment, but suggested that he asked the very charming and pretty young saleslady. Frank explained he wanted the underwear for his wife and asked if these were the best on offer? He was assured these were the very best. Still wanting to be convinced, Frank asked: "Would you wear these?"

The young lady said: "I am wearing some like these."

She quickly raised her dress to shoulder height to show a full set of undies.

Frank quickly concluded the purchase and we hurried from the shop. That was the most convincing saleslady I had ever met.

While we were lying on the beach at the Lido one afternoon, Field Marshal Alexander and General McCreery paid us a visit. They stopped to chat with us, and with other men on the beach. We later learned it was due to Field Marshal Alexander's insistence the 'Excelsior Hotel' was reserved for a British troops leave centre, despite American demands.

On 11th July, we left 'The Excelsior Hotel' on the Lido, at 9.30am and sailed for St Mark's Square for the last time. It had been a very good leave. We had enjoyed the comfort, being lazy, sightseeing, shopping, and visiting a cinema.

We had to wait until 3pm for our transport. We travelled as far as Mestre, where we spent the night in the Army Transit Camp. We arrived back in Arnoldstein the next day at 4.30pm.

CHAPTER TWENTYONE

The road home

After our return to Austria I was quickly back to duty. The day after my return, I was on 'The LIAP Run'. This was a leave scheme with the title 'Leave in Lieu of Python' and was for men who had been overseas for three years or more. Men going on LIAP met at a special camp at Villach and were taken, by lorries, via Germany, Luxembourg and France to Calais. From there they were taken by ship to Folkestone, and went home for 28 days leave. The return journey was by the same route.

I travelled in the cab with Bill Aish, my friend for many years, who was driving the lorry. We went to the first camp on the route, which was at Villach and was called 'El Alamein'. On Monday 18th July 1945, we began our journey across Europe: the long awaited journey home for some fortunate men. Our first day's journey took us through Spittall, Radstadt, Salzburg and Traunstein, covering 150 miles. We stayed the night at Traunstein at the camp called 'Enfideville'.

The next day we had our first experience of driving on the autobahn. In places, the road had been used as a runway for aircraft. Wide sections in the middle of the roadway had been painted green to make it look like a hedge, or grass dividing the two sections of the motorway. A large number of German aircraft were on the side of the road, in the fields alongside the road, or under trees bordering the road. All these aircraft were damaged or burnt out.

Our journey took us through Munich, which showed grim evidence of the effectiveness of the raids by the RAF. The buildings were very badly damaged. Many of them were totally destroyed. Rubble was everywhere. Railway lines had been laid in the main streets and railway trucks had been used to carry away the mountains of rubble. Some railway trucks were still there, partly filled with rubble and debris. The railway station was in ruins.

Later, we by-passed Augsburg and, after covering 150 miles, we arrived at Ulm, and stayed at the camp called 'Tunis'.

Ulm had suffered from four raids by the RAF. We were told that an estimated 5,000 people had been killed or injured in those raids. The streets were a mass of rubble. In the evening, we visited the cathedral, but were not allowed inside. There was one hole in the roof, caused by a small bomb. Otherwise, the building was undamaged except for blast marks. This was remarkable since the buildings around the cathedral were in ruins. It was as if the RAF had been ordered to spare the cathedral.

At Ulm, I saw the river Danube for the first time and was very disappointed to discover that it was a muddy brown, not blue as Strauss had portrayed it.

● Jack Kenworthy in Austria, 1945.

During our journey to Ulm we had passed within a few miles of Dachau, the site of one of the Nazi horror camps, but we did not see it. We also passed near Berchesgarten, Hitler's mountain retreat, but we were too far away to see much detail. The scenery looked very nice, however.

We left Ulm on Wednesday 20th July at 8am and travelled through Stuttgart, Mannheim - which had been very badly damaged - and Darmstadt. We also passed within a few miles of Worms; so I thought of the great church reformer, Martin Luther.

We saw a great deal of war damage on our journey but the place that stood out in my memory is Karlsrhue. There was hardly a house undamaged there and, as we travelled on a road above Karlsrhue, it seemed as if every house had lost its roof. It looked as if the town had suffered a tremendous incendiary bomb raid. As we travelled along the road overlooking the town, we had almost an aerial view, and it looked like a lot of shoeboxes with the lids off. It must have been a terrible experience for the inhabitants.

At Opperheim we crossed the river Rhine over a bridge named 'President Roosevelt in Memoriam', which had been built by the USA Army. The river is 250 yards wide at this point.

We went on to Mainz, where we re-crossed the river Rhine, and entered the transit camp called 'Centuripe'. We had covered 196 miles.

Each of the Transit Camps were named after places connected with the history of the Eighth Army, and each was staffed by members of the Divisions in the Eighth Army:

* Villach was 'El Alamein'. 7th Armoured Division. Sign: Desert Rat.
* Traunstein was 'Enfideville'. 56th Division.
* Ulm was 'Tunis'. 6th Armoured Division. Sign: Mailed Fist.
* Mainz was 'Centuripe'. 78th Division. Sign: Golden Battleaxe.
* Sedan was 'Salerno'. 46th Division. Sign: Oak Tree.
* Calais was 'Cassino'. 13th Corps troops. Sign: Leaping Gazelle.

Each of the camps' names represented a battle honour of the unit staffing it. The 7th Armoured Division played a very important part in the battle of El Alamein. The 56th Division took a prominent part in the battle at Enfideville. The 6th Armoured Division did exceedingly good work in the advance on Tunis. The 78th Division, specially trained for mountain warfare, made a tremendous contribution to the horrific battle for Centuripe, in Sicily, and it is one of the battle honours of the division. The heroic work of the 78th Division artillery played such an important part in the victory at Centuripe, and so brought about the victorious end to the Sicilian campaign. The 46th Division suffered very heavy casualties at Salerno and Anzio, and so they staffed the camp called 'Salerno'. The final camp at Calais was called 'Cassino' to represent all members of the Eighth Army involved in the battles for Cassino. The staff was from 13th Corps troops.

At Mainz, in the transport camp 'Centuripe', we received the best treatment of our long journey. When we arrived, men took our lorries and filled the tanks with petrol, and checked everything, and then parked the vehicles. We found sleeping bags provided in our bedrooms, and a hot shower was available before dinner. The dinner was the biggest cooked meal I had seen for a very long time, and this was followed by a large dish of fresh fruit, raspberries, gooseberries and cherries, covered in custard; followed by cups of tea.

We were now in British Liberation Army (BLA) territory. The BLA were otherwise known as 'The D-Day Boys'. The rivalry between the BLA and MEF (Middle East Forces: 'our lot') was very keen and had been made worse by remarks made by Lady Nancy Astor. This Member of Parliament had referred to men of the Eighth Army as 'D-Day Dodgers'. It was also reported that Lady Astor had said that all men who had served in the Eighth Army should be made to wear yellow ribbons when they returned to England so that women would know to beware of them because they were sex crazy and suffering from VD.

The Eighth Army's feelings were expressed in slogans scrawled on the sides of our lorries: 'BLA - Britain's Luckiest Army. MEF - Men England Forgot'; 'D-Day Dodgers: leave every three and a half years - if you are lucky'. This was a reference to the fact that members of the BLA were alleged to have leave every six months. Another caustic slogan was a list of about 20 names of places once famous in the advances of the Eighth and First Armies, followed by the words, 'These were D-Days'.

Perhaps the best comment on all this feeling of resentment was expressed by an unknown soldier in the words of a song that became extremely popular with troops of the MEF. It was sung to the tune of 'Lili Marlene':

THE D-DAY DODGERS

We're the D-Day Dodgers, out in Italy,
Always drinking vino, always on the spree,
Eighth Army skivers, and the Yanks,
We live in Rome; we laugh at tanks,
For we're the D-Day Dodgers, in sunny Italy.

We landed at Salerno, a holiday with pay.
Jerry brought the bombs down to cheer us on our way,
They showed us sights and gave us tea,
We all sang songs; the beer was free,
To welcome D-Day Dodgers to sunny Italy.

Naples and Cassino, taken in our stride,
We didn't go to fight, we just went for the ride.
Anzio and Sangro are just names,

We only went to look for dames,
The randy D-Day Dodgers in sunny Italy.

On the way to Florence we had a lovely time,
We ran a bus to Rimini, right through the Gothic Line,
Soon to Bologna we will go,
And after that, we'll cross the Po.
We're still the D-Day Dodgers in sunny Italy.

Once we heard a rumour we were going home,
Back to dear old Blighty, never more to roam.
Then someone said, "In France you'll fight."
We said: "No fear. We'll just sit tight."
The windy D-Day Dodgers in sunny Italy.

Dear Lady Astor, you think you know a lot,
Standing on your platform talking Tommy rot.
You - England's sweetheart and its bride
We think you mouth's too bleeding wide,
That's from the D-Day Dodgers in sunny Italy.

Look around the mountains in the mud and rain,
See the rows of crosses, some without a name.
Heartbreak, toil and suffering gone,
The boys beneath them slumber on.
They were the D-Day Dodgers who stayed in Italy.

Both the words and the song are still sung today at reunions and at concerts - and whenever our comrades who stayed in Italy are remembered. Another comment heard today when D-Day is mentioned, is, 'Which D-Day are they talking about? We had so many before they went into Normandy.'

Before we left the camp 'Centuripe' we were ordered to remove all slogans because we were going further into BLA territory.

On Thursday 21st June, we left Mainz at 8am and travelled through Germany into the State of Luxembourg; then into France. Some of the towns we passed through were Stromberg, Rawer, Trier and Luxembourg, which was a very pretty town. We eventually reached the Transit Camp at Sedan, after covering 205 miles. As we entered the town of Sedan, a dance band on a lorry, met us and led us into the Transit Camp 'Salerno'.

Our journey had shown us many contrasts. The change from Germany to Luxembourg was most marked. The devastation of Germany, the style of buildings, and even the appearance of the people changed as we crossed into Luxembourg. The town of Luxembourg looked so neat and clean, with gardens and streets filled with flowers.

Then, in France, people lined the streets and waved to us. On the road, Field Marshal Montgomery passed us. He sounded the car horn and waved to the men as he passed.

The lorries carried the sign of the Eighth Army so he probably said, 'There goes my Army', as he did when talking to us in North Africa just before the invasion of Sicily - which was another D-Day for the Eighth Army.

When we arrived at the Transit Camp we found it was in an old French Cavalry Barracks. Our 'beds' were in horse stalls that, at least, had been cleaned out.

On Friday 22nd June, we left Sedan at 8am. It was interesting to see places that were associated with World War I, of which I had read. We saw several cemeteries from that War, which looked neat and well cared for. It was an impressive sight to see so many gravestones in orderly rows. We travelled through Cambrai, Arras, St Omer and on to Calais: a journey of 185 miles.

After leaving Arras, we saw slagheaps on the skyline and, just before entering Bithune, we came to the coal-mining villages. They looked dreary and drab with slagheaps towering above the dirty houses; the coal-miners sitting around the front doorsteps and the children playing in the road.

On arrival in Calais, we took our passengers to the Transit Camp 'Cassino', but we went to 121 Transit Camp. The 'Cassino' Camp was for leave personnel only. Our journey from Villach to Calais was 972 miles.

Saturday 23rd June was our 'rest day', so Bill Aish and I looked around the town during the morning and afternoon, and in the evening we went to the camp cinema.

We all wore our khaki-drill uniforms, and this caused some surprise and a lot of questions. In one of the bars, a member of the BLA asked some of our lads if they were American troops. On being told they were British, they then asked how they could get a uniform like ours. The reply was: "You only get this uniform when you fight overseas."

That started a mini-battle.

One of our drivers caused some consternation in a NAAFI canteen by paying for his purchases in North African francs. The coins were clearly marked 'one franc' and the inscription was in French, but the design was different from the French franc, and they were accepted very reluctantly.

On Sunday 24th June, we began our return journey to Villach, following the same route but in reverse order, and stopping at the same transit camps. We arrived in Villach at 5.30pm on Thursday 28th June and went to our billet in Arnoldstein, and so rejoined our platoon.

On arrival at our platoon location, I was told I would be on the Calais run again on the following Saturday - 30th June. On Friday 29th June, our platoon officer, Lt Baker, told me that I had been invited by the senior chaplain to attend a 'quiet afternoon' for chaplains and ordination candidates at Spittal on Saturday 30th June. So I was taken off the Calais detail. He also said that he had already arranged transport for me.

When I arrived in Spittal for the 'quiet afternoon', I found several men there whom I had met on previous occasions. The ordination candidates were now getting to know each other. There were two services, both conducted by the Rev C W H Storey, who was the assistant deputy army chaplain general, 5th Corps. The services were both enjoyable and helpful.

During the 'quiet afternoon' it was announced that the newly appointed temporary chaplain for my unit was the Rev H C C Lannigan, which pleased me a great deal. I knew Harry well. He was a Methodist chaplain and I previously benefited a great deal from his sermons and Bible Studies at chaplain's conferences I had attended. We had become very friendly and enjoyed good fellowship.

Another important announcement was that ordination candidates were now allowed to conduct services for their own units in the absence of a chaplain, but permission of the commanding officer had to be obtained first. This was good news, because I had been conducting services for the men of my platoon whenever possible and acting as unofficial chaplain since we had landed in North Africa. Now I could do so with official sanction, and so confirmed my appointment by the senior chaplain, the Rev Ivor Phillips.

While in Spittal on another occasion, I met two very good comrades of Cassino days. They were RSM Skinner and RQMS Dixon of the Kensington Regiment, with whom I had worked closely when in the 78th Division Jeep Platoon. It was good to know they had survived the war.

● RASC billet on the shore of Wörthersee in Austria, 1945.

The Canvas Chapel

CHAPTER TWENTYTWO

Change of duties

About a week after the 'quiet afternoon' at Spittal, I was appointed liaison NCO for the group of German POWs attached to our platoon for general working party duties, including helping in the preparation of rations for German POWs in our area. My interpreter was Henry Viereck.

On 5th July 1945, Lt Baker told me to go with him on a special job, and to bring Henry Viereck with me.

This was to be a rather embarrassing task. We inspected houses in the Arnoldstein area to see what would be suitable for winter billets for British troops. I was sorry to see the fear on the faces of the women when they saw us, and the distress when they learned the purpose of our visit. Some of the houses were beautifully decorated and tastefully furnished. Some of the walls were decorated with large paintings: beautiful scenes painted directly on to the walls. This house hunting continued for several days, but I don't think that any of the houses were actually requisitioned.

Among the German POWs I discovered Karl Schwitters who, before the war was a Lutheran pastor. He was conscripted into the German Army as an ordinary soldier; later becoming a clerk, which he had been for the past five years. He spoke very little English, so Henry interpreted for us. Karl asked for a New Testament in English, which I obtained for him.

The senior chaplain for the 78th Division, the Rev Ivor Phillips, had asked chaplains and ordination candidates to look out for any clergymen, pastors or ministers among the German POWs. I therefore informed him about Karl Schwitters. Within a few weeks, Karl was sent to Lienz, for a period of testing and questioning and was soon returned to his home in Hanover, where he resumed his duties as a Lutheran pastor.

In 1946, while I was in college at Rawdon, I was able to arrange with a Baptist Church in Bradford to include Karl in a scheme they had instituted for sending food parcels to needy people in Germany. Karl wrote letters of heartfelt appreciation for the food parcels.

On Thursday 19th July, Major Carpenter, commanding officer of 237 Company RASC, gave me permission to conduct a weekly church service. He also told me that I was appointed as one of the education instructors for the company under a new scheme to be instituted. This would mean promotion to sergeant.

It all depended on whether my 'B' release came before the scheme started.

Our platoon moved to a new billet, a Gasthaus outside of Arnoldstein on the road to Italy. It was about a mile or so from the Italian border and was surrounded by beautiful scenery including the mountains in Yugoslavia - which were only a few miles away - and the Italian Alps. It was in that billet that I conducted my first official church service for the platoon on Sunday 29th July.

During this service we sang the hymn, 'Glorious things of thee are spoken, Zion, city of our God.' We sang it to the tune that all knew and associated with that hymn: 'Austria'. Before we had finished singing the hymn, a number of Austrians crowded at the open windows and thronged the open doorway, all looking in amazement at us. I later discovered that the Germans had forbidden the playing or singing of the tune 'Austria'. The local people probably thought a revolution was starting or a new nationalist party had come into being. At least, it showed them that freedom was returning to Austria.

After this, the local Austrians addressed me as 'Herr Pastor'. Later I was addressed as 'Herr Doktor' because I had successfully treated an Austrian lady who was suffering from a very badly infected wound in her right ankle, and the whole of her right leg had been badly poisoned.

On Thursday 2nd August, I joined a group of men at 78th Division Signals, and we began our journey to Assisi to attend a 'moral leadership course'. We travelled in an open truck via Udine and Pordonone, and spent the night at the transit camp at Mestre, near Venice. The next day, we continued our journey via Bologna, Florence, Arrezzo, Oerugia and on to Assisi. It was interesting to see the scenes of some of our old battles - and some of the places looked the same as when we had left them.

The moral leadership course was held at the Chaplains' Centre, and we were billeted there. We attended lectures and discussion groups, visited churches and sites associated with St Francis, and attended several church services. There was also time for private walks and activities. Many of the lectures were thought provoking. Some of the lectures were disturbing with new ideas but all of them were very helpful.

On the last day of the course, each 'student' was interviewed by his group leader. Each of the tutors was also a group leader, and my group leader was the Rev W Neil, MA, BD, PhD. He spoke to me about entering the ministry. I told him, briefly, why I felt called to enter the ministry; how the sense of call had developed, plus my activities in Christian work before and during the war, and also told him the story of the Canvas Chapel in Bizerte. I also mentioned the difficulty of serious study during my time overseas, and my concern about the prospect of continuous study in college, now I had been accepted as a student by Rawdon College in Leeds.

I wrote down his reply. He said: "It is definite that you are really called of God. There is no shadow of doubt in the call being given you. You have been led in a marvellous way.

"The sequence of events in your life shows the reality of the call. You are admirably suited for the ministry.

"Don't worry about education, but do your best in your studies and efforts. Don't worry about degrees. Thirty degrees will not make a man a preacher. Don't let the fact of age worry you. The studies are the same if you are 22 or 32, but it may be harder moulding the mind at 28 than at 22. Don't look back but press on, doing the best you can to fit yourself for the life of a minister."

Dr Neil greatly encouraged me and strengthened my sense of call to the Christian ministry that was, again, confirmed. This was a further advance on my spiritual pilgrimage.

I wrote to my parents about Dr Neil saying: 'I have a great regard for Dr Neil. He has a brilliant brain and a keen sense of humour, and is a striking personality. He always seems to have a suitable joke for every occasion, but can also be very serious. His depth of thought and clear perception is something to marvel at. He greatly impressed me and his lectures are a joy to listen to.'

I owe a great deal to Dr Neil.

On 13th August, we left Assisi and travelled back to Austria via Perugia, Cessena, Forli, Argenta, and stayed the night at Consondola. All of these were places that I remembered. It was at Argenta that I had watched flame-throwers in action and saw the horrible results of their work. These were sights that I will never forget.

The next day, we passed through Ferrara, Padua and went on to Venice, where we had a quick tour before spending the night at Mestre. The next day, we arrived in Austria and returned to our units.

Two days after returning to my platoon, Bill Aish - my friend and companion for five and a half years - left for demob under the 'B' release scheme. Before the war, Bill was a first-class carpenter and was released on these grounds. He was the first man in 237 Company to leave on 'B' release but others soon followed; plus older men who left for demob.

And so things began to change. Men who had spent many years together were now parting company. Soldiers were becoming civilians. There was a certain sadness at parting with good comrades, but also a sense of excitement and expectation at the thought that the return to 'Civvy Street' was coming nearer. Also, there were changes of jobs and living conditions.

It was my custom in an evening, when not on duty, to walk on the hillside and in the woods near our Gasthaus and enjoy the scenery and appreciate the quietness. I often went to the same spot and sat on a fallen tree trunk. There, I would read my New Testament and pray, and prepare my sermon for the Sunday service. Every evening, two little girls came by, bringing in two or three cows. I spoke to them, but since they did not understand English, all I received was a shy smile. One evening, I gave them a bar of blended chocolate - part of my NAAFI ration. They shyly and hesitatingly accepted my gift. Later, as I walked past the house in which they lived, their mother came out to speak to me. She told me that her daughters, aged seven and five, had never seen chocolate before and had asked her what had I given them. She expressed her gratitude and gave me three fresh eggs.

On Sunday 26th August, I conducted a church service for the whole of 237 Company, RASC, and it was held in the school in Arnoldstein. In the evening, I preached the sermon in the service at the British Church in Villach. Troops from around the area came voluntarily to this service. Some Austrian civilians also attended; so it was a large congregation.

The Rev Ivor Philips, our senior chaplain, organised the 78th Division Christian Fellowship for 28th to 31st August. Ivor Phillips led the event and the lecturers were chaplains from the 78th Division. I was pleased to see the Rev Harry Lannigan again. While Harry had been on leave in England, I had conducted the services for the platoon and also for the company each Sunday. Some services had been held in our Gasthaus; some in 'B' platoon canteen, and some in the school in Arnoldstein. I was especially pleased to see the Rev Kenneth Tyson, a Church of Scotland minister, whom I had met a long time ago. I was with him at Cassino for a short while before he was wounded.

The course was held at the Strand Hotel at Techendorf on the Wiessier See (The White Lake). The hotel staff were Latvians. One girl on the staff was a committed Christian and attended the services, including attending the Communion Service.

Among those present were Fred Udall and Private Kimberly of the Canvas Chapel days. There was also Tom Truman and Private Vesty, both of whom were on the course at Assisi. Another man present remembered me singing solos at the YMCA Canteen in Alyth, Scotland, just before we left for North Africa. There were 24 men and four chaplains present, and we all greatly appreciated the fellowship.

When my friend, Frank Davis, was told that he was to go home on leave, he asked me to preach a special sermon for him on the day before he left for home. After much thought, I prepared a sermon called, 'The Journey Home', basing it on the 'Calais trip' route. This sermon created a deep impression on all who heard it, because they knew the route well. Until the time of his death, about 20 years later, Frank always referred to that sermon as 'that was my sermon' and often spoke about it. The written notes of that sermon are in appendix 3.

With men going on leave or on demob, we had more lorries than drivers, and also more duties per man, for those who remained. My change of duties included having a 15 cwt truck for my own use because I was platoon quartermaster. I collected rations, clothing, NAAFI supplies and then issued them, collected and distributed the mail. I was also medical orderly, acted as a general taxi service and was chaplain's assistant. I had full and free use of the 15 cwt truck for my duties as chaplain's assistant, including taking men to church services - including those at the British Church in Villach - and for any other use I thought proper. I also took men to Villach on the first stage of their journey home for demob. Added to this, I was frequently guard commander.

When Frank Davis went on leave, I should have gone with him, but postponed it in the hope that my 'B' release would arrive. But it did not come. Then, in October, I received news from Dr A C Underwood that my 'B' release should arrive in January 1946.

The number of men remaining in 'A' platoon was so reduced that we were moved. This meant that we shared the company HQ billet at the Railway Station Hotel, Arnoldstein. I retained my 15 cwt truck and carried out all the duties and conducted church services each Sunday. Some of the men had accepted me as their chaplain, and said: "If you go on leave, we will have no padre."

On Friday 12th October, our commanding officer, Major Carpenter, told me that I was to go on leave on Sunday, otherwise I would lose my leave. If my 'B' release arrived while I was away, he would send it to me.

At last I was going home after three years - all but four weeks - since leaving Scotland for North Africa. I had been in nine countries: Algeria, Tunisia, Egypt, Sicily, Italy, Austria, Germany, Luxembourg and France. I had seen many sights - some pleasant and some hideous - and had had a variety of experiences. All of them had prepared me for my entrance to college and for my training for the Christian ministry. Later, I also realised how these experiences had contributed to my work as a minister of the gospel.

CHAPTER TWENTYTHREE

Home again

Together with a few men from my own unit, we reported to El Alamein Camp in Villach on Sunday 14th October 1945. The next day, we went by passenger train, via Udine, to Milan and spent the night at 311 transit camp in Milan. On Wednesday 17th October, we boarded a train at 5.30pm, with six men and their kit to each compartment. We travelled through the 15 mile long Simplon Tunnel, and through Switzerland and France, arriving at Calais at 9.30am on Friday 19th October.

On our arrival at Calais station, we were taken to a transit camp, where we remained until taken to the docks. We embarked at 5.30pm but remained in harbour for a while. Our crossing of the Channel was uneventful and we saw the white cliffs of England in the early light of dawn. We docked at Folkestone at 6.50pm and we quickly boarded a special train, which took us to Victoria in central London. From there, I shared a taxi with an officer to get to Paddington station. I left Paddington at 9.20pm and arrived at Newport, in Monmouthshire at 2.20am. I waited for the early train at 7am and I eventually arrived home at 8.30am on Saturday 20th October.

On 20th November, I received a telegram from Army Records stating my 'B' release had been authorised. This was the last day of my leave. I left the next day to begin my journey to Folkestone, only to be told at Newport railway station, by the railway transport officer that, due to bad weather in the Channel, ships sailing for Calais were delayed. So I was given a 24 hour extension of leave. I returned home, to spend my birthday with my parents.

On Thursday 22nd November, I returned to the Folkestone transit camp, having met up with men from 237 Company RASC at Victoria station, and we travelled together to Folkestone. The next morning, my comrades returned to Austria, while I waited at Folkestone for my papers and travel warrant. At 8.30am I reported to the office to collect my papers and was told to come back later. After several visits to the office I received my

● Rawdon College staff and students, 1946.

documents at 6pm. The corporal had been aggressive and awkward each time I had called at the office, and was aggressive and rude when he handed me my documents. He ordered me to proceed immediately to the station. This caused a somewhat heated discussion and I refused to leave Folkestone at that time of night to travel to a demob camp in Cheshire. The journey, which involved changing trains at several places, notably Crewe - a very cold, dark and unpleasant station on which, several times I had spent most of the night.

A young officer heard our discussion and intervened. I told this officer that I had been waiting since 8.30am for my documents and the corporal had not co-operated, so I refused

● Rawdon College cricket team, 1948.

The Canvas Chapel

to travel through the night, spending hours waiting on stations during the night when I could have travelled during the day - especially since the corporal had said that my documents would be ready at 10am that morning. The officer blamed the corporal for the delay and sanctioned my stay overnight at the transit camp.

The next day, I travelled to Beeston Castle station, about eight miles from Chester. With other men, I was taken to No1 Holding Company, Oulton Park Camp, at Little Budworth, Tarporley, Cheshire. There, I met men with whom I had served at various stages of my Army career. It was like a reunion and I was glad to know they had survived the war.

As I found a bed-bunk I heard a voice I recognised, and the man was telling a real tale. I called out: "Tell the truth, Coffin." There was a moment's silence then the cry: "Who's that?"

I walked around to where the group of men were standing. It was Coffin, the man who used to bring our water ration to the front line at Cassino. That evening, we went to the camp cinema together.

During the week that I spent at Oulton Camp there was little to do, except undergo medical examinations, complete documentation and hand in kit. For almost six years I had looked after my kit. I had 'blancoed' the webbing, cleaned the brasses, cleaned the mud from it, brushed out the sand, and now it was contemptuously thrown on an ever growing heap. When I handed in my battered tin hat I was truly sorry to part with it. We had been through a lot of exciting times together. It had been a very good companion and a faithful shield to me.

Then came the great day: 28th November 1945. A group of us were taken by lorry to a large warehouse in Ashton under Lyme, where we received our demob suit, shirts, socks, a hat, and a brown cardboard box to put all these items in. Then we were taken to the railway station and 'Civvy Street'.

● In Aberconway Place, Oakdale, July 1948.

On 30th November, I wrote a letter to Dr Underwood at Rawdon College, to say that I had been demobbed. On Monday 3rd December, I received a telegram asking me to report to Rawdon College the next day. This I did and my studies began the next day.

It had been a long pilgrimage from lay preacher in Bournemouth in 1936 to a theological student at Rawdon College, some nine years later. Many and varied were the experiences on the way, yet all of them had contributed in some way to moulding me for the

● In later years.

next part of my journey through life.

I remained at the Baptist Theological College, at Rawdon, until June 1948, when I completed my college course.

Then I began a life ministering to Baptist churches. I was minister of three Baptist churches, and stayed at each one for 11 years: Halesowen, Worcestershire (1948-59), Kings Langley, Hertfordshire (1959-70) and London Colney, Hertfordshire (1971-82). When I retired, in 1982, I had a few months of freedom before becoming part-time free church chaplain at Hill End hospital, St Albans, where I remained for 11 years before retiring for the second time.

Since my retirement from pastoral charge in 1982, I have continued to conduct services in various churches, including Baptist, Methodist, United Reformed and other free churches, as well as in a few Anglican churches, including midweek lunchtime services in St Albans Abbey.

My experiences as an ordained minister would fill another book, if it was ever written!

APPENDIX I

Wings of Flight or Wings of Faith

Psalm 55:6: 'Oh, that I had the wings of a dove! Then would I fly away and be at rest.'

Isaiah 40:31: 'They that wait upon the Lord shall renew their strength: they shall mount up with wings as eagles.'

Psalm 55, verse 6 is the expression of David's despair, while Isaiah 40, verse 31 is an expression of Isaiah's faith. The first represents man's desire and the second represents God's answer. David wanted to escape from his present position. Isaiah states how adversity and difficulties can be met.

1. The Wings of a Dove suggest the Wings of Flight

David was in despair. Everything had gone wrong. He had been let down by his friends and attacked by his enemies. He had a strong desire to escape from it all.

The desire to escape from things is quite natural. Man's instinct is to escape from what he does not understand. Flight is instinctive from things that frighten, and comes from a sense of self-preservation. When we are worried, we have a desire to get away from the cause of our worry. When we feel life is becoming too difficult; that our responsibilities are becoming too great, or temptations are becoming stronger and we feel unable to stand against them, then we long to get away from it all. Then we say with David, "Oh, that I had the wings of a dove" - the wings of flight. Those who evade problems or difficulties by running away are using the wings of a dove, the wings of a fugitive.

Yet the wings of flight are not much use.

The dove is capable of flying long distances but not of reaching great heights. The dove must fly fairly near the ground, always near the earth. Those who try to fly from worries, responsibilities and duties can never get very far from them. However far we go to escape we find we have taken our problems with us. The wings of flight may change our place on earth but cannot take us away from earth. As a man once said: "I began drinking to drown my sorrows, but I found that they float."

The wings of flight cannot solve our problems. The best they can do is to change the problems: exchanging one set of difficulties for another set of difficulties. Flight cannot bring real peace and rest.

Long ago, the prophet Elijah ran away from the threats of a wicked queen, and suffered despair in the very place that he thought would be a haven of refuge. One cause of despair was exchanged for another.

2 The Wings of an Eagle suggest the Wings of Faith

The eagle is unlike the dove in that it has greater wing power and is capable of stronger and rapid flight. It is capable of flying long distances and to great heights, remaining on the wing with unwearied energy.

When we are troubled and perplexed; when we are assailed by trials and temptations, we do not need the wings of a dove, but the wings of an eagle: the wings of faith which will enable us to soar to great heights, so that we can rise above our problems and difficulties. By our faith in God we can rise above our problems and see them in the right perspective.

Without the wings of faith we are shut in by mountains of difficulty. We are able to see only a small portion of the countryside around us. Our vision is restricted. We can only see life as it affects just us at that moment. With the wings of faith, we can see the larger meaning of life. We can see our problems as they really are, against the larger perspective. When we are above the object, we can see it all - and then it is often smaller than we think.

When walking through the streets of York, it seems that we are shut in by the houses and overwhelmed by the size of the Minster. But, if we climb to the top of the Minster, we look down on the narrow streets, and look upon the expanse of the countryside, and everything is changed. From above, the outlook is so different.

With the wings of faith, we can rise above our problems, and they will not seem so large. The mountains of despair will be seen to be molehills. Floods of grief will be seen as streams. Our difficulties and problems appear smaller when seen through the eyes of faith, and when they are measured against God's power and love. When we use the wings of faith, we see that our problems are not so bad as we first thought. When we look at life as a whole, from the heights to which faith can take us, we can see that our difficulties are not so terrible as we first thought. We see that we can conquer trials and temptations that had seemed to be too big for us.

With the wings of faith, we can see beyond and around our difficulties. Without the wings of faith we remain on the same level as the obstacles, which seem to fill our vision. With the wings of faith, we rise above them and see beyond the immediate present.

If we can live by faith in God our strength will be great. We shall be able to mount up with wings as eagles and be able to view life from different angles, and shall see beyond our present trials and problems.

3 Faith is obtained by waiting on the Lord

The experiences of life seem to sap our energy - our physical, mental and spiritual energy - so that we often feel too weak to carry on. We need some way of renewing our energy, or receiving a spiritual boost. Just as rest and relaxation can renew our physical and mental energy, so we can renew our spiritual energy by waiting upon God.

We often spend more time telling God what we want - or what we want him to do for us - than we spend quietly listening to God. It is not easy, but if we can learn to be quiet before God, just enjoying the peace of his presence, allowing his peace and strength to flow into us, we would be rejuvenated.

God plants faith in our hearts, but we have to cultivate it. A weak and wavering faith will produce a weak and wavering spiritual life, and will result in defeats by life's experiences. To obtain the faith that will enable us to rise above difficulties we must spend time with God; by reading the Bible; by giving time to prayer; by meditation on God's Word; by being quiet before God.

The Psalmist spoke out of his own experience when he said: "Wait on the Lord; be of good courage, and he shall strengthen thine heart: wait, I say, on the Lord." (Psalm 27:14). Again, the Psalmist said: "My soul, wait thou upon God; for my expectation is from him." (Psalm 62:5).

We can face the present and the future with greater confidence by using eagles' wings: the faith that will enable us to rise, triumphant, over all circumstances. Trust in God and you will renew your strength, and will mount up with wings like eagles.

APPENDIX II

The Military Medal

No, T/161809 Lance Corporal Brinley Little, RASC.

At approximately 21:00 hours on the night of April 17th 1944, L/Cpl Little was in charge of five Jeeps and trailers for delivery to Monte Cassino area. Arriving in the area of enemy shelling he found that the Mortar Dump at the side of the road had been hit, set alight and was brilliantly lighting the whole area. Notwithstanding enemy shelling and flying shrapnel from exploding mortar bombs, he continued on and reached 'Mortar Corner'. There he found, pinned down, some men, one of who was wounded. Although the area (still lighted by the blaze) was under shell fire he first ascertained if the wounded man had received first aid, and then continued to organise the ferrying forward to Battalion H Q of the trailer- loads, the hill from 'Mortar Corner' being too steep for trailers. Taking up the last load he sought out the Medical Officer and ascertained that his previous message (by his driver) for an ambulance had been received and that action had been taken. After collecting his Jeeps and trailers he returned to his location.

At 19:30 hours on the 18th April 1944, the enemy commenced shelling the area of the Jeep Platoon at San Michele. L/Cpl Little was thrown to the ground by the blast of the first shell. Picking himself up he ran to the first man he saw injured, ascertained the wound was superficial, and went to the next two men who were seriously wounded. Throughout the shelling that followed, L/Cpl Little did all he could by way of first aid to ease these men until the arrival of the ambulance. Throughout these incidents L/Cpl Little showed complete disregard for his own personal safety. His sole actions were devoted to the job in hand and rendering assistance to his comrades. His calmness, efficiency, and example without loss of time, was an inspiration and encouragement to all around him.

The following announcement appeared in the Daily Part 1 Orders of 237 Company RASC.

Daily Orders Part 1. No. 125 for Friday 12 :5 :44. Major J.S.Dorling, Commanding 237 Infantry Brigade Company, R.A.S.C.

No, 446 - DECORATIONS

It is published for information of all ranks that the following immediate award has been notified in 13 Corps letter 1279/12/A dated 9th May 1944; Military Medal to t//161809 L/Cpl E.B.Little.

Field 11/5/44

APPENDIX III

Echoes of the Canvas Chapel

At various times and in strange places during the Battles for Cassino I met men who had attended the Canvas Chapel. All of them looked back to that simple place of worship as an important point in their lives, and still drew courage and comfort from the memories of those days. Many of them went on to show a Christian witness among their comrades, although some of them had little or no Christian fellowship to sustain them.

In a letter to my parents dated 30th May 1944, which was Whit Monday, I gave them news of some of those who had attended the Canvas Chapel.

Jim was converted to Christianity at the last meeting held in the Canvas Chapel. He was a self-confessed communist, and very earnest in those beliefs. Four of us prayed for his conversion and rejoiced when he changed his faith from communism to Christ. When he returned to his unit he began telling others what Jesus Christ meant to him. When he was posted to another unit he continued telling others of his Christian faith, and many of the men were helped by him.

Joe Colley, a member of the Salvation Army, was modest and humble, with a child-like trust in God. In a letter he sent to me he wrote: 'It can be summed up in the story of the talents. God knows I am only capable of handling one of his little jobs, so I must be content to sit at the bottom of the table.'

Joe worked in the workshop section of an RASC company, and was greatly respected by his workmates. He often spoke to them of his Christian faith, sometimes gathering them together for discussion groups, or to share in a Christian service. I met him again in 1948 and he still talked of the wonderful effect the Canvas Chapel exercised on those who attended the services, or knew about them.

Frank Utley was a member of the Church of England, and lived in Weymouth. When he returned to his unit, a RAOC Company, he continued to tell others of the Canvas

Chapel and of his own Christian faith. He helped to arrange services, discussion groups, and occasionally speaking to the men in the groups about his faith, though Frank always said he would be a better secretary than a speaker.

Fred Udall served in the London Irish Rifles. His home was in London. He accepted Jesus Christ as his Lord and Saviour when in hospital in North Africa, through the witness of a Christian who was in the bed next to Fred's. He was a sergeant in the mortar platoon, and, when he returned to his unit after base details, he was told that he was posted to another platoon. To be able to remain with the mortar platoon he relinquished his rank at his own request and became a private. He did so to be able to remain with the men who had known him before he became a Christian, so that he could show them the difference trusting in Jesus Christ had made in his life.

I saw Fred as he and his comrades moved up into the front line at Cassino, and we had a brief time together. Some of the men in his section told me what a grand man he was, absolutely fearless in battle, walking about and encouraging the men. His faith gave him a calm mind. He spoke to anyone who would listen to him about his Saviour, during a battle, in a slit trench or dugout, on the road or when resting. His one passion was to preach the Word of God to the saving of souls. He often said: "Why did no one tell me of Jesus Christ, of His great love for me, and that he died for me?"

Fred wanted everyone to know about Jesus and the difference that trusting in Jesus Christ made. We met again in Austria.

Many years after the War ended, a message reached me that a man named Norman Parker had met a friend of mine and wished me to know that he had never forgotten the Canvas Chapel and the messages there. Those memories had helped him during the war and afterwards. Similar messages reached me many years after the Canvas Chapel had disappeared in the activity of war. But the spirit of the Canvas Chapel lives on.

APPENDIX IV

The journey home

The New Testament reading is found in Luke Chapter 15, verses 11 to 32.

TEXT: Luke 15:18 The prodigal son said: "I will set off and go to my father."

Ever since we landed in North Africa we have thought of the day we would go home. For some that day has arrived, and others have already gone on the journey home. Some of us have had the experience of driving the trucks that took many men from Villach to Calais, as the first stage of their homeward journey.

You will remember the route and the procedure. Pick up the men going on leave at the transit camp, 'El Alamein' in Villach, here in Austria, then begin the long journey. The route took us through Innesbruck, Salzburg, Ulm, where we saw the river Danube, Trier, Luxembourg, Sedan and Arras to the transit camp 'Cassino' in Calais. The men on leave left us there and went by boat to England, and home to their families.

That journey is an illustration of our journey through life, with Europe representing the pages of history. It is easy to see the road to Calais across Europe as representing our life through history. As we now travel that road in our imagination we can note the similarities to events in our lives.

We began the journey by driving through the maze of streets in Villach, and very early on the journey outside of Villach we encountered the first of many hills. Some people have found the hills of difficulty very early on life's road. Experience has revealed to all of us that the hills of life, the problems, the worries, the bad times we encounter, vary in their intensity and length, but none go on forever.

The road to Calais was not all hills, and life is not all difficulties and troubles. In places the road dropped down into a valley and ran alongside a river. Villages on the route relieved the monotony, and the villagers with their colourful costumes brought added brightness. Life too, has its pleasant times, and friends and family bring colour and interest into our lives. How grateful we ought to be for them.

The road goes on, twisting over hill and dale, through woodland and meadow, beneath mountains whose peaks rise in grandeur, and whose slopes are clothed with a mantle of trees. The valleys are bejewelled with lakes and festooned with ribbons of rivers. All these are God's handiwork in nature, provided for our enjoyment and inspiration, reminding us of life's beautiful days, filled with pleasure, given to encourage us.

This road to Calais had scenes of beauty, but there were also drab scenes. You will remember the shock as the scene changed when we drove through the mining area of France, it was drab and drear. Life too, has its dull and drab periods, which depress us. But even these unpleasant days and experiences have their value. They help us to appreciate the good days, the beautiful experiences.

The contrasts of life serve their purpose, for when we are in the valley we can best appreciate the majesty and grandeur of the mountains. From the mountain-top we learn to appreciate the tranquillity of the valley. The days of pleasure and peace prepare us for the times of difficulty and distress.

Life would be a poor place if it were all pleasure, and we would soon lose our sense of appreciation. If life consisted of all trouble we would soon be overwhelmed. As God, in nature, has arranged different types of scenery, so in life He allows us to experience both joy and sadness, ease and difficulty.

The road to Calais passes through forests, which are places of beauty, though they can become places of terror for those who may become lost in them. We are told the way to find the way out of a dark forest is to follow the shafts of light.

This is a lesson on how to deal with times of doubt that comes to most people at some time or another. Painful experiences darken our life, we feel shut in, questions arise and we feel overwhelmed by doubts, and bewildered. We feel we have lost our way.

If we can learn from our doubts and fears we can make use of them. If we become lost in doubts and fears that would be a tragedy. We must work our way through our doubts following the light as we see it until we arrive at the place where we can believe again, where we can accept the facts, and put them into practice.

Along the route to Calais there are many signs to show the way. They are placed there by the military police to help travellers, to give direction to those in doubt. On the road the military police are there to help and advise. On the Road of Life God is ready to help and advise us when we need such help. He provides maps and a Guide Book to help us on our journey through life. In the Bible we find His plans and wishes plainly set out.

We have been familiar with the signs saying 'Safe Lane' to guide us through minefields. God has similar signs telling us to follow certain paths and all will be well. He has other signs, similar to those we used to see, saying, 'Mines', warning us of danger. God has signs like that warning us of spiritual and moral danger. God has given the names of these mines, Greed, Lust, Pride, Temper, Selfishness, Self-will, and many others that wreck many lives.

It is possible to render mines harmless, and then to remove them. God has a process to render the mines of life harmless and to remove them. When we invite Jesus Christ to come into our lives and share our life with Him, He renders all those mines harmless.

On our journey between the transit camps there were brief halts and at mid-day we were provided with tea and sandwiches. Then at night we had a cooked meal and a bed. This was an opportunity to rest and relax. The camps are places of rest and refreshment, and we are grateful for them.

On the Road of Life there are also places of rest and refreshment. Sunday is a milestone on the way, a place to halt and find spiritual help and refreshment in church services. Both the Sunday services and the midweek activities of the church help us along the Road of Life.

If we wished, we could ignore the midday halts and the transit camps on the road to Calais, but if we did so we would find the journey hard and tiring. In life, we can ignore the help offered by the Christian church, but it would make life more difficult. If we neglect food and rest for the body, it becomes weak. If we neglect spiritual food and help then our spiritual life becomes weak.

We cannot afford to miss the halts and camps on the road to Calais. We are very unwise to miss opportunities of help and refreshment and encouragement available for the Christian life. We need the fellowship of the church of Christ here on earth.

The road to Calais sweeps on, sometimes over mountains, sometimes around mountains and along a valley. Sometimes it sweeps through forests and, at other times, along plains. Eventually we arrive in Calais, the end of the road across Europe. Home is not far away now. The lorries remain at Calais but the men on leave go on home, crossing the English Channel. The vehicles in which they travelled return whence they came.

One day we shall reach a place in history where life's road ends. Our times of ups and downs will be over. Our bodies, the vehicles in which we have travelled through life, will return whence they came. But the real you and I cannot stop at this point.

Death is not the end.

The Romans had the idea of calling death the river Styx, the dark river. Christians sometimes refer to death as crossing the river Jordan into the Promised Land. The poet Tennyson refers to death as 'Crossing the bar', suggesting death is like putting out to sea. I want to suggest it is 'Crossing the Channel'.

The journey to England will cause no fear if we are in a good ship with a good pilot. Death need not cause us any fear if we are travelling in the ship called 'Christian Faith' or 'Faith in God's love and mercy'. And if we are trusting the pilot, Jesus Christ.

When the men on leave arrive in England they will quickly reach home and be reunited with their family and friends. When we pass from this life, trusting in the love and mercy of God, we go to our real home. The body is of the earth - material - but the soul is eternal and spiritual. It comes from God and returns to God. In God's presence, our heavenly home, there will be a reunion with those from whom we have been parted by death. We will be home at last.

We all travel the Road of Life as best we can, according to our understanding and faith. This is the moment to ask ourselves: 'How are we doing?' Are we using the best Guide Book with 'Hints on how to deal with all situations'? It is worth trying to follow this Guide Book and sharing life with Jesus Christ. It makes travelling on the Road of Life much easier.

On the Road Home, the soldiers have to carry their own kit. On the Road of Life, Jesus Christ will carry our load of worry and trouble, and He will carry our load of sin.

Have you booked your passage in the right ship to cross the Channel?

Are you trusting in the right Pilot, Jesus Christ?

Jesus is the best Guide for Life's journey, as well as for crossing the Channel at the end of the road. We are all travelling the Road of Life, but how are we travelling?

INDEX